ALIVE-ALIVE O!
Flann O'Brien's *At Swim-Two-Birds*
Edited by Rüdiger Imhof

THE APPRAISAL SERIES
Irish and English Literature in Context
General Editor: Maurice Harmon

FOR KARIN WITH LOVE

APPRAISAL

IRISH AND
ENGLISH LITERATURE
IN CONTEXT

SERIES

The APPRAISAL series presents, in one volume, *the key essays* — critical, inter-pretive or contextual — dealing with specific works of literature. These essays may be entirely original, being specially commissioned for the series where the editor considers existing material to be inadequate; or may bring together in a re-edited and structured volume, the most important essays for a full, and up-to-date, evaluation of the work; or, the APPRAISAL volume may combine both of these approaches, in order to achieve the best result.

Individual volumes in the APPRAISAL series are researched, edited and introduced by writers whose academic and scholarly expertise on their own subject is already established.

The General Editor for the series is Maurice Harmon of University College, Dublin.

Published in the series:
The Way Back: George Moore's The Untilled Field *and* The Lake
Editor: Robert Welch, University of Leeds

Alive-Alive O! Flann O'Brien's At Swim-Two-Birds
Editor: Rüdiger Imhof, University of Wuppertal

Forthcoming
Reading Maria Edgeworth's Castle Rackrent
Editor: Coilin Owens, George Mason University

Alive-Alive O!

FLANN O'BRIEN'S
AT SWIM-TWO-BIRDS

Edited by
Rüdiger Imhof

Wolfhound Press, Dublin
Barnes & Noble Books, Totowa, New Jersey

First published 1985 WOLFHOUND PRESS, 68 Mountjoy Sq., Dublin 1.
Co-published in the USA 1985 by BARNES & NOBLE BOOKS, 81 Adams Drive,
Totowa, N.J.

British Library Cataloguing in Publication Data

Alive alive O': Flann O'Brien's At Swim-Two-Birds.
— (Appraisal series: v. 2)
1. O'Brien, Flann. At Swim-Two-Birds
I. Imhof, Rüdiger   II. Series
823'.914   PR6029.N56A8

ISBN 0-905473-95-7 Wolfhound Press
ISBN 0-389-20581-8 Barnes & Noble Books

ISSN 0790-0775

Library of Congress Cataloging in Publication Data

Alive alive O'; Flann O'Brien's At Swim-Two-Birds.
— (Appraisal series, ISSN 0790-0775)
1. O'Brien, Flann, 1911-1966. At Swim-Two-Birds
I. Imhof, Rüdiger   II. Series
PR6029.N56A932 1985   823'.912   85-13423

ISBN 0-389-20581-8

Typesetting: Photo-set Ltd.
Printed in Britain by Billing & Sons Ltd.

CONTENTS

ACKNOWLEDGEMENTS

The editor and the publishers wish to thank the following who have kindly given permission for the use of copyright material:

The Journal of Irish Literature for "Scenes in a Novel", extracts from O'Brien letters, and Miles Orvell's "Entirely Fictitious: The Fiction of Flann O'Brien".

The Irish Times for "On *At Swim-Two-Birds*".

Timothy O'Keeffe for Graham Greene's comment.

The Times Literary Supplement for "Nest of Novelists".

The Observer for Frank Swinnerton's "Right Proportions" and Philip Toynbee's "A Comic Heir of James Joyce".

The New Statesman for Anthony West's "New Novels", V. S. Pritchett's "Death of Finn" and Timothy Hilton's "Ireland's Great Cyclist".

The Dublin Magazine for the 1939 review of *At Swim-Two-Birds*.

The Spectator for John Coleman's "The Use of Joyce".

Hibernia and John Jordan for his "The Saddest Book ever to come out of Ireland!"

Benedict Kiely and Golden Eagle Books Ltd for the extract from *Modern Irish Fiction: A Critique*.

Bernard Benstock and *Eire-Ireland* for "The Three Faces of Brian Nolan".

Martin Brian & O'Keeffe for the extracts from Niall Sheridan's "Brian, Flann and Myles" and J. C. C. Mays's "Brian O'Nolan: Literalist of the Imagination".

Anthony Burgess and Faber & Faber for the extract from *The Novel Now*.

Anthony Cronin and the *Irish Times* for "An Extraordinary Achievement" and "After *At Swim*".

Stephen Knight and Angus & Robertson for the extract from "Forms of Gloom: The Novels of Flann O'Brien".

Anne Clune and Gill and Macmillan for the extracts from *Flann O'Brien. A Critical Introduction to His Writings*.

Ninian Mellamphy and *The Canadian Journal of Irish Studies* for "Aestho-Autogamy and the Anarchy of Imagination: Flann O'Brien's Theory of Fiction in *At Swim-Two-Birds*".

Anglo-Irish Studies for "Two Meta-Novelists: Sternesque Elements in Novels by Flann O'Brien".

Alf MacLochlainn for "De Selby Discovered".

The editor has made every effort to trace copyright holders. If he has inadvertently overlooked any he will be pleased to make the necessary arrangements at the first opportunity.

INTRODUCTION

Brian Moore, in a recent article entitled "English Fame and Irish Writers"[1], refers to Flann O'Brien's masterpiece *At Swim-Two-Birds* as "a book as Irish as it was vanguard and written in a language that the strangers do not know". Certainly, *At Swim-Two-Birds* is immensely and disarmingly Irish. Yet, as with any profound work of literature or art, it is not as an outstanding specimen of a particular national literature – as a supreme instance of the Irish comic tradition, for example – that the novel is likely to be appreciated in times to come. Despite its unequivocal references to Ireland and Irish literature, *At Swim-Two-Birds* should find its proper context as a brilliant artistic achievement in the international tradition of innovative fiction. The present casebook is intended to reduce the number of strangers to O'Brien's language.

A work of literature, it may be argued, follows the dynamics of aesthetic purpose in the organisation of its constitutive materials.[2] The result is an aesthetic object capable, in its deployment of language, of arousing different aesthetic experiences. Any one of these experiences is the outcome of a particular reader's imaginative realisation of the suggestive stimuli inherent in the text. An Irish critic may look at *At Swim-Two-Birds* through different eyes from, say, an English, an American or a German colleague. But, as there is no such thing as one correct approach to a piece of literature or art, who is to say which response is the more appropriate? The articles and writings collected here are all very different in their approaches and results, thereby testifying to the almost inexhaustible richness of O'Brien's novel.

An Introduction to a study that unites appreciations and

exegeses of a specific work of literature is naturally expected to comment on the selection of items offered. This invariably amounts to a last-ditch justification on the part of the editor. But before this justificatory "egg-dance" commences, the non-specialist on O'Brien, might benefit from information which could not be gained from these reprints, but which may better his understanding of O'Brien and his exemplary novel. Therefore we begin with a brief account of O'Brien's life and activities as a writer. Next follows a short interpretative discussion of the novel. Then main trends in the criticism of the novel will be outlined and the pieces selected for reprinting will be dealt with in order to highlight the salient aspects of their interests. Lastly, an attempt will be made to point to the significance of *At Swim-Two-Birds* for post-war innovative fiction, an aspect not previously covered in any study of the novel. The tremendous impact the book seems to have exerted – and is still exerting – on post-war writers as different as B. S. Johnson, Anthony Burgess, Gilbert Sorrentino, Raymond Federman and Alastair Gray is only beginning to be noticed by critics.

*

Flann O'Brien, Myles na gCopaleen, Brother Barnabas, Count O'Blather, John James Doe, George Knowall, Oscar Love, West-Briton Nationalist, Hazil Ellis, Matt Duffy, Brian Nolan – these are only some of the *noms de plume* Brian O'Nolan adopted in the course of his multifarious activities as a writer, tragically ended by O'Nolan's untimely death from an incurable disease.[3] The plethora of pen-names protected his privacy and gained him immunity from possible retaliatory attacks which, above all, his scathingly satirical pieces might have provoked. At least, this is Myles na gCopaleen's explanation as given in "De Me".[4] With evident under-statement, O'Nolan regarded himself as no more than "an accomplished literary handyman".[5] His critics, on the other hand, have, almost unanimously, crowned him "Ireland's greatest modern satirist and fantasist".[6]

Brian O'Nolan was born in Strabane, Co. Tyrone, on 5 October 1911.[7] In 1930 he entered University College, Dublin. Niall Sheridan was then in charge of editing the students' magazine *Comhthrom Féinne*, and he asked O'Nolan to write a series of short pieces dealing with contemporary life in Dublin, some kind of Dublin *Decamerone*. O'Nolan agreed but only on condition that he be allowed to write in Old Irish. Furthermore, he argued, he would be addressing merely a very small audience, as only few Irishmen had as much as a smattering of Old Irish, presumably just an audience of three, that celebrated trio of scholars: Osborn Bergin, D. A. Binchy and Richard Best. Because of this obviously limited readership, he asserted, there could be no question of any form of editorial censorship. Sheridan did not raise any objections and let O'Nolan have his way. Soon after the first instalment of this curious and, as it turned out, juicy Boccaccio adaptation had appeared, Sheridan, to his surprise, found himself summoned before the President of the College and charged with publishing obscene matter, written in Old Irish, in a semi-official University organ.[8] Henceforth O'Nolan dealt with a myriad of different topics in his pieces for *Comhthrom Féinne*, signing them from the second one, "Brother Barnabas".

In 1934 he assumed the fictitious personality of "Count O'Blather" and published his own magazine, *Blather. Blather* was devoted to parody, satire, short stories, limericks, all sorts of word-games, lessons in Irish as well as the propounding of fantastic and hilarious notions and inventions. His work for the two magazines anticipated *in nuce* a good deal of what he was later to exploit in his *Cruiskeen Lawn* columns.

In 1935, having obtained his MA with a study on "Nature in Irish Poetry", O'Nolan became a junior administrative officer in the department of local government. He remained a civil servant until 1953, when the minister in charge of the department gave orders for the summary dismissal of O'Nolan, now in the position of principal officer of town planning. It is often argued, with a liberal dash of euphemism, that the minister took great exception to the devastating and un-compromising criticism Myles na gCopaleen was in the habit of launching against administrative and bureaucratic idio-syncracies in the *Irish Times*. It is more likely that the real reason for the ministerial decision was O'Nolan's fondness of intoxicating beverages. In the end, though, owing to the inter-vention of, presumably, John Garvin,[9] it was arranged that O'Nolan would be permitted to retire on a partial pension on grounds of ill-health.

Around 1937, while pursuing his work in the department of local government five and a half days a week with what could not be regarded as exuberant enthusiasm, O'Nolan began work on his first full-blown piece of fiction, which, after several changes, was later called *At Swim-Two-Birds*. With the help of Niall Sheridan, who apparently took out one-fifth of the text before the manuscript was sent to Longmans,[10] the novel was completed some time in 1938 and was published by Longmans on 13 March 1939, without causing any great stir. According to one of Myles's eccentric views, reprinted in this collection, the book's lack of success was connected with the alleged fact that Adolf Hitler took offence and, in order to torpedo it, started World War II.

In January of the same year O'Nolan and his friend Sheridan started a controversy with Sean O'Faolain and Frank O'Connor in the *Irish Times*. O'Connor's play *Time's Pocket* had been staged in Dublin in December 1938 and had, by and large, met with sharp disapproval from the critics. O'Faolain drafted a letter to the editor of the *Irish Times* in defence of his friend O'Connor. In reply, O'Nolan and Sheridan began to bombard the *Irish Times* editor with a series of letters over a period of several weeks. On this occasion, O'Nolan used the pen-name "Flann O'Brien" for the first time. When the controversy was over, he and Sheridan, who had immensely enjoyed themselves, decided to stir up another controversy. This time, using a rich variety of different fictitious names, they managed to keep it alive for more than a year. The hoax appealed greatly to the readers of the *Irish Times,* and the editor of the paper, R. M. Smyllie, asked Sheridan to arrange a meeting with O'Nolan for him. The outcome of that meeting was an offer for O'Nolan to write a regular column for the *Irish Times*. On 4 October 1940, the first *Cruiskeen Lawn* (the full jug) article appeared; from the second one onwards, they were signed by one "Myles na gCopaleen". At first, Myles's interest was predominantly focused on the Irish language; with pungent cynicism he lashed out at those supporters and critics of the Gaelic Revival Movement who arrogantly debated the pros and cons of the movement without themselves possessing a reasonably sufficient knowledge of the language, those people whom Myles later, in a letter to the editor of *Kavanagh's Weekly*, called "the Gaelic League type of

moron (few of whom know Irish properly at all)".[11]
Subsequently, Myles's *Cruiskeen Lawn* attacks developed an
almost inexhaustible thematic variety. Myles grew into the
role of a *miles gloriosus* of satire, indefatigably engaged in a
merciless war fought on four fronts. He became an omniscient,
omnipotent, ubiquitous personality, who had studied under
Scarlatti, entertained Kreisler with his inimitable performance
on the violin in 1931, assisted Clemenceau in re-establishing
rule and order in France, and had tutored Einstein and a
number of leading European philosophers. He was, all in one,
Dublin gutty, world-famous journalist, art-expert,
archaeologist, ornithologist, linguistic analyst, horse-doctor,
lawyer, judge, Regius Professor of Potheen, TCD, President of
Ireland, Irish Disraeli, in short: "a greater Man than God",
who was prepared to accept and acknowledge only one other
authority beside himself – one Leonard O'Davinci. With the
exception of a short break in 1962, necessitated by an illness,
O'Nolan kept his *Cruiskeen Lawn* columns alive for nearly
twenty-six years. It is pre-eminently on the strength of these
articles, in which he pilloried all imaginable human follies,
that O'Nolan can claim a place in the illustrious ranks of the
famous Irish wits: Thomas Sheridan, Jonathan Swift, John
Philpot Curran, "Father Prout" (Francis Mahon), James
Joyce and Oliver St John Gogarty.

During the second bogus controversy, O'Nolan was working
on two further novels. *An Béal Bocht* (The Poor Mouth) came
out in 1941. Originally written in Irish and later translated
into English by Patrick C. Power, the book presents a biting
satire upon – among other things – the excesses of the Gaelic
Revival Movement and the romantically veiled Abbey-image
of the Irish peasant. It quickly sold out, and after only a few
weeks a second impression was published. Work on the second
novel, *The Third Policeman* (originally entitled "Hell Goes
Round and Round"), was completed in 1940. O'Nolan could
not find a publisher and so spread the rumour that, while he
was motoring in Donegal with a friend, the manuscript had
been lying loose in the boot of the car; at every stop the boot
had been opened and the wild winds of the North had
whipped away a page or two, until the entire novel had
vanished page by page over the Bloody Foreland.[12] *The Third
Policeman* was posthumously published in 1967, O'Nolan it

seems, took the apparent failure of his third novel very badly, and at the instigation of William Saroyan he now turned to the theatre. Three plays, *Faustus Kelly, Thirst,* and *The Insect Play*, resulted from his efforts in 1943.

The years between 1947 and 1952 were overshadowed by illnesses and what Anne Clissmann, no doubt euphemistically, calls "accidents" – involving, more likely than not, a few "jars" too many. But no matter by what sort of accidents O'Nolan was victimised, the frequent illnesses and the mishaps he was subject to during those years impaired his creative abilities and seem to have been responsible for the decline in the quality of his writings to the level of journalistic pot-boilers. In addition to his articles for the *Irish Times,* he wrote in the fifties, as "John James Doe", "A Weekly Look Around" for the *Southern Star* (Skibbereen) and as "Mat Duffy" for the *Sunday Review* and as "George Knowall" in "George Knowall's Peepshow" for the *Nationalist and Leinster.* In May 1959 Timothy O'Keeffe, who was then with MacGibbon & Kee, suggested to O'Nolan a republication of *At Swim-Two-Birds.* The reissue of the novel in 1960 seems to have triggered off in O'Nolan a fresh creative interest. In the same year he wrote *The Hard Life,* the manuscript of which reached MacGibbon & Kee in January 1961 ready for the press, and before the year was out the novel had been published. Moreover, since 1960, O'Nolan had begun to write for television. In swift succession he churned out *The Flight* (1962), *The Time Freddie Retired* (1962), *The Man with Four Legs* (1962), *The Dead Spit of Kelly* (1962) – an adaptation of his short story "Two in One" – and a revised version of *The Boy from Ballytearim* (1962), originally written in 1955. He also devised two television series: *The Ideas of O'Dea* (1963-64) and *Th' Oul Lad of Kilsalaher* (1965). A third one, *The Detectional Fastidiosities of Serjeant Fottrell,* on which he worked in 1966, never got beyond the initial stage of conception. All of O'Nolan's creative forays into the literary province of drama demonstrate, in their occasionally severe compositional shortcomings, that he never managed to exploit the potentials of the histrionic media in a qualitatively satisfactory manner.

Around 1962 O'Nolan began work on his last complete novel, *The Dalkey Archive.* MacGibbon & Kee brought the book out in 1964. In the autumn of that year O'Nolan drafted yet another narrative project, which was intended as "a comic but unmistakable attack on the Kennedy family".[13] When Brian O'Nolan died on April Fool's Day 1966, after a long and excruciatingly painful time suffering from cancer of the skin, only seven chapters of what, after many changes of title came to be known as *Slattery's Sago Saga,* had been written.

*

During his time at UCD, when O'Nolan and his cronies Niall Sheridan, Denis Devlin, and Donagh MacDonagh, were yet again busy "putting glasses of stout into the interior of [their] stomachs"[14] in the snug of Grogan's pub in Leeson Street, O'Nolan submitted a fantastic plan for an unorthodox literary venture:

> . . . nobody had yet produced the Great Irish Novel. The time had come when it must be written or, rather, manufactured .... Brian proposed that he, Devlin, MacDonagh and [Sheridan] should write the book in sections and then stick the pieces together in committee .... Existing works would be plundered wholesale for material .... *Children of Destiny* would be the precursor of ... the Ready-Made or Reach-Me-Down School.[15]

This Great Irish Novel never materialised; in its stead O'Nolan created *At Swim-Two-Birds,* which securely belongs to the "quirky comic tradition"[16] of Irish literature, the tradition which accommodates the works of such celebrated writers as Dean Swift, James Joyce, Samuel Beckett and, as more recent representatives, Brian Coffey's *The Big Laugh,* Alf MacLochlainn's *Out of Focus,* Patrick McGinley's *Bogmail,* and Michael Mullen's *Kelly* and *Festival of Fools.*[17]

At Swim-Two-Birds is a parodic symposium of textual strategies and stylistic conventions which, borrowed from a huge variety of different narrative genres, are wrought into a highly original Chinese-box construct. This involuted fictional fabrication is to be classed as metafiction since it overtly questions the validity of the respective compositional schemes and their linked themes, and, furthermore, reflects, either explicitly or implicitly, on the conditions for the production of fictional texts. O'Nolan thought, as one of the extracts from his letters in this collection shows, that his narrative *tour de force* was "harder on the head than the worst whiskey"[18] for most readers. In retrospect, he pooh-poohed the book as "juvenile nonsense"[19], conceding, though, that "those birds must have some unsuspected stuffing in them".[20] In fact, because of its wealth of thematic matter and originality in compositional design, *At Swim-Two-Birds* is a long way from being a mere "belly laugh or high-class literary pretentious slush".[21]

The nameless narrator in *At Swim-Two-Birds* counts among his favourite books those of "Mr. A. Huxley" (p. 11). Interestingly, Huxley's novel *Point Counter Point* provides the concept for the Chinese-box structure of O'Nolan's book. Philip Quarles, in one of his notebook entries, deliberates on "the musicalization of fiction", and he hits upon the following idea:

> Put a novelist into the novel. He justifies generalization . . . . He also justifies experiment. Specimens of his work may illustrate other possible or impossible ways of telling a story . . . . But why draw the line at one novelist inside a novel. Why not a second inside his? And a third inside the novel of the second. And so on to infinity, like those advertisements of Quaker Oats where there's a quaker holding a box of oats, on which is a picture of another quaker holding another box of oats, on which etc. etc.[22]

On a first inspection, *At Swim-Two-Birds* appears to consist of three different "books", to which the three different beginnings and endings seem to correspond. The "biographical reminiscences" of the UCD-student/protagonist represent the frame-story, the largest Chinese-box, as it were. Intercalated therein and generated through the "spare-time literary activities" (p. 9) of the narrator is the narrative of the fictitious author Dermot Trellis, which is introduced partly resultatively, partly inchoately. The despotic attitude of Trellis towards his characters leads to an open rebellion, which Trellis's son, Orlick, who is the product of an illegitimate union between Trellis and the heroine of his *opus*, notes down as a story within Trellis's story. But this is not all. There, too, is O'Nolan, who weaves the various stories into an aesthetic whole, which constitutes the fourth "book", so to speak, and which takes on the form and thematic objectives of a meta-novel. This intricate "story-teller's book-web" (p. 19) is held together by a complex net of thematic parallels, motif echoes, stylistic correspondences and contrapuntal arrangements. The converging point for the different novels within the novel, as well as the more than thirty parodic exercises in styles and modes of narration,[23] is, comparable to the situation in *Tristram Shandy,* the prescience of the UCD student.

The frame-story is taken up by an account given in the first-person singular and divided into ten "biographical reminiscences". It covers in parts the final year the narrator spends at UCD, and it does so by exploiting the thematic as well as compositional conventions of three fictional genres. There are, to begin with, those conventions of fictional biography; and as the protagonist is a writer or artist, even if only of sorts as some may remark, the outer narrative may be considered as the memoirs of an artist, utilising, as it does, strategies of the *Künstlerroman.* Anne Clissmann *et al.* have pointed out a great number of parodic references to Joyce[24], in particular to *A Portrait,* which fully substantiate the assumption that O'Nolan may have intended his principal character to be a transmogrified version of Stephen Dedalus. The series of biographical reminiscences corresponds, in the random arrangement of its narrative units and the possibility of its being continued indefinitely, to narrative conventions associated with the picaresque or neo-picaresque novel. The opposition of the UCD student to his social environment, represented notably by the student's uncle, is reminiscent of the social conflict in narratives of this kind. Further, as in a picaresque novel, the frame-story deals, to some extent, with the development of the principal character from a simpleton to a worldly-wise person (or *Schelm*). It also observes, if liberally, some of the compositional rules of the *Bildungsroman.*

The favourite occupation of the narrator, which in large parts consists in his retiring "into the privacy of [his] mind" (p. 9), is responsible, among other things, for the Trellis *opus.* The "philosopher and moralist" Trellis is planning a melo-dramatic novel that will "show the terrible cancer of sin in its true light and act as a clarion-call to torn humanity" (p. 36). But "purely a moralizing tract" (p. 35), Trellis is aware, would not reach the public to anything like the extent he desires. Consequently, he decides to incorporate "plenty of smut" (p. 35) into his book. Trellis's approach as a writer reveals itself, on closer inspection, as a travesty of the approach adopted by the traditional omniscient narrator in fiction, who, as a rule, exercises "absolute control" over his characters. The customary attitude of the omniscient narrator towards the personages of his own making is flaunted by Trellis's compelling his characters to live with him in the Red Swan Hotel, "so that he can keep an eye on them and see that there is no boozing" (p. 35). The creation of Furriskey, who is projected as the central villain of Trellis's piece, is likewise a travesty, namely of the biblical act of creation. "A voice came from the interior of the cloud. 'Are you there, Furriskey', it asked" (p. 50). The voice is Trellis's, and Trellis is thereby brought into proximity with God when creating and calling Adam. The omniscient narrator is thus unmasked as a narratorial god of creation.[25] The *reductio ad absurdum* of the concept of the god-like omniscient narrator is coupled with yet another, comparable *reductio*. Trellis composes his book largely in the style associated with the socio-realistic tradition of the novel. This is to say that he aims at verisimilitude, that he seeks to create the illusion of the "realness" of the characters and events, as in the Victorian novel to whose general thematic intentions Trellis's "moralizing tract" is indebted. Trellis wants Furriskey to be "a man of unexampled depravity" (p. 35). Following Horace's basic rule of the *ordo artis,* he creates him *ab ovo et initio* (p. 35) by means of what in *At Swim-Two-Birds* is termed "aestho-autogamy" (p. 40) and alleged to be "a familiar phenomenon in literature". Now with the help of fake "press extracts", the birth of Furriskey is presented as if Furriskey were a real person. Trellis "out-realists" the realist; the illusion of the "realness" of a fictional character is given a last absurd twist. On the other hand, Trellis betrays himself to be a ruthless plagiarist. He borrows, nay steals his characters, as if grotesquely following T. S. Eliot's dictum "mature poets steal", wherever he can find them, the mythological hero Finn MacCool and Mad King Sweeny as well as the Pooka MacPhellimey, the Good Fairy from folk literature, and, in addition, a bunch of cow-punchers from the Western romances written by one William Tracy.

To any of these characters, or groups of characters, certain independent narrative units are attached, each rendered in the specific style of narration pertaining to the genre from which the respective character or characters have been lifted. The

legendary Finn MacCool serves as an opportunity for a
"humorous or quasi-humorous incursion into ancient mythology"
(p. 13); written in the stilted, poetic diction as employed by
Kuno Meyer in his translations of Gaelic legends, this episode
describes, for instance, the heroic, extraordinary appearance of
Finn. Finn himself figures as narrator in Trellis's *opus* when he
recites, "with honey-words" (p. 64), the romance of King
Sweeny, that middle-Irish pseudo-saga from the so-called
"King Circle". The cowboys from Tracy's Westerns introduce
the narrative style of the familiar Western romance, for
instance through Shanahan's account of the gunfight in
Ringsend, itself yet another *reductio ad absurdum* of the phrase
"horse-play of cornerboys". A similar contrastive arrangement
of historical and modern literary forms can be found when
Finn, incorporating into his recital the lays of mad King
Sweeny, is interrupted by Shanahan, who argues self-assuredly
that the literary form of the lay, "the real old stuff of the native
land" (p. 75), has not only now become a preposterously
anachronistic sort of poetic expression, but, more is the pity, is
of inferior artistic quality when compared with the contemporary "working-man's pome" by Jem Casey, such as
"Workman's Friend", which culminates in the pithy
observation: "A PINT OF PLAIN IS YOUR ONLY
MAN"[26]. The genre of folk and fairy tales, with its
characteristic narrative style and subject-matter, is exploited
in the strand of action featuring the Pooka MacPhellimey and
the Good Fairy. Here again, as with the other literary modes,
the parodic intention of O'Nolan is predominant, in this case
the leprechaun tradition in Irish literature, which ranged from
such ancient sagas as the one about Fergus Mac Léti, King of
Ulster,[27] to James Stephens's *The Crock of Gold,* Eimar
O'Duffy's *King Goshawk and the Birds* or Mervyn Wall's Fursey
novels, and to which Ned Nicholl, at least as far as the
implications of the title of his novel go, tried to put an end with
No More Leprechauns. The various literary incursions which
Trellis's *opus* undertakes into mythological legend, the
medieval romance, the twentieth-century Western romance,
the ancient lays, the working-man's "pomes" and fairy tales
are held together, structurally as well as thematically, in two
ways: firstly, by the fact that the characters associated with the
incursions are fellow-travellers on a mutual journey through

Ireland with the aim of being present at Orlick's birth, and
that, recalling the pilgrims in *The Canterbury Tales,* they take it
in turns to tell a story in order to while away the time; and,
secondly, by Trellis's bringing them together in the Red Swan
Hotel.

Trellis's uncompromising, tyrannical stance as god-like
author is reason for the Pirandelloesque revolt of the
characters, which is responsible for Orlick's story within the
story within the story. The idea of a mutiny by fictional
characters against their creator has its origin, or so it seems, in
an article O'Nolan, as "Brother Barnabas", wrote for
Comhthrom Féinne.[28] It can be understood as a further *reductio ad
absurdum,* especially if viewed in connection with the following
theoretical observation by E. M. Forster:

> The characters arrive when evoked full of the spirit of
> mutiny. For they have these numerous parallels with people
> like ourselves, they try to live their own lives and are
> consequently often engaged in treason against the main
> scheme of the book. They 'run away', they 'get out of
> hand' ...; if they are given complete freedom they kick the
> book to pieces.[29]

This is precisely what happens to Trellis's book. With a
Luciferian *non serviam* on their lips, the characters hatch a plot
against Trellis in order to be able to live their own lives.
Having found out that in his sleep Trellis cannot retain
"absolute control" over them, Finn and Shanahan keep him in
a comatose condition by means of drugs. Furriskey, designated
villain of the piece, decides not to rape Sheila Lamont, as
intended by the "philosopher and moralist", but instead to
marry "a domestic servant" (p. 61) and lead a virtuous life "in
a little house in Dolphin's Barn" (p.101). Not before long,
though, Shanahan and Lamont suspect that the drugs may
lose their effect, and they persuade Orlick, who has inherited
his father's "gift for literary composition" (p. 164), to compose
"a story on the subject of Trellis, a fitting punishment indeed
for the usage he has given others" (p. 164). Orlick has it in
mind to pierce the authorial malefactor "with a pluperfect"
(p. 168), but this is deemed by the other characters too lenient
a punishment; instead they request a "simple story with plenty
of the razor" (p. 169). After several starts, Orlick conceives of a

revenge-plot modelled on the Sweeny legend. The mutiny finds its climax when the characters put Trellis on trial for his "crimes", taking the roles of judge, jury, witnesses and prosecutor at the same time. Each witness prefers a different charge against Trellis. With only a few notable exceptions, all these accusations are connected with Trellis's capacity as omnipotent and omniscient author/narrator, and they can *in toto* be read as a critique of this literary convention.

Yet in addition to debunking the concept of the omniscient narrator, *At Swim-Two-Birds* puts forward reasons why the work of such a story-teller can no longer come into its own. That he does not perish at the hands of his rebellious characters Trellis owes to a servant girl employed in the Red Swan Hotel, who, while putting Trellis's room to rights, inadvertently burns those pages of the manuscript which made and sustained the existence of Furriskey and his friends. Torn and tattered, Trellis returns to the Red Swan and mutters, "ars est celare artem ... doubtful as to whether he had made a pun" (p. 216).

The fourth book within *At Swim-Two-Birds,* finally, comes about inasmuch as O'Nolan does not adhere to the classical demand *ars est celare artem,* but pursues the very opposite by paying homage to the conviction which lies at the root of all metaliterature: *artis est patefacere artem.* Like Beckett's fictional texts, *At Swim-Two-Birds* belongs primarily to what, for lack of a more precise term, is frequently called "imaginative" literature, a kind of literature that has freed itself of the obligation to represent reality. The dominant textual strategies of metafiction are those which make the reader aware that a novel is nothing but an artefact made up of words, or – to adopt one of Beckett's dicta — that telling stories is telling lies. It must suffice her to mention only some of the metafictional strategies in *At Swim-Two-Birds.*[30] They all serve the purpose of what the Russian formalist Shklovsky has termed *die Blosslegung des Verfahrens* (the laying bare of the literary process).[31] There are, for instance, the numerous *reductiones ad absurdum,* the explicit authorial comments upon the artificial nature of the matters presented, the unorthodox way of delineating a character through providing a list clearly separated from the rest of the text instead of allowing the data to become integrated parts of the narrative flux. Or there are the games played on the expectation of the reader, reminiscent of the games in *Tristram Shandy:* the use of typographical signs to express thematic issues, the narrator's admission of certain difficulties in dealing with a particular aspect in the account, which may frequently entail an abrupt break in the narrative or lead to an omission of an intended narrative unit, as when the UCD student divulges his inability to render Orlick's birth (p. 114); or the casting doubt on the validity of specific generic conventions, as in the case of Trellis's morally realistic novel of Victorian provenance, the parodying and burlesquing of styles and modes of fiction, and also the contrastive juxtaposition of literary forms, which may result, as happens in the case of Sweeny's lays and Casey's "pomes", in an open debate on the advantages and disadvantages of these forms, so to speak in "a battle of the books".

The two most outstanding metafictional elements in *At Swim-Two-Birds* are the self-conscious narrator[32] and the theory of the novel advanced by him within the pages of his work. The UCD student succeeds in employing all the various compositioinal strategies and in weaving a "story-teller's book-web" only because, as pointed out at the very beginning of the novel, he is continually reflecting on his own method and process of composition: "Having placed in my mouth sufficient bread for three minutes' chewing, I withdrew my powers of sensual perception and retired into the privacy of my mind ... I reflected on the subject of my spare-time literary activities ... (p. 9)."

If one felt tempted to define *At Swim-Two-Birds* as a typically Irish piece of literature, the motif of the teller-within-the-tale could be a possible criterion. For, as Thomas Kilroy has argued, since *Castle Rackrent,* "the distinctive characteristic [of Irish fiction] has been the imitation of a speaking voice engaged in the telling of a tale".[33] At any rate, the reflections of the narrator lead to quite an unusual theory of the novel:

> . . . a satisfactory novel should be a self-evident sham to which the reader could regulate at will the degree of his credulity. It was undemocratic to compel characters to be uniformly good or bad or poor or rich. Each should be allowed a private life, self-determination and a decent standard of living .... Characters should be interchangeable

as between one book and another. The entire corpus of existing literature should be regarded as a limbo from which discerning authors could draw their characters as required, creating only when they failed to find a suitable existing puppet. The modern novel should be largely a work of reference. Most authors spend their time saying what has been said before – usually said much better . . . (p. 25).

It should be evident that *At Swim-Two-Birds* represents an exact concretization of this quirky theory as also of Philip Quarles's in *Point Counter Point*. The theorising of the narrator likewise includes the view "[that] one book, one opening, was a principle with which I did not find it possible to concur" (p. 13). To demonstrate his conviction, the narrator offers three different beginnings to his story, which find their counterparts at the close of the novel in the three different "Conclusions". These endings, more easily than the beginnings, can be related to different thematic levels in *At Swim-Two-Birds*. The first one belongs to the fictional memoirs of the UCD student, the second one brings the Trellis *opus* to an end and the third pertains to the meta-frame of the book. The *"Conclusion of the book, ultimate,"* is part of the meta-level insofar as the theme of truth and untruth, essence and appearance, which dominates this level is reflected through various instances of sanity and insanity. Moreover, those three "good-byes" that the poor German, who was very fond of three "scrawled with a dying hand on a picture of his wife" (p. 218), is a final allusion to the triadic Chinese-box structure of the novel.

The fate suffered by *At Swim-Two-Birds,* as far as its critical reception is concerned, is comparable to the fate of most innovative pieces of literature, namely: initial neglect and misunderstanding have very slowly been replaced by recognition and open-hearted admiration. When the book came out on 13 March 1939, it all but set the Liffey on fire. To be true, it managed, for one glorious week in April, to triumph over *Gone with the Wind* as top of the bestseller list in Dublin,[34] but such a success could hardly be the foundation for a lasting reputation. Most critics and reviewers either ignored or panned the book, even though Graham Greene, as the extract from his comment shows, had spoken highly of it and recommended it for publication as "a book in a thousand". If one tries to determine reasons for the book's initial lack of success one can presumably disregard Myles na gCopaleen's self-mocking explanation. The war may have been, and presumably was, inimical to the book's fame, as some have maintained. The times, with so many more urgent and pressing concerns for the people to attend to, may have prevented any potential masterpiece from being given its due. Then there was the publication of Joyce's *Finnegans Wake*. Joyce's colossal fabrication did not appear until 4 May 1939, some six weeks after *At Swim-Two-Birds*. But then six weeks is certainly not long enough to make a reputation, especially since after these six weeks everyone appears to have been busy trying to solve Joyce's gigantic literary puzzle. The most plausible explanation would seem to be that the book was ahead of its time and that critics and reviewers simply failed – or were too blind – to recognise the intrinsic artistic merits of the novel.[35] At least this is the firm impression one gets from considering the reviews of 1939 reprinted here. They are, by and large, representative of what was written about the book at that time.

Until it was re-issued in 1960, *At Swim-Two-Birds* was confined to an underground existence, as Timothy Hilton puts its in his review "Ireland's Great Cyclist", with treasured copies lent only to trusted friends. It remained the property of isolated groups of cognoscenti. Then in 1960 influential reviewers, such as Philip Toynbee and V. S. Pritchett, wrote extremely favourable notices, and, what is more, they began to pay tribute to the book's artistic achievements. The slow process of recognition was thus gradually set in motion. Presumably as a result of the attention it attracted in the sixties from reviewers and readers, *At Swim-Two-Birds* managed to secure for itself a place in the Penguin gallery of "Modern Classics", to which it was admitted in 1967. But in spite of this decisive promotion, critics remained adamant in neglecting it. If it was mentioned in critical studies, it was so pre-eminently as a comic work, as yet another instance of the Irish comic tradition, or, in the words of Dylan Thomas, as "just the book to give your sister, if she's a loud, dirty, boozy girl".[36] *At Swim-Two-Birds* is, of course, a hilarious *tour de force,* yet that does not preclude its being an immensely important artistic achievement. As late as the seventies, things began to take a distinctive turn for the better. Within a short period of time, an impressive number of studies were published which have left no doubt that the book is a major work of fiction and that its author has to be judged alongside Joyce and Beckett as one of the most noteworthy Irish writers of the century.

There can also be no doubt that *At Swim-Two-Birds* is quintessentially Irish; its exploiting of multifarious forms of Irish literature is ample proof of this. But, as argued here, the thematic use to which the various modes of Irish literature are put is metafictional or, at least, parodic, so that the novel may, with justification, be classed with the international tradition of the parodic novel, or of metafiction. It would be fruitless to quarrel about which of the two possible traditions – the Irish comic tradition and the international tradition of parodic literature or metaliterature – is the more appropriate one for *At Swim-Two-Birds.* Whereas, however, most studies to date have viewed the book against the background of the Irish tradition, perhaps attempts should now be made to shift the focus to the larger and older tradition and investigate the possible role and significance of the book within this. After all, as early as 1938, Graham Greene drew attention to its affinity with *Tristram Shandy,* itself an exponent of this international tradition. More recently, a few investigations have been undertaken along these lines, yet they do not seem to have as yet established the full significance of *At Swim-Two-Birds* as an innovative novel.

When in 1974 *The Journal of Irish Literature* devoted an entire issue to Brian O'Nolan, another decisive step was taken in the slow process of recognition. Although the items in this issue are of mixed quality, the number makes available a good deal of material hitherto unpublished. A year later Anne Clissmann's voluminous monograph, *Flann O'Brien: A Critical Introduction to His Writings,* appeared. It is certainly an indispensable source of information about the man and his diverse literary as well as journalistic activity, but some feel, and have said so in reviews, that the book lacks critical acumen. This may be so, yet it will remain a standard work on O'Nolan. Two further sets of publications should probably be mentioned for their contribution to the fame of O'Nolan and thereby to the fame of *At Swim-Two-Birds*. One is the series of books that offer a wide selection of Myles na gCopaleen's *Cruiskeen Lawn* columns. With one exception, namely *The Various Lives of Keats and Chapman and The Brother* – which was put together by Benedict Kiely – the books have been edited by Brian's brother Kevin. They are: *The Best of Myles, More of Myles, Further Cuttings from Cruiskeen Lawn*, and *The Hair of the Dogma*. It would doubtlessly have enhanced the value of the collections if the editors had deemed fit to index the items with source references. The second set of publications is a result of the decision taken by Pan Books to bring out *The Best of Myles* as well as O'Nolan's novels – including a translation of *An Béal Bocht* but excluding *At Swim-Two-Birds*, which is still published by Penguin – in their Picador series as paperbacks.

*

The selection of material for this casebook was made so that the main trends and aspects of criticism on *At Swim-Two-Birds* would be represented in their historical perspective. Any choice is bound to be grounded in the interests of the chooser. Since no two people entertain exactly the same interests, this selection will certainly not please all readers. It is hoped, though, that it is sensible enough to please many.

The O'Brien letters reprinted here either in full or in extract, which formed a part of "A Sheaf of Letters" compiled by Robert Hogan and Gordon Henderson for the O'Nolan issue of *The Journal of Irish Literature*, supply some information as to how the title of the novel was arrived at. Additionally, they testify to Joyce's reception of the book and reveal the author's somewhat derogatory attitude towards his creation. Brother Barnabas's account of certain unusual "Scenes in a Novel" will probably be helpful in throwing some light on the origin of some of the outstanding, quirky ideas which are responsible for a good many of the thematic obsessions as well as the specific compositional design of *At Swim-Two Birds*.

Bernard Benstock's "The Three Faces of Brian O'Nolan" may seem slightly out of place in a casebook devoted entirely to O'Nolan's first novel, as Benstock also takes into account the other books in English and deals with more general aspects of O'Nolan's writing. But the article merits reprinting for its succinct, sensible assessment of O'Brien's achievement and because it opens up the deliberately narrow focus of the study. Two of the main aspects singled out by Benstock are O'Nolan's catholicism and the role of drinking. Benstock maintains that the O'Nolan canon is supersaturated with Catholic theology, while at the same time regarding the serious lack of commitment in any direction that emerges from the books as a severe drawback. The novels are said to offer a purposefully myopic view of the world as a result of the author's addiction to the happy ending and his use of fantasy. Benstock contends that O'Nolan's fame will rest on *At Swim-Two-Birds*, since the later books, *The Hard Life* and *The Dalkey Archive*, are rather flat and prosaic; they are inferior literary products because they lack O'Nolan's strongest attributes: his fanciful manipulation of language and his ability to structure a complex novel to exist on four or more levels simultaneously. Benstock is rather unfair on *The Third Policeman*, which he mentions merely in passing. The posthumously published *The Third Policeman*, though not equal in brilliance to *At Swim-Two-Birds*, is a novelistic *tour de force*, indubitably possessing those two O'Nolan attributes, and being one of the very first pieces of absurdist literature in the twentieth century.[37]

Niall Sheridan, who – as has frequently been pointed out, among others by Sheridan himself – served as a model for the character of "Brinsley Sheridan" in *At Swim-Two-Birds*, offers some clues in his "Brian, Flann and Myles" to the origin and genesis of the novel. He also provides some enjoyable pieces of background information on the period in which the idea for the as-yet-unwritten "Great Irish Novel" took shape. The extract from Anne Clissmann's monograph, while making use of Sheridan's account, adds further details.

J.C.C. Mays's article, "Brian O'Nolan: Literalist of the Imagination", suggested itself for inclusion because, within the limited scope of an essay, Mays covers an extraordinary number of different aspects of the utmost relevance for O'Nolan's *œuvre*. Some of the conclusions submitted are certainly open to disagreement, but unlike many other studies, Mays's abounds in stimulating suggestions for further investigations. Mays deals with the compositional texture of the book, which he sees as a result of the "method of counter-point". In addition he makes the point, on which critics are still divided, that Finn MacCool is "the least satirized" of the three narrators and that his songs have "no parody in them", a contention also made by Anne Clissmann in the extract from her monograph and by Stephen Knight in his "Forms of Gloom: The Novels of Flann O'Brien". This, with the assertion that, though its construction is intricate, the book gives little sense of shape, is debatable, for O'Nolan would seem to have shown a masterful ability to infuse a brilliant compositional harmony and rhythm (in Joyce's sense of the terms established by Stephen Dedalus in *A Portrait)* into his fiction.

In the extract from *The Novel Now,* Anthony Burgess discusses O'Nolan's novel together with those by two other Irishmen, who, it may well be argued, have contributed most influentially to the novel form in the twentieth century – Samuel Beckett and Joyce Cary. (The question of whether Cary is an Irish writer is beside the point here.) To a greater extent, perhaps, than English writers, Irish writers seem preoccupied with the nature and use of language in literature. If this appears to be an unwarrantable generalization, a look at Beckett's fictional texts will establish that there is at least some truth in the contention. According to Burgess, the idio-syncratic compositional organization of *At Swim-Two-Birds* is intended to shift the narrative interest away from story and plot and thereby to achieve an extension of the use of language in fiction writing.

In his two articles for the *Irish Times,* Anthony Cronin deals – among other aspects – with the initial reception of the novel, stressing that it was overshadowed by misconceptions as to the creative intentions and artistic merits of the book. One such misconception he sees, quite rightly, in the attempt by certain critics to evaluate *At Swim-Two-Birds* in the context of post-Joycean literature, rather than in the wider and far more appropriate context of the "modern movement in general". Perhaps, as suggested earlier, even that literary province is too narrow. My own article, "Two Meta-novelists: Sternesque Elements in Novels by Flann O'Brien", has been included to substantiate this suggestion. Cronin also contends that much of the confusion around *At Swim-Two-Birds* has stemmed from the "deluded" notion that the novel is a parody of Joyce. The extract taken from Anne Clissman's monograph would seem to prove him wrong.

Stephen Knight sees the novel as an attack on the reader's epistemological certainties. Discussing the nature of the fictional characters with the premise "that the characteristics and actions of literature are as real as any of 'real' life", Knight argues that in *At Swim-Two-Birds* O'Nolan set out to question our ideas of reality.

Miles Orvell emphasises the metafictional intentions underlying the novel. He selects two aspects which show how O'Nolan flaunts the artificiality, the "book"-quality of his fabrication. Firstly, the reader-response is controlled by (a) distancing the reader from the "content" of the story in order to make him attend to the telling of it, which is a typically metafictional operation and (b) by playing with the reader's normal empathy for fictional characters. Secondly, O'Nolan makes the author-character relationship in various forms the overriding theme of the book.

Among the most lucid and illuminating studies of *At Swim-Two-Birds* to have appeared within recent years must be counted Ninian Mellamphy's "Aestho-autogamy and the Anarchy of Imagination: Flann O'Brien's Theory of Fiction". The article persuasively demonstrates that O'Brien's Pandora's box of a novel is a significant aesthetic document. As Mellamphy correctly observes, *At Swim-Two-Birds* anticipates a good deal of what has been attempted in contemporary experimental fiction, for instance in the post-war preoccupations of Robbe-Grillet and the craftsmen of *le nouveau roman,* in its attack upon "the sacred-cow conventions of mimetic fiction". The problem most extensively dealt with in the novel is that of the artist as he shapes his artefact. Mellamphy wrongly thinks however that the nameless undergraduate is involved in the composition of a *magnum opus* "that has as its subject the agonies of an artist involved in writing an experimental novel". Trellis's inchoate book is not at all experimental. One of the thematic issues connected with Trellis's moralising tract derives precisely from the fact that it is meant to represent the conventional class of fiction.

Perhaps some may have hoped to find in this collection at least an extract from John Wain's appreciatory essay "'To

write for my own race': Notes on the Fiction of Flann
O'Brien", which appeared in the *Encounter* issue of July 1967.
It is clearly among the first to draw attention to the
importance of O'Nolan's achievement as a novelist. The
reason why a decision against Wain's piece was taken is that,
on closer scrutiny, almost 99 per cent of it turns out to be a
mere plot summary, recounting in great detail the events
taking place on the different narrative levels in *At Swim-Two-
Birds* and making liberal use of lengthy quotations.

The selection is completed by an article from the pen of
none other than the savant de Selby, or De Selby. Even though
the curator of de Selby's work, Mr Alf MacLochlainn, calls it a
"fugitive piece", the untitled essay, it is seriously believed,
which shows de Selby performing a dazzling and daring foray
into Celtic mythology, will be an invaluable source of
information for anyone working on *At Swim-Two-Birds,* and
likewise on O'Nolan's entire *œuvre.* In fact, it would not be
surprising at all if de Selby's profound study inaugurated a
reworking of the *Buile Shuibhne* myth together with a new
branch of literary criticism.

*

If the extract from Ben Kiely's *Modern Irish Fiction: A Critique*
has not been remarked upon, this has been quite a deliberate
move. For the point Kiely raises leads conveniently over to the
last issue to be considered here: the influence of *At Swim-Two-
Birds* on more recent novelists. According to Kiely, O'Nolan's
book provides an answer to the argument that James Joyce
drove the European novel into a cul-de-sac. And indeed there
is persuasive reason for embracing Kiely's suggestion without
any reservations. In many ways, *At Swim-Two-Birds* may be
said to stand, together with the narratives of Samuel Beckett,
at the beginning of a new and, proportionally, sensational
interest in metafiction, an interest of particular consequences
for the sixties and seventies of this century. Just as O'Nolan
was undoubtedly indebted to Laurence Stern, so many
contemporary experimental novelists are undoubtedly
indebted to O'Nolan.

Take, for example, the English novelist B. S. Johnson,
without question an interesting and innovative writer in his

own right, and his novels *Travelling People* and *Christie Malry's Own Double-Entry*. The narrator in *Travelling People* begins his account in a manner strikingly similar to that of the UCD student:

> Seated comfortably in a wood and wickerwork chair of eighteenth-century Chinese manufacture. I began seriously to meditate upon the form of my allegedly full-time literary sublimations.[38]

The statement unmistakably, or so it seems, recalls the opening of *At Swim-Two-Birds*:

> Having placed in my mouth sufficient bread for three minutes' chewing, I withdrew my powers of sensual perception and retired into the privacy of my mind .... I reflected on the subject of my spare-time literary activities (p. 9).

Johnson's narrator goes on to theorise about the novel just like the UCD student. He, too, is dissatisfied with established norms of novel writing. Whereas O'Nolan's protagonist finds it impossible to concur with the principle that a novel should have only one opening and one ending, Johnson's decides "that one style for one novel [is] a convention that [he resents] most strongly" *(TP*, p. 11). The decision that a novel should employ a diversity of styles is likewise anticipated in *At Swim-Two-Birds*. The narrator in *Christie Malry's Own Double-Entry* attempts a story concerning God's creation of the world and the fall from grace of Adam and Eve. But before he has gone far into it, he discontinues his efforts because "this sort of thing has been done before" and much better at that.[39] There is an echo here of the UCD student's belief that "most authors spend their time saying what has been said before – usually said much better" (p. 25). Lastly, the narrator in *Christie Malry* has a discussion with his hero about the very story in which the latter is involved. Christie voices a theory of the novel which, because of the idiosyncracies of its contentions, matches perfectly the theory in *At Swim-Two-Birds*. Some might even argue that this theory has much to be said in its favour.

> . . . who wants long novels anyway? Why spend all your spare-time for a month reading a thousand-page novel, when you can have a comparable aesthetic experience in the

threatre or cinema in only one evening? The writing of a long novel is in itself an anachronistic act: it was relevant only to a society and a set of social conditions which no longer exist . . . . The novel should now try simply to be Funny, Brutalist, and Short *(CM,* p. 106).

Anthony Burgess has paid a short, but unmistakable tribute to *At Swim-Two-Birds* in his stupendous novel *Earthly Powers* by incorporating a brief quotation from the theory of the novel as expounded by O'Nolan's writer-protagonist:

'A novelist friend of mine', Diana Cartwright said, 'affirmed that a satisfactory novel should be a self-evident sham to which the reader could regulate at will the degree of his credulity.[40]

The same quotation is used by Raymond Federman, experimentalist *extraordinaire,* as an epigraph for his *Take It or Leave It,* a fiction that purports to be nothing but "a spatial displacement of words".[41] *Take It or Leave It* is permeated with speculations about the nature of fiction as well as of literature in general. However, as a result of exasperatingly whimsical typographical gimmickery and the mind-boggling quality of its thematic preoccupations, most people are likely to leave it.

A final example is Gilbert Sorrentino's *Mulligan Stew.*[42] Like O'Nolan's novel, *Mulligan Stew* presents a symposium of a multitude of different styles and narrative modes. Almost all the compositional as well as thematic features that have come to be associated with books as quirky and metafictional as *At Swim-Two-Birds* are there, from the novel-within-the-novel construction – despite the belief of the fictitious novelist Antony Lamont, whose name bears a close resemblance to the name of one of the cowboys in *At Swim-Two-Birds,* that "the idea of a novel about a writer writing a novel is truly *old hat"* *(MS,* p. 224) – down to ambivalent typographical illustrations. The salient thematic units in *Mulligan Stew* would appear to be these: (1) Antony Lamont's attempts, of clearly dubious merits, to compose an absurdist whodunnit, as reflected by the novel-within-the-novel; (2) a psychogram of Lamont; (3) Lamont's opinions on the present state of the novel, in particular on recent experimental fiction, that emerge from a host of entries in his scrapbook and notebook; and (4) what, for the sake of brevity, may be called the revolt and private life to the main characters involved in Lamont's novel.

As can be seen, *Mulligan Stew* is indebted to *At Swim-Two-Birds* in a number of ways. In addition to aspects already mentioned, the idea of Halpin, the protagonist, stepping out of the novel he is "working" in and expressing his utter discontent with what he is designated to do, corresponds to the revolt of Furriskey and company against their author, Dermot Trellis, in *At Swim-Two-Birds*, which culminates, of course, in the project of Orlick writing a counter-tale. This creative activity on the part of the characters finds its parallel in *Mulligan Stew*, where Lamont notes in his scrapbook that the celebrated novelist George "bingo" Pompson, one day after taking his "usual mid-afternoon 'nap' " *(MS,* p. 240), discovered the manuscript of a novel written not by him, but by his characters. In *At Swim-Two-Birds*, the theory of the novel suggests that, because everything worth the telling has already been told, all there is left to discerning authors is to steal and borrow from existing works of literature. Dermot Trellis, as will be remembered, is eventually also put on trial for stealing his characters from various books by other writers, for instance from the Western romances of William Tracy. In *Mulligan Stew* is another Dermot Trellis, also a writer, who is engaged in writing "some sort of 'Western' that takes place in, of all places, Ireland" *(MS,* p. 28). And like the Dermot Trellis of *At Swim-Two-Birds*, who decides that a purely moralising tract would fall on deaf ears with the reading public, which is why he spices it with plenty of smut, the Dermot Trellis in *Mulligan Stew* spices up his opus "with plenty of smut in order for publisher to even consider doing it" *(MS,* p. 28). Further, Sorrentino's Trellis has also written a novel, called *The Red Swan*, which recalls the Red Swan Hotel where O'Brien's Trellis lives with his characters.

In addition to these parallels, there are a number of references to other writings by O'Nolan, some in the form of titles of fictitious novels Halpin comes across when exploring a cabin in the mountains:

Red Flanagan's Last Throw by William Tracy
Country Album by Nicholas de Selby
Born to Be Italian by Myles na gCopaleen

What the Vice-President Eats by "du Garbandier"
A Pint of Plain Is Your Only Man by Jem Casey
Stick It under My Oxter by Finn MacCool
Omar Bulbul, The Persian Nightingale by P. MacCruiskeen

Having mentioned Jem Casey's "A PINT OF PLAIN IS YOUR ONLY MAN", it may be recalled that in *At Swim-Two-Birds* Lamont and his friends praise the "pome" for its permanence. In *Mulligan Stew* the critic-and-novelist McCoy arrives at an identical judgement: "there are things in Casey's work that make for what one might, with justice, call permanence" *(MS,* p. 42f.). Probably of greater importance than these references, which have no real artistic consequences for Sorrentino's book, is the striking resemblance in the narrative flow of O'Nolan's *The Third Policeman* and Lamont's absurdist mystery story. *The Third Policeman* begins thus:

> Not everybody knows how I killed old Phillip Mathers, smashing his jaw in with my spade; but first it is better to speak of my friendship with John Divney because it was he who first knocked old Mathers down.[43]

The narrator starts his account *post factum,* and then promises to go backwards in time to explain how he came to murder the old man. Similarly, Martin Halpin begins after he has lodged two bullets in the body of a man called Beaumont, and Halpin, too, promises to tell the whole story by going backwards in time. This is how Halpin begins his story:

> It is I who have killed my best friend and associate, Ned Beaumont, I and no other, no matter what is said later, by me or anyone else *(MS,* p. 294).

Much of the fascination of *The Third Policeman* is due to the weird, amusing theories of the idiot-savant de Selby. Sorrentino has changed the name to Da Salvi, but has retained de Selby's notion that "night is simply an insanitary condition of the atmosphere due to accretions of black air" *(MS,* p. 30). Moreover, he has incorporated a number of grotesque theories that may have come straight out of *The Third Policeman,* or, for that matter, out of Myles na gCopaleen's "Research Bureau", on which O'Nolan rode one of his hobby-horses in his *Cruiskeen*

Lawn columns. Lastly, in *Mulligan Stew*, Sorrentino alludes to Myles's, Keats and Chapman stories: "Keats and Shelly never had any of the conversations that the slanderous Miles [sic] O'Nolan attributes to them" *(MS*, p. 245).

Mulligan Stew is without doubt the most extensive tribute to Brian O'Nolan in a fictional form. This book would like to share its dedication: "to the memory of Brian O'Nolan – his 'virtue *hilaritas*'' '.

PART I

SCENES IN A NOVEL

By Brother Barnabas

(Probably Posthumous)

I am penning these lines, dear reader, under conditions of great emotional stress, being engaged, as I am, in the composition of a posthumous article. The great blots of sweat which gather on my brow are instantly decanted into a big red handkerchief, though I know the practice is ruinous to the complexion, having regard to the open pores and the poisonous vegetable dyes that are used nowadays in the Japanese sweat-shops. By the time these lines are in neat rows of print, with no damn, over-lapping at the edges, the writer will be in Kingdom Come.[1] (see Gaelic quotation in 8-point footnote). I have rented Trotsky's villa in Paris, though there are four defects in the lease (three reckoning by British law) and the drains are – what shall I say? – just a *leetle* bit Gallic. Last week, I set about the melancholy task of selling up my little home. Auction followed auction. Priceless books went for a mere song, and invaluable songs, many of them of my own composition, were ruthlessly exchanged for loads of books. Stomach-pumps and stallions went for next to nothing, whilst my ingenious home-made typewriter, in perfect order except for two faulty characters, was knocked down for four and tuppence. I was finally stripped of all my possessions, except for a few old articles of clothing upon which I had waggishly placed an enormous reserve price. I was in some doubt about a dappled dressing-gown of red fustian, bordered with a pleasing grey piping. I finally decided to present it to the Nation. The Nation, however, acting through one of its accredited Sanitary Inspectors, declined the gift – rather churlishly I thought – and pleading certain statutory prerogatives, caused the thing to be burnt in a yard off Chatham Street within a stone's throw of the house where the Brothers Sheares played their last game of *taiplis*. Think of that! When such things come to pass, as Walt Whitman says, you re-examine philosophies and religions. Suggestions as to compensation were pooh-poohed and sallies were made touching on the compulsory acquisition of slum property. You see? If a great mind is to be rotted or deranged, no meanness or no outrage is too despicable, no maggot of officialdom is too contemptible to perpetrate it ... the ash of my dressing-gown, a sickly wheaten colour, and indeed, the whole incident reminded me forcibly of Carruthers McDaid.[2] Carruthers McDaid is a man I created one night when I had swallowed nine stouts and felt vaguely blasphemous. I gave him a good but worn-out mother and an industrious father, and coolly negativing fifty years of eugenics, made him a worthless scoundrel, a betrayer of women and a secret drinker. He had a sickly wheaten head, the watery blue eyes of the weakling. For if the truth must be told I had started to compose a novel and McDaid was the kernel or the fulcrum of it. Some writers have started with a good and noble hero and traced his weakening, his degradation and his eventual downfall; others have introduced a degenerate villain to be ennobled and uplifted to the tune of twenty-two chapters, usually at the hands of a woman – "She was not beautiful, but a shortened nose, a slightly crooked mouth and eyes that seemed brimful of a simple complexity seemed to spell a curious attraction, an inexplicable charm." In my own case, McDaid, starting off as a rank waster and a rotter, was meant to sink slowly to absolutely the last extremities of human degradation. Nothing, absolutely nothing, was to be too low for him, the wheaten-headed hound ....

I shall never forget the Thursday when the thing happened. I retired to my room at about six o'clock, fortified with a pony of porter and two threepenny cigars, and manfully addressed myself to the achievement of Chapter Five. McDaid, who for a whole week had been living precariously by selling kittens to foolish old ladies and who could be said to be existing on the immoral earnings of his cat, was required to rob a poor-box in a church. But no! Plot or no plot, it was not to be.

"Sorry, old chap," he said, "but I absolutely can't do it."

"What's this, Mac," said I, "getting squeamish in your old age?"

"Not squeamish exactly," he replied, "but I bar poor-boxes. Dammit, you can't call me squeamish. Think of that bedroom business in Chapter Two, you old dog."

"Not another word," said I sternly, "you remember that new shaving brush you bought?"

"Yes."

"Very well, You burst the poor-box or its anthrax in two days."

"But, I say, old chap, that's a bit thick."

"You think so? Well, I'm old-fashioned enough to believe that your opinions don't matter."

We left it at that. Each of us firm, outwardly polite, perhaps, but determined to yield not one tittle of our inalienable rights. It was only afterwards that the whole thing came out. Knowing that he was a dyed-in-the-wool atheist, I had sent him to a revivalist prayer-meeting, purely for the purpose of scoffing and showing the reader the blackness of his soul. It appears that he remained to pray. Two days afterwards I caught him sneaking out to Gardiner Street at seven in the morning. Furthermore, a contribution to the funds of a well-known charity, a matter of four-and-sixpence in the names of Miles Caritatis was not, I understand, unconnected with our proselyte. A character ratting on his creator and exchanging the pre-destined hangman's rope for a halo is something new. It is, however, only one factor in my impending dissolution. Shaun Svoolish, my hero, the composition of whose heroics have cost me many a sleepless day, has formed an alliance with a slavey in Griffith Avenue; and Shiela, his "steady," an exquisite creature I produced for the sole purpose of loving him and becoming his wife, is apparently to be given the air. You see? My carefully thought-out plot is turned inside out and goodness knows where this individualist flummery is going to end. Imagine sitting down to finish a chapter and running bang into an unexplained slavey at the turn of a page! I reproached Shaun, of course.

"Frankly, Shaun," I said, "I don't like it."

"I'm sorry," he said. "My brains, my brawn, my hands, my body are willing to work for you, but the heart! Who shall say yea or nay to the timeless passions of a man's heart? Have you ever been in love? Have you ever —?"

"What about Shiela, you shameless rotter? I gave her

dimples, blue eyes, blond hair and a beautiful soul. The last time she met you, I rigged her out in a blue swagger outfit, brand new. You now throw the whole lot back in my face . . . . Call it cricket if you like, Shaun, but don't expect me to agree."

"I may be a prig," he replied, "but I know what I like. Why can't I marry Bridie and have a shot at the Civil Service?"

"Railway accidents are fortunately rare," I said finally, "but when they happen they are horrible. Think it over."

"You wouldn't dare!"

"O, wouldn't I? Maybe you'd like a new shaving brush as well." And that was that.

Treason is equally widespread among the minor characters. I have been confronted with a Burmese shanachy, two corner-boys, a barmaid and five bus-drivers, none of whom could give a plausible account of their movements. They are evidently "friends" of my characters. The only character to yield me undivided and steadfast allegiance is a drunken hedonist who is destined to be killed with kindness in Chapter Twelve. *And he knows it!* Not that he is any way lacking in cheek, of course. He started nagging me one evening.

"I say, about the dust-jacket —"

"Yes?"

"No damn vulgarity, mind. Something subtle, refined. If the thing was garish or cheap, I'd die of shame."

"Felix," I snapped, "mind your own business."

Just one long round of annoyance and petty persecution. What is troubling me just at the moment, however, is a paper-knife. I introduced it in an early scene to give Father Hennessy something to fiddle with on a parochial call. It is now in the hands of McDaid. It has a dull steel blade, and there is evidently something going on. The book is seething with conspiracy and there have been at least two whispered consultations between all the characters, including two who have not yet been officially created. Posterity taking a hand in the destiny of its ancestors, if you know what I mean. It is too bad. The only objector, I understand, has been Captain Fowler, the drunken hedonist, who insists that there shall be no foul play until Chapter Twelve has been completed; and he has been over-ruled.

Candidly, reader, I fear my number's up.

*

I sit at my window thinking, remembering, dreaming. Soon I go to my room to write. A cool breeze has sprung up from the west, a clean wind that plays on men at work, on boys at play and on women who seek to police the corridors, live in Stephen's Green and feel the heat of buckshee turf....

It is a strange world, but beautiful. How hard it is, the hour of parting. I cannot call in the Guards, for we authors have our foolish pride. The destiny of Brother Barnabas is sealed, sealed for aye.

I must write!

These, dear reader, are my last words. Keep them and cherish them. Never again can you read my deathless prose, for my day that has been a good day is past.

Remember me and pray for me.

Adieu!

From *Comhthrom Féinne*, Vol. XIII, No. 2 (May 1934), pp. 29-30, reprinted in *The Journal of Irish Literature*, III, 1 (January 1974), pp. 14-18.

EXTRACTS FROM BRIAN O'NOLAN'S LETTERS

To A. M. Heath & Co.   3rd Oct., 1938

. . . I have given a lot of thought to the question of a title and think SWEENY IN THE TREES quite suitable. Others that occurred to me were The Next Market Day (verse reference); Sweet-Scented Manuscript; Truth is an Odd Number; Task-Master's Eye; Through an Angel's Eye-lid; and dozens of others.

To A. M. Heath & Co.   19th October, 1938

I'm rather surprised that Longman's don't like the title SWEENY IN THE TREES. It certainly seems preferable to AT SWIM-TWO-BIRDS, which I now like less and less. Surely it is defective from the commercial view-point.

I would be very glad if you could persuade them to part forthwith with the advance. I desire to buy a black hat and other accessories. I suppose you have no information as to when the book is likely to appear.

To Longman's Green & Company, Ltd.   10th November, 1983

I have been thinking over the question of a pen-name and would suggest FLANN O'BRIEN. I think this invention has the advantage that it contains an unusual name and one that is quite ordinary. "Flann" is an old Irish name now rarely heard. I am leaving the title of the book in the hands of your firm. I have not since thought of anything more suitable than the few I communicated through Heaths. I have no objection to "At Swim-

Two-Birds" being retained although I do not fancy it much except as a title for a slim book of poems.

To *The Irish Times*   1st May, 1939

. . . By the way, a friend of mine brought a copy of "At Swim-Two-Birds" to Joyce in Paris recently. Joyce, however, had already read it. Being now nearly blind, he said it took him a week with a magnifying glass and that he had not read a book of any kind for five years, so this may be taken to be a compliment from the fuehrer. He was delighted with it – although he complained that I did not give the reader much of a chance, "Finnegans Wake" in his hand as he spoke – and has promised to push it quietly in his own international Paris sphere...

Joyce was very particular that there should be no question of reproducing his unsolicited testimonial for publicity purposes anywhere and got an undertaking to this effect.

To Ethel Mannin   10th July, 1939

A friend of mine Mr Kevin O'Connor mentioned to me that you might read a book I have written so I have asked the publishers to send you a copy. It is a belly-laugh or high-class literary pretentious slush, depending on how you look at it. Some people say it is harder on the head than the worst whiskey, so do not hesitate to burn the book if you think that's the right thing to do.

To Brian Inglis   17 August, 1960

First, I think I should thank you for publishing that very favourable review of AS2B. It was at least more reasonable than Toynbee's, who I think went off his rocker in the OBSERVER. The book is, of course, juvenile nonsense but I understand that sales are enormous and that it is "going like a bomb".

From "A Sheaf of Letters" ed. Robert Hogan and Gordon Henderson, *The Journal of Irish Literature*, III 1 (January 1974), pp. 67-9, 76.

ON *AT SWIM-TWO-BIRDS*

By Myles na gCopaleen

In the year 1939, a book curiously named AT SWIM-TWO-BIRDS appeared. Adolph Hitler took serious exception to it and in fact loathed it so much that he started World War II in order to torpedo it. In a grim irony that is not without charm, the book survived the war while Hitler did not.

From the *Cruiskeen Lawn* column in the *Irish Times* (4 February 1965); repr. in Anne Clissmann, *Flann O'Brien: A Critical Introduction to His Writing* (Dublin: Gill & Macmillan, 1975), pp. 78f.

A BOOK IN A THOUSAND

By Graham Greene

. . . I read it with continual excitement, amusement and the kind of glee one experiences when people smash china on the stage . . . . It is in the line of *Tristram Shandy* and *Ulysses:* its amazing spirits do not disguise the seriousness of the attempt to present, simultaneously as it were, all the literary traditions of Ireland – the Celtic legend (in the stories of Finn), the popular adventure novels (of a Mr Tracy), the nightmare element as you get it in Joyce, the ardent poetry of Bardic Ireland and the working-class people poetry of the absurd Harry [sic] Casey. On all these the author imposes the unity of his own humorous vigour, and the technique he employs is as efficient as it is original. We have had books inside books before but O'Nolan

takes Pirandello and Gide a long way further: the screw is
turned until you have (a) a book about a man called Trellis
who is, (b) writing a book about certain characters who, (c) are
turning the tables on Trellis by writing about him. It is a wild,
fantastic magnificently comic notion, but looking back
afterwards one realises that by no other method could the
realistic, the legendary, the novelette have been worked in
together . . . .

From the original Longmans jacket of *At Swim-Two-Birds*. The text was
kindly quoted to me by Mr Timothy O'Keeffe of Martin Brian & O'Keeffe
Ltd.

NEST OF NOVELISTS

Mr Flann O'Brien will hardly be surprised if a reviewer is at a
loss how to describe this book of his. No doubt it is to be
described as fiction, though perhaps nothing would be lost if it
is not. Mr O'Brien seems to have attempted two things. First,
he has carried a little farther than others the idea of the novel
within a novel. He presents us with a Dublin student, who is
writing a novel about a Dublin publican, who is writing a
novel about various loungers in his own bar parlour. Either the
student's novel or the publican's is also concerned with
characters taken from the novels of somebody else. The
enthusiastic testimonial quoted on the wrapper says further
that some of the publican's characters are engaged in writing
about the publican, and there is no reason why this should be
questioned. Anyhow, there are two, three or more
manuscripts, fragments of which are interlarded with the
spoken or written comments of the student upon them, the
fruit of researches which have not yet been incorporated into
one or other of the manuscripts.

This is not all. Mr O'Brien's second purpose is to provide
stylist samples of every Irish literary tradition. Accordingly
there are sections of *At Swim-Two-Birds* which reproduce Celtic
myth and legend in prose and in verse, other sections given up
to the Irish adventure story, odds and ends of Irish proletarian

doggerel and a fragment modelled on the *Walpurgisnacht* manner of Mr Joyce. It is all as clever as paint and by no means without interest, more particularly for the reader with an inside knowledge of Irish literary controversies at the present time. Mr O'Brien has clearly a taste for, among other things, the recondite, and he offers a miscellany of scraps of out-of-the-way information. Probaby the richest part of the book is concerned with the travels of the Pooka MacPhellimey, though the best judge in these matters would be a devotee of the literature of fairy twilight and leprechauns. Altogether this is something of a *tour de force,* in which the only exceptionable thing is a schoolboy brand of mild vulgarity. Whether Mr O'Brien has achieved what he set out to achieve it is difficult to say. At the beginning his preoccupation seems to have been with the proper material and method of the modern novel, and possibly this stayed with him as he proceeded to write. At any rate, having all but exhausted, with the exercise of much ingenuity, the subject of Irish content and Irish style, will he not now sit down and try his hand at writing an Irish novel?

From the *Times Literary Supplement* (18 March 1939).

RIGHT PROPORTIONS

By Frank Swinnerton

I see that *At Swim-Two-Birds* has been compared to *Tristram Shandy* and *Ulysses.* It is not equal to either. It reads as if it were the work of an Irish undergraduate, familiar, indeed, with those books and others of recent appearance, but uncertain of anything except his own humour and his wish to produce a work of fiction. So we have the author writing rather pompously, in the following style:

> The subject-matter of the dialogue in question was concerned (as may be inferred) with the turpitude and moral weakness of Mr Furriskey. It was pointed out to him by the voice that he was by vocation a voluptuary concerned

only with the ravishing and destruction of the fair sex. His habits and physical attributes were explained to him in some detail. It was stated, for example, that his drinking capacity, speaking roughly and making allowance for discrepancies in strength as between the products of various houses, was six bottles of stout; and that any quantity taken in excess of such six bottles would not be retained. At the conclusion of the interview, the voice administered a number of stern warnings as to the penalties which would befall him should he deviate, even in the secrecy of his own thought, from his mission of debauchery.

Within the novel as so written are, first, some tales and poems in the manner of the old Irish, an amusing fantasy recalling Mr James Stephens (it is the best thing in the book), the account of a novel written by an imagined character whose life is largely spent in bed and whose inventions are thereby freed for a life of their own, the account of the punishment planned for him by these inventions, extracts from various old books, and a good deal of talk which I tried to think funny but which I found in fact rather gaseous. Mr O'Brien has plenty of words, and writes with an immense sense of sportiveness. I did not notice, however, that he had a single original idea to express; and I should reluctantly put him among the bores.

From *The Observer* (19 March 1939).

INSPIRED NONSENSE

by Anthony West

At Swim-Two-Birds is a self-conscious work heavily under the influence of Joyce. Long passages in imitation of Joycean parody of early Irish epic are devastatingly dull, passages slavishly following Joyce's love of snotgreen squalor are worse still. But for each one of these there are two or three that are very funny and very good reading. The main story, out of a crowd which the author has not bothered to tie up with any great care, is about an author who is writing a Zolaesque novel. He stays with his characters in a public house and has great difficulty in keeping them in order; they realise he is writing a book about them and they become determined to avoid the sticky ends to which his plot will bring them, so they club together to write a book about the author which will bring him to a sticky end before the he finishes them off. It is inspired nonsense that makes one laugh a great deal; it carries on another level a good deal of witty and intelligent criticism of the structure of novel that gives one pleasure of another sort.

From 'New Novels', *The New Statesman and Nation* (17 June 1939).

STRUTS AND PROPS

This book is mostly fantasy, with a basis of realism, which is also shot through with a curious freakish whimsy. Its construction is most unusual, apparently meaningless, almost chaotic and in the hands of a less deft writer would be dreadful. But Mr O'Brien has the knack of inveigling even a stick with fantasy, and so it happens that the absurd struts and props of his literary construction help rather than hinder his mirage of the bizarre, and for all its incomprehensibility the thing runs free and easily and with a distinctive life of its own. There is nothing here for lovers of the conventional or classical. But for all who think and dream a little out of normal focus it holds a wealth of surprise and delight. For his flags of fancy fly cheerfuly from beginning to end.

The title gives no indication or clue as to the author's intentions. He mentions it on page 95. It is "the church of Snamh-da-en (or Swim-Two-Birds) by the side of the Shannon." That is all – whether real or fictitious is not mentioned, and it is the only help we get from him.

There are episodes that flow with fluency and freedom, one of the best concerned with mad King Sweeney's wanderings through Erin, with its delicious and entirely unoffensive satire of Celtic folk tales – or what one of the characters in the book calls "the real old stuff of the native land." Some of his characters are elusive and impalpable, but others stand out with the vivid intensity of unmistakable magic. One of his most enchantingly capricious conceptions is the conventionally named "Good Fairy," who is a voice only, but a voice "sweeter by far than the tinkle and clap of a waterfall and brighter than the first shaft of day." But it is only the tone of the voice that is suave, for the contents of the conversation is startling, entertaining, malicious, and the personality vivid as lightning.

Though *At Swim-Two-Birds* is externally incoherent it is fundamentally held together in essence by a pervading atmosphere, and it is the accomplishment of this on the part of the author that makes it such a remarkable literary feat. For his charm is irresistible and makes itself felt even in places that seem somewhat silly, affected or offensive. And it may be in the reconcilement of the opposing factors of fantasy and realism in his own mind that the mystery of his writing finds its flight.

From *The Dublin Magazine*, XIV, 3 (July-September 1939), pp. 102f..

THE USE OF JOYCE

By John Coleman

The reissued *At Swim-Two-Birds* defies classification. It might be described as an extremely funny one-man symposium on Irish literature. It shows as one of the very, very few books to have successfully drawn some kind of inspiration from *Ulysses*. And it's the first work I've found that gives any meaning whatsoever to that fashionable label, the 'anti-novel.' For, when Mr Flann O'Brien (a pseudonym, apparently, for a Mr Brian Nolan: I hadn't heard of either before) wrote this remarkably original farce over twenty years ago, he seems to have been out to destroy our conventional expectations of fiction with every weapon to hand. And Joyce was to hand.

His student-narrator, a sort of spoof-Dedalus, much given to drowsy meditation in his bedroom and to alcoholic sorties with low companions, is writing a novel about one Trellis, who is in turn writing a novel about a group of improbable characters (lifted from Tracy, another novelist), and these in turn revolt and compose several chapters about Trellis, drugged asleep, in an attempt to kill him off. There might be symbolism and to spare, here, but one doesn't feel Mr O'Brien's heart is really in that. In ways too devious to report, he further enlivens all this with some disturbingly accurate pastiches of bardic lays, Celtic legend . . ., and popular blood-and-thunder – as well as a superb account of the Pooka MacPhellimey ('a member of the devil class') and his disputations with the Good Fairy. There are cowboys, a working-class poet (with poems), and a court scene of nightmare illegality. Notoriously, Irish humour has its black, satiric aspects. Swift came down on the side of his abstract Houyhnhnms; and somewhere in the distances that both Joyce and Beckett set between themselves and their matter, with all that arrogant erudition playing over bawdry and squalor, a positive distaste for life as a state – and not just for some particular manifestation of it – is communicated. Mr O'Brien just misses this by holding resolutely to his norm of fantasy: the Augustan periphrasis and earthy deflations, the mock-scholastic debate of *At Swim-Two-Birds* result in something peculiarly wild and sweet. Only the prolonged pains inflicted on Trellis at the end begin to move out of comedy on to uglier ground.

From *The Spectator* (22 July 1960).

A COMIC HEIR OF JAMES JOYCE

By Philip Toynbee

This extraordinary book was first published in 1939, and what is no less extraordinary is that it should have received so little attention at the time. (In this newspaper Mr Frank Swinnerton dismissed it as "pompous", "gaseous" and "boring.") Its resurrection is timely. The author's real name is Brian Nolan, and he is a distinguished Dublin journalist who has also written books in Irish. Joyce described him as "a real writer with the true comic spirit."

Mr Graham Greene has endorsed and expanded this enthusiasm and has spoken of *At Swim-Two Birds* as "a book in a thousand." He goes on to describe it in terms of such succinct accuracy that I shall take the easy option of quoting his words. (Confronted with this unclassifiable and elusive document reviewers will be alert for easy options.):

> We have had books inside books before now (writes Mr Greene) and characters who are given life outside their fiction, but O'Brien takes Pirandello and Gide a long way further; the screw is turned until you have (a) the narrator writing a book about a man called Trellis who is, (b) writing a book about certain characters who (c) are turning the tables by writing about him.

But these comic devices would be nothing by themselves. What Mr O'Brien seems to have set out to do is to adapt and extend the parodical method which Joyce used so freely throughout *Ulysses*. I can detect no section or fragment of the book which is not a partial and entirely conscious parody of some previous style in verse or prose. The narrator, idle but inventive student, periodically describes his own life in a mixture of grotesquely pompous journalese and that pseudo-scientific pedanticism which Joyce had used in the question-and-answer section of *Ulysses*. Into the book which the narrator is writing appear, at one or more removes from the account of his own life, parodies of the Finn legends and of the ancient poetry of Bardic Ireland; parodies of working-class poetry and heroic couplets; parodies of popular adventure novels, popular scientific manuals and contemporary realism. There are certainly other elements which I have failed to notice, but it might be added that the whole plan of the book is a parody of conventional fiction – or at least a deliberate assault on its methods.

But *At Swim-Two-Birds* is more than an ingenious piece of destructive fun: it is the question of how much more which is likely to divide critics. It is more, I would say, because the language itself is more than parody, although it is never without an element of parody. There is that exuberant personal inventiveness for which the Irish and the Welsh have long been famous or notorious. There is a plangent eloquence which is also associated with a peculiarly Celtic inspiration. What is needed to explain all this is 2,000 words of quotation. Less than that will be misleading, for it is Mr O'Brien's legitimate pride that he can alter his manner to suit his material. Yet there is a dominant manner, and the following quotation at least has the merit of marking a transition from the dominant to one of the subordinates:

> I put the letter with care into a pocket at my right buttock and went to the tender trestle of my bed, arranging my back upon it in an indolent horizontal attitude. I closed my eyes, hurting slightly my right stye, and retired into the kingdom of my mind. For a time there was complete darkness and an absence of movement on the part of the cerebral mechanism. The bright square of the window was faintly evidenced at the juncture of my lids. One book, one opening, was a principle with which I did not find it possible to concur. After an interval Finn MacCool, a hero of old Ireland, came out before me from his shadow. Finn, the wide-hammed, the heavy-eyed, Finn that could spend a Lammas morning with girdled girls at far-from-simple chess-play.

*

Mr Greene mentions *Tristram Shandy,* and to this I would add *Gargantua and Pantagruel.* The book is Rabelaisian in the literal sense, as well as being mildly so in the popular sense. It seems undeniable to me that it is a very funny book indeed; that it is full of magnificently extravagant passages of writing and that the underlying idea – the rebellion of characters against their creator – is full of rich comic possibilities which Mr O'Brien has generously exploited. If I were cultural dictator of England – and I would like to be that for a period of six weeks – I would make *At Swim-Two-Birds* compulsory reading at all our universities. I infinitely prefer this version of the student imagination to those with which the last decade has made us so wearily familiar. Mr O'Brien is at least as funny as Mr Amis, which is saying a lot, and he was not restrained, twenty-one years ago, by the cultivated drabness of language and imagination which the School of Amis has inflicted on us for so many years.

*

But the book has its faults. I was heartily bored, after a page or two, by the Finn MacCool passages, which are also the most pretentious passages. Mr O'Brien had not at this time acquired the gift of knowing when to stop. We often receive the impact of his jokes in a line or two only to find that he intends to continue them for several pages. There is a good deal of Irish boloney scattered through these pages, and it is not enough that this is often turned against itself. There is too much horseplay, and too much ingenuity for its own sake.

Yet this book shows us that there is more than one way of being heavily in debt to Joyce. Most of his imitators chose to make use of the interior monologue, which was perhaps the least rewarding, as well as being the least original of Joyce's methods. Mr O'Brien preferred to exploit the extravagant humour in *Ulysses*, and he learned his lesson well. Without *Ulysses* this book would have been scarcely conceivable; but this doesn't mean that it is imitative in any pejorative sense. Like a character in his book Mr O'Brien was born to his creator at the age of twenty-five. Sired by Joyce he emerged fully grown as a writer. He might perhaps be described as the sunny younger brother of the Cimmerian Mr Beckett.

From *The Observer* (24 July 1960).

THE SADDEST BOOK EVER TO COME OUT OF IRELAND

By John Jordan

The literary reputation of Mr Brian Nolan (or is it O'Nolan?) as distinct from any legendary accretions – for like the other few men of distinction who live most of the time in Dublin, he is the victim of popular myth-mongering – is based chiefly on the following work: in Irish, *An Béal Bocht,* which is hard to classify, in Irish and English his contributions to *The Irish Times* for which he uses a splendidly traditional pen-name "Myles na gCopaleen" (see Gerald Griffin's *The Collegians* and Boucicault's masterpiece *The Colleen Bawn)* and which are even harder to classify; and in English, and quite unclassifiable, *At Swim-Two-Birds,* now republished on its twenty-first birthday (MacGibbon and Kee 21/-).

There are also several minor works including the play *Faustus Kelly* and a rewarding anecdote called "The Martyr's Crown" published originally in *Envoy.* But the above works are Mr Nolan's chief call on our attention.

AN BÉAL BOCHT

I have often been asked by members of that large and motley crew who affect disdain for the Irish language why, if it's so good, so acute etc., *An Béal Bocht* has not been translated. The answer is simple. It is a bookish book. Appreciation of it requires some familiarity with the spate of autobiographical treatises which form a very large part of the literature produced by the movement for the revival and preservation of the Irish language. Some of these books have literary merit, some have not. Even the best are a bit dubious.

To savour *An Béal Bocht* you need to have savoured the threnodic and complacent elements of say, *Peig* or *An t-Oileánach* and perceived that they can harden into cliché.

I've called it "bookish" but then Mr Nolan is a very "bookish" man. He once called himself, in his horse-dealer's capacity, (see Griffin's *The Collegians)* a "spoiled Proust." He might more properly be called (I'm not up to an equivalent splendour in punning) a foiled scholar. Every other day in *The Irish Times* he demands from his readers a range of literary and historical reference not unlike that required by the more allusive kind of academic. He also requires some knowledge of Latin, Irish and the major European tongues. What then does he *do* in *The Irish Times?* This is best answered perhaps by considering the *persona,* not always *grata* of "Myles na gCopaleen."

MYLES MYTHOLOGY

First of all, this individual seems to live in Santry. He has a house there, a housekeeper and a well-stocked cellar. Though he is of extreme age and often incapacitated, these disabilities are offset by the possession of gifts normally attributed to Merlin (and to others less and more respectable). He has a bird's-eye view of everything that's going on everywhere. This faculty is accompanied by the gift of multi-location.

HIS 'PLAIN PEOPLE'

How, and for what purpose does he employ these gifts? Well they enable him to send out bulletins to the Plain People of Ireland (one of his few weaknesses) on every conceivable (or printable) subject at home or abroad, and to direct their wandering attention to folly in high places, local or universal codology, cant (in Dr Johnson's sense), mis-prints, mis-translations, mis-appropriations, and many other serious things in which the Plain People have not the slightest interest.

Why does he undertake this most thankless of tasks? For it would seem that he would be happier with his buddies Keats and Chapman, of whom he occasionally records charming anecdotes and *boutades*.

NO MARTYRS

I think the answer to this final question is that the creator of "Myles", Mr Nolan, as well as being a foiled scholar, is a spiritual disciple of Savonarola, diverted from martyrdom by two facts: (a) martyrs, unless political, are out of fashion in Ireland (b) no-one takes him seriously. He might do better in Russia, or even in America. Even as the bard of the strange and complex workings of the Dublin Mind, he is largely underestimated.

"Did you read Myles this mornin?" "God yes, he's a gas man."

A MISSION

To be a little graver, it seems to me that behind the gCopaleen mission of bad tidings, there is a genuinely sombre, even bitter, mind, and that to call him a "humourist" thus placing him in the category of D. B. Wyndham Lewis or J. B. Morton, is both insulting and foolish.

SADDEST BOOK EVER

And perhaps that mind is at its most melancholy in the book I'm supposed to be reviewing, *At Swim-Two-Birds.* Of course it is a very funny book, and technically a tower of strength. Of course it is linguistically a triumph. But whether or not he intended it to be so, it is one of the saddest books ever to come out of Ireland.

Consider the narrator. This is a young student in his final year at an easily identifiable "College." The greater part of his time is spent either in bed or in some easily identifiable pubs. He lodges with his uncle, a brilliantly realised figure of unimpeachable authenticity. He is writing a book about a publican (who spends even more time in bed) who himself is writing a book about a marvellous collection of Dublin Men (and others), who come alive while he is sleeping and write a book about him (the publican). I haven't the space to examine the virtuosity of execution in this complicated scheme.

What strikes me as important is the way in which so cerebral a plot seems to figure the exact mental condition of the narrator. It is the kind of plot we might expect from Oblomov, that character of Goncharov who, it will be remembered, spent his life in bed until overtaken by nothing more dignified than ejection and a pathetic end.

And the narrator himself might well stand for a symbol of the terrible Irish vices of talking and not doing, of planning and not completing, of scoffing and not contributing, of dreaming, dreaming, dreaming. This boy is better evidence than any actual data why Joyce found it necessary to leave Dublin, and his creator has invested him with the tragic significance of the Irish intellectual, of every age group and every degree of talent, who fails to fight off lethargy and canalize bitterness into creation.

SADISTIC INTENSITY

I have touched only on one aspect of the book, and on that one in particular because it is likely to be over-looked. But on the symbolic level, the book is immeasurably rich. For instance, the fate allotted to the publican Trellis by his characters, while verbally very funny, is in fact peculiarly horrible in its brutality and sadistic intensity: here we might see a fable of the fate of Irish writers in their own country. And in Mr Nolan's use of the story of Mad Sweeny, we might see a parable of the relationship in Ireland between the writer and the Church.

But *At Swim-Two-Birds* is the kind of book in which it is possible for each reader to find his own level and I would not deny that there are many passages which are quite crazily funny. Mr Nolan knows, to every inflection and turn of phrase, the idiom of spoken English in Dublin and in that, and in his linguistic virtuosity, he is the only true heir of Joyce. "Tell me, do you ever open a book at all?" is the recurrent question of the student-narrator's uncle. All our young men should open *At Swim-Two-Birds*, and it would not do some of the older ones any harm to re-open it.

From *Hibernia* (5 August 1960).

DEATH OF FINN

By V. S. Pritchett

This brilliant and wicked book was first published in 1939, a bad year for originality and laughter. In spite of praise from James Joyce – who was parodied in it – and Mr Graham Greene, and from the best critics, it reached only a small public. Let us hope the prospects are brighter now, for Mr O'Brien's is one of the funniest "novels" to come out of Ireland. To describe it is difficult. One could say that the author designed to reduce the total Irish literary tradition to farce and to make hay of the modern novel, but his irreverence is not journalistic. The book is not a skit. It is scholarly, vigorous and creative. The narrator is a slothful, verminous and drunken Dublin student who deceives his pious uncle and, while supposedly reading for his exams, is either fast asleep or working out a destructive theory of the novel. By now novelists merely copy one another. The only intellectually respectable thing to do is to pot, pillage, rearrange and summarise available literature and its techniques. But while he is writing a novel about a novelist called Trellis, the characters of Trellis's book – maimed by inadequate treatment – avenge themselves on their author by making up a grotesque yarn about him.

That is the ballast of the book; it hardly keeps on an even keel, but at any rate, it rolls along comically half-capsized; in its course, it picks up a lot of Joyce, breaks into Celtic legend – Finn MacCool – Bardic exercises, Irish realism and Wild West yarning and fills up with the conceits, fantasies and enormities of talk in lecture halls, Law Courts and Dublin pubs. If Mr O'Brien had waited ten years he could have taken Beckett on board and so reduced a whole tradition to laughter. But, as I say, Mr O'Brien is not out to kill a culture; by his vitality and impudence he adds to it. Even Finn MacCool, whose adventures get rather boring, can be seen bombinating again as a grotesque:

> Three fifties of fosterlings could engage with a handball against the wideness of his backside, which was wide enough to halt the march of warriors through a mountain pass.

And if Finn palls, he is splendid taken a page at a time.

Mr O'Brien's gifts are startling and heartless. He has the astounding Irish genius for describing the human animal, its shameless and dilapidated body, its touching and proliferating fancy, its terrible interest in useless conundrums. On top of this he has an extraordinary freedom of the English language, perhaps because the Elizabethan tradition has survived in Ireland. His people are either seedy Dubliners or ludicrous giants, but their wits are alight; they live in language, in comic image, rather than in life. It looks as though his idea was to knock the regionalism out of Irish literature by magnifying it. Since Joyce, the nose-picking, truculent porter-and-Guinness-swilling Dublin student has been an established figure in Irish literature, pre-dating our own post-war Jimmies and resembling, in their unemployable way, the over-educated rogues of the Elizabethan universities and the picaros of Salamanca.

The sloth of Mr O'Brien's sulky, superior narrator who, despite his beatnik behaviour, triumphs with cynical ease in his examinations at the end, is an enjoyable quality. I became tired of the joke only when Mr Trellis's characters started writing about him, simply because of the excess. This kind of fantasy is apt to be self-destructive. But I shall often return to

Mr O'Brien's diverting brainstorm and shall often brood about one of his deluded characters who feared to sit down because he imagined his bottom was made of glass.

From *The New Statesman* (20 August 1960).

IRELAND'S GREAT CYCLIST

By Timothy Hilton

Brian O'Nolan, alias Flann O'Brien (for novels), alias Myles na gCopaleen (in his newspaper column) died in Dublin on April Fools' Day last year. Universally mourned in the city he had delighted for so long, his death went almost unremarked in England or anywhere else. Like his life; few people outside Ireland have ever heard of his work. Astonishingly, *At Swim-Two-Birds*, the most purely comic book of this century, remained out of print for years. It gained itself only a very limited circulation when rescued in 1960; and its latest edition as a Penguin Modern Classic carries a biographical blurb that is full of errors. *At Swim-Two-Birds* has been one of those books doomed to an underground existence, with treasured copies lent only to trusted friends (much the same thing, apparently, happened to *Murphy*). It remains the property of isolated bunches of cognoscenti. They hold readings from it round kitchen tables. They huddle giggling, in the corners of bars. They – quite literally – know extensive passages by heart, and use it for hours of jesting . . . .

Literary historians will no doubt examine all those pieces, (the articles he wrote as "Myles na gCopaleen" for the *The Irish Times*), and note that beneath the fun is that quality of desperation that often goes with the most devoted punsters, that the nonsense is often the thin ice above despair, that the methods of his humour have their prototypes, if not their origins in the macabre Irish humour of the sheela-na-gig, the violence, fantasy, and grotesquerie of Swift *et al*. One sees this most clearly in a book like *At Swim-Two-Birds*, part of whose subject is the Irish literary tradition. It's a mistake to think of it as an amiable book, or a romp, but an easy mistake to make because one is so likely to skip its Irish epic parts. 'It is Caolcrodha MacMorna from Sliabh Riabhach, said Conan, it is Calecroe MacMorney from Baltinglass.' We read that, see what's coming, and over go the pages to the next easy bit. But the way that the legend of the mad King Sweeny is recounted is the pith of the book. In that he seems to be alive at the end, he is the novel's one great exemplar of its much-discussed 'aestho-autogamy', holding together the real and the fantastic, cementing different levels of its structure. He is from the medieval Irish *Buile Suibhne*, a document unparalleled for the vicious oddity of its hero's mishaps, a frenzied king forced to live up trees, naked, pierced with thorns, snow packing his wounds, subsisting on watercress and milk from heel-holes in cow-dung, duped by a loud-snoring miller, forever hounded by an abbot, by hags and goblins. Luckily, he can fly. The point about these frightful privations is that they're all terribly funny, O'Brien's sense of humour is a sharp instrument; it penetrates the myth, its inexplicable and implacable violence and desolation, leaves it intact and makes it comic. His translations from Sweeny's lamenting poems are brilliant, transfixed. They are chill, pared, and with just that clipped quality that one immediately recognises as belonging to old British and Celtic epic poetry:

> Sweeny the thin-groined it is
> in the middle of the yew;
> life is very bare here
> piteous Christ it is cheerless.

That is funny, but it is a truthful rendering, not a parody. For in that myth, and at its purest in the poems which form part of it, O'Brien hit on precisely the subject of his best, early work, a strange union of laughter with beauty and pain.

From *The New Statesman* (8 December 1967).

THE HERO AT HOME IN THE STREETS
OF DUBLIN

By Benedict Kiely

The summarising of such a book [*At Swim-Two-Birds*] is very nearly as thankless a task as that undertaken by the two zealous Americans, Joseph Campbell and Henry Morton Robinson, in their attempt to write a précis of *Finnegans Wake* [*A Skeleton Key to Finnegans Wake* (London, 1947)]; and indeed Flann O'Brien's book could be portion of an answer to the argument that James Joyce drove the European novel into a *cul-de-sac*. Not only the dream-sequences of Joyce, but the tricks of Sterne, the visions and stories of the ancient Gaelic World and the humours and fantasies of modern Ireland, and the theories of Luigi Pirandello have been used in *At Swim-Two-Birds* by a very original genius. The hero that O'Grady saw haloed in light is here as comic as he can be in bawdy tales still told by Gaelic-speaking people. Even if O'Grady had had access to those tales it is unlikely that his mood would have allowed him to sketch Fionn MacCool in this way: "Fionn MacCool was a legendary hero of old Ireland. Though not mentally robust, he was a man of superb physique and development. Each of his thighs was as thick as a horse's belly, narrowing to a calf as thick as the belly of a foal. Three fifties of fosterlings could engage with handball against the wideness of his backside, which was large enough to halt the march of men through a mountain pass." All around this figure of fun circle drunken undergraduates and Dublin jocksers, domestic servants, policeman, Gaelic Leaguers, devils and good fairies. Seventy years after O'Grady's *Bardic History* the hero has been made at home in the streets of Dublin.

Benedict Kiely, *Modern Irish Fiction: A Critique* (Dublin: Golden Eagle Books Ltd., 1950), pp. 76f.

PART II

THE THREE FACES OF BRIAN NOLAN

By Bernard Benstock

"No man, said the Nolan, can be a lover of the true or the good unless he abhors the multitude; and the artist, though he may employ the crowd, is very careful to isolate himself."[1] The Nolan paraphrased here is of course Bruno of Nola (not Brian O'Nolan), the Nolan pressed into service by the young James Joyce to expound in "The Day of the Rabblement" the Flaubertian creed of the consummate artist. For the succeeding forty years Joyce remained diligently loyal to that creed, flying by nets, and practicing articulate silence, self-imposed exile, and inverse-jesuitical cunning. The same cannot be said of Brian Nolan (or O'Nolan, as he later acknowledged himself), the one Irish writer of the generation following Joyce's who in many ways most resembled a disciple of Joyce. Born in 1911, O'Nolan came of age as a writer in the thirties, when Joyce was already too old to learn anything from him.

In most ways O'Nolan was his own man, or more precisely three men divided against themselves. A hard drinker and Dublin pub wit, he was consubstantially closer to his journalistic self, the Myles na gCopaleen of the *Irish Times*, than he was to his artistic self, the Flann O'Brien who produced his literary masterpiece *At Swim-Two-Birds* in 1939, the year Joyce published *Finnegans Wake*. Neither of these two books, Joyce's last and O'Brien's first, received at the time the critical attention it deserved (it has become habitual for critics to blame the war, but the fault lies in both cases with the critics). The death which soon after claimed James Joyce had its counterpart in the twenty-year suppression of the talented Flann by the irrepressible Myles. (Unless of course we find that Ireland was to blame).

The delightful excellence of *At Swim-Two-Birds* (re-issued in London in 1960 by MacGibbon and Kee and published in the United States in 1967 by Viking Compass Books) has withstood the test of time, the shortsightedness of critics, its own limited Irishness and wild obscurities, as well as the kiss of death of being credited as a Joycean imitation. To praise *At Swim-Two-Birds* is not sufficient: to appraise it is no easy matter. John Wain recently attempted to do both,[2] and although his welcome tribute does much to assure us that Flann O'Brien really did exist and is not just a figment of some Pooka's Celtic imagination, he managed to do little more than offer a plot summary and copious excerpts. Nor did his sporadic indications of Joycean influence[3] contribute much more: What is significant about the novel is O'Brien's inventiveness, his refreshing originality. Had the book appeared a year later, after the availability of the complete *Wake,* we would have been saddled with the necessity of either proving or delimiting Joyce's influence, but as it stands, with only fragments and set-pieces from *Work in Progress* in print at the time O'Brien was at work, it is something other than direct influence that is primary – it is a shared background, an environment in common to an unusual degree. Joyce and O'Nolan were Irish-Catholic, Irish *and* Catholic, to an extent unique among twentieth-century writers. Both exploited their conditions as educated members of the Dulbin Catholic bourgeoisie, and as much as they rebelled in their individual ways against the limitations of religion and class, both knew enough to make capital of their circumstances.

Wain has as much difficulty placing O'Nolan's "Catholicism" as a generation of earlier critics have had with Joyce's. O'Nolan's position as such is both complicated and simplified by the non-existence of any evidence of a rebellion against the Church. There is no protestation of apostasy available in print, no autobiographical statements of complex personal ambivalence, and no semi-autobiographic character accused of having a "cursed jesuit strain . . . injected the wrong way." Wain contents that "O'Brien, whether or not he was a Catholic, *croyant et practiquant,* was deeply interested in Catholic doctrine and church organisation." This is surely the most important observation. The O'Brien canon, like Joyce's, is supersaturated with Catholic theology, with a fascination for a history of heresies (some as yet untried), and with a particular preoccupation with the Jesuits. The literary result borders on travesty: In *At Swim-Two-Birds* saints Ronan and Moling pronounce curses with gusto, advocating multiple tortures for those who crossed them; but it is not until the two later novels, *The Hard Life* (1961) and *The Dalkey Archive* (1964), that Catholicism figures so importantly. (Both novels were published in London by MacGibbon and Kee. *The Hard Life* was published in the United States by Pantheon and *The Dalkey Archive* by Macmillan.) In the first Mr Collopy spends his evenings with a German Jesuit named Father Kurt Fahrt, attempting to get a rise out of him by maliciously maligning the Society of Jesus, and a Jesuit-arranged audience with the Pope results in an angry denunciation of Collopy and Father Fahrt by the Holy Father. In the other book a demonic physicist with theological pretensions conjures up Saint Augustine and other Church Fathers (they are all distinct disappointments under cross-examination); one character named Hackett is attempting to rehabilitate Judas Iscariot, and another named James Joyce is attempting to infiltrate the Society of Jesus in order to exorcise the Holy Ghost out of the Trinity. Yet where does Flann O'Brien (or Brian O'Nolan) stand in relation to these burlesques of Catholic matters? His hands are clean and he is paring his fingernails, nicely refined out of existence, having opted for the authorial prerogative of remaining non-committal.

It is the serious lack of commitment in any direction that limits Brian O'Nolan and ensnares him with the second rank, below Joyce and Yeats and Seán O'Casey – nor does the reader find the sort of sincere despair to which Samuel Beckett is so vitally committed that he can find no other commitment. There is little chance of discerning where O'Nolan stands in regard to the Church or to Ireland or to the social conditions in which his characters find themselves. Outside the realistic tradition of the novel, and with no directed satirical thrust to his brand of fantasy, he relies exclusively upon irony – an irony without a center of gravity – for his dominant tone. His people bear the burden of their own convictions: It is Mr Collopy who chances an attack of Jesuits, and Father Fahrt who undertakes to counter his allegations. And neither of the combatants wins a decisive victory. Collopy is well-grounded in his facts, but these are all past history; nor does he ever become the kind of person who can positively enlist the reader's sympathy or regard. The Jesuit priest, on the other hand, permits himself the luxury of personal irritation in his attempt to cut Gordian knots with his annoyance. We can neither condemn the Pope for his anger and amazement at having the issue of public conveniences for women made the subject of a papal audience, nor can we credit him with handling the bizarre Collopy with tact or even bemusement. In the final analysis Flann O'Brien's fictional characters live self-contained existences in a fictional world which bears interesting resemblances to the real world of Brian O'Nolan's life, but without actually enlisting their author in their problems or becoming involved with concerns which may have been his.

Crediting O'Nolan with being a Catholic writer is as exact as crediting Joyce. Both have Catholic backgrounds and are immersed in Catholicism, but what must be considered are O'Nolan's religious attitudes, and as a Catholic novelist he betrays none. In fact, a ball of malt or a pint of plain porter takes on the proportions of a creed in the Flann O'Brien books. This in itself does not imply a moral judgment; it is merely an observation of attitudes beginning with the witty mock-caveat found early in the first novel, where the protagonist reports that "innumerable persons with whom I had conversed had represented to me that spirituous liquors and intoxicants generally had an adverse effect of the senses and the body and those who became addicted to stimulants in youth were unhappy throughout their lives and met with death at the end of a drunkard's fall, expiring ingloriously at the stair-bottom in a welter of blood and puke."

Needless to report that the protagonist pays little heed to such self-admonitions, and the book's progress is his own rakish acceptance of Kelly's invitation into a pub, and the warning itself, originally credited to "innumerable persons," leads into an absurd tract on the subject issued by the Christian Brothers. The hero of *At Swim-Two-Birds* makes the effortless transition from the safely warned to the casual habitué of the public house, without any noticeably deleterious effects. In *The Hard Life* his counterpart is young Finbarr, whose older brother Manus evolves into a hard drinker, a process that keeps step with his shady business successes; by novel's end Manus has weaned Finbarr away from half-pints to whiskeys: "In a daze I lifed my own glass," Finbarr narrates, "and without knowing what I was doing did exactly what the brother did, drained the glass in one vast swallow. Then I walked quickly but did not run to the lavatory. There, everything inside me came up in a tidal surge of vomit." This is Finbarr's rite of initiation into manhood, the "hard life" (but there is something of a suggestion that for him it will not necessarily be the callous one of Manus's cut-throat mercantilism). The "blood and puke" of the initial caveat represent the ritualistic elements of the religion of drink, although for Flann O'Brien there is rarely any blood: Vomit is as close to reality as he allows for his fiction, the comic aspect remaining predominant. This is not only the condition that the author places upon his material, but it is also his strongest asset as a writer, his ability to create a perfect, ludicrous vignette which capsulizes the events of the narrative. When the drunken Kelly is stopped by the expounding Rousseau enthusiast, he "made a low noise and opened his mouth and covered the small man from shoulder to knee with a coating of unpleasant buff-coloured puke."

Like religion, drinking can lead to excess, a fanatical complement to its more basic components. But it seems to surpass religion in Flann O'Brien's Ireland by succeeding where religion fails, in bringing together in a state of harmonious grace diverse individuals – often when fractious religions dispute tends to set them at each other's throat instead. The debates between such friends as Mr Collopy and Father Fahrt threaten to erupt into genuine animosity, except that Collopy's handy crock of Kilbeggan whiskey is always at hand. What rescues such set-pieces from becoming digressions of unrelated colloquy is the manner in which the antagonists immediately drop their quarrel or any semblance of anger for the libation ceremony. As in a slapstick film all action stops momentarily while the contestants step out of character for the pleasant lull of filling glasses and exchanging concomitant small talk: "You're annoying me, Collopy," says the Jesuit, and in the next breath he adds. "Here, play with this glass," requesting a refill. After another round of friction they join in a toast to the Society of Jesus, and the controversy commences immediately after. Religion does not bring these two Catholics, lay and clerical, together – the whiskey does that.

In *The Dalkey Archive* it assumes almost total control. De Selby's plan to exterminate the human race is placidly accepted by Mick Shaughnessy because he is in the process of downing glass after glass of De Selby's excellent whiskey. For Mick to deny the insane scheme to reverse the process of time would in effect deny the existence of the week-old whiskey that De Selby has manufactured and is now dispensing, and both the heavy-drinking Hackett (a Kelly-Manus continuation) and the more moderate Mick are loathe to shatter the pleasant social interaction cemented by the miraculous liquor. In order to be able to plan a counter-attack against De Selby, it becomes important for Mick to refuse the next morning's invitation to a whiskey breakfast. This resolution becomes so fixed in his mind with sobriety and self-denial that Mick links his counterplan for foiling De Selby with a determination to abstain from whiskey and to enter a Trappist monastery – and thus abstain from conversation. The constant barrage of theological dispute is mere digression compared to Mick's determined effort against whiskey – the central thread of the novel.

Again it is an element of Flann O'Brien's comic irony, since there never seems to be any real drinking problem in Mick Shaughnessy's case. Mick is actually a well-balanced character, surpassing the two first-person protagonists of *At Swim-Two-Birds* and *The Hard Life*. Unlike them he is energetic and well-directed, with no luxurious proclivity for remaining endlessly in bed which characterizes his predecessors (If whiskey is the religion, taking up the horizontal is the philosophy that governs Flann O'Brien's heroes: a character named Byrne expounds it; the narrators of the first two books practice it; the righteously bourgeois uncles denounce it; and Dermot Trellis of *At Swim-Two-Birds* almost dies of it when it backfires). But in this instance also, when the author seems close to making a moral judgment, either supporting the established contention that indolence is a vice or advancing the rebellious cause of *dolce far niente,* he does neither. The characters themselves carry the responsibility for their own behaviour, and it is no simple matter to determine from a novel's "hero" what course of action his narrator advocates for him. The hero of *At Swim-Two-Birds* wallows in sloth, yet triumphs over his uncle by passing his examinations with distinction. His extension, the Finbarr of *The Hard Life*, collects a tidy inheritance when the active Mr Collopy dies ignominiously after being chastised by the Pope; while Mick reverses the trend and is successful in destroying De Selby's destructive potential through diligent action.

What emerges from these novels is a realization of their author's basic naiveté, his addiction to the happy ending (although it is always shot through with irony). His selection of fantasy precludes the necessity of grappling with reality, but to insist upon such "satisfactory" conclusions to these fantasies tends to indicate more than just a poetically comic vision. It denotes rather a purposefully myopic view of the world. This need not deny O'Nolan his wild sense of irony; yet it does seriously qualify his ironic attitudes. If the uncle's pomposity is his target, that sentimental singer of opera and deliverer of sanctimonious messages is aptly torpedoed by the slothful nephew's success at his examinations. But the uncle takes his "defeat" very much in stride, graciously congratulates the victor and presents him with a watch for his achievement, sharing genially in the triumph. The evil Pooka is certainly a far more lovable creature than the bad-tempered Good Fairy, and his victory in the fight to gain control of Orlic Trellis is intended to win the reader's approval. Yet the Good Fairy survives the encounter unscarred and seems more Pooka's ally than adversary during the trial of Dermot Trellis.

The Hard Life contributes to the tendency: a neat touch of irony is no match for a major reliance on fairy tale solutions. Despite his complicity in his half-uncle's death, Manus goes off to continue his successful business shenanigans; he can accept his disinheritance nonchalantly, having enough money from his previous inheritance to pursue his role as good samaritan and evil genius. Finbarr, in his turn, now has enough money to qualify as a drop-out from the Christian Brothers' school and have his breakfast served in bed by Annie. He might even accept Manus's suggestion and make the situation permanent by marrying Annie, although it is the mere suggestion of it rather than the whiskey that caused his vomiting. Brian O'Nolan's Luciferism, that tendency to glamorize small evils in the name of a rebellion against the hypocrisy of the self-proclaimed good citizens, is rather tame – certainly when compared with Joyce's. The strong sense of the outrageous

found in Shem the Penman and the determined individualism
of Stephen Dedalus are much watered down by Joyce's
"successor."[14]

Even *The Dalkey Archive*, commended by its own book-jacket
blurb for its daring irreverence, stays carefully within the pale.
The publisher advertises that "since writing this book, Mr
O'Brien claims to have been persecuted by St Augustine. He
has become disaster-prone and says that he has no reason to
think that the saint has yet finished with him." This is
tempered by Mr O'Brien in his Dedication: "I dedicate these
pages to my Guardian Angel, impressing upon him that I'm
only fooling and warning him to see to it that there is no
misunderstanding when I go Home." The only evidence
available from the book itself is that the author is "only
fooling," and it is rather safe fooling. Every character is
permitted his hobby-horse, each one wildly unorthodox and
even heretical (Hackett's defense of Judas; Joyce's case against
the Holy Ghost; Sergeant Fottrells anti-bicycle theory; De
Selby's panoply of heresies, only a minor one of them that
Jonah's whale was actually a shark). But except for the
dangerous De Selby, each operates safely within a socially
accepted framework – it is all merely talk after all, like
Collopy's diatribe against the Jesuits, and even the police
sergeant's larceny and vandalism are venial enough. Joyce is
handed over to the Jesuits, and the reader is free to decide for
himself whether they succeed in disabusing him of his misconception regarding the Third Person of the Trinity or he
manages to reform the Roman Catholic Church. De Selby is a
major threat, however (a threat against everything, not just
the Church), and against this menace Mick mounts a
legitimate campaign, to everyone's satisfaction. Mick versus
De Selby is no contest: A threat to the human race subsumes
all other controversies.

It is only with Hackett that Flann O'Brien has an opportunity to flaunt an unconventional attitude, and his ironic tone
brings him close to awarding the victory to heterodoxy. When
Mick's supposed fiancée, whom he intends rejecting in favour
of a monastic vocation, announces her plan to marry the
shiftless, crass, hard-drinking Hackett, O'Brien's safe world
appears to be in jeopardy. But Mary relents and gives up
Hackett for Mick, who is then left with having involuntarily

chosen Mary in lieu of the Trappist life. The final irony is of course Mary's casual announcement of her pregnancy (Mick has taken Mary's virginity for granted, so the child is obviously not his); yet as much as this contributes to the constant jostling of Mick's fixed universe, it does little to offset his monumental heroism as mankind's benefactor. Mary is his logical, if somewhat imperfect, reward, the spoiled spoils of his victory.

It would be unjust to overlook Brian O'Nolan's constant desire to set the smug world on its ear, but he does exhibit a perpetual tendency for last-minutes cold feet. He is not the first to manifest such ambivalence, but his particular case history does much to corroborate James Joyce's fear that the integrity of the Irish artist is always in danger as long as he chooses to remain in Ireland.[5] Like Gabriel Conroy and Robert Hand, O'Nolan remained in Dublin, like them making his living as a journalist. It was Myles na gCopaleen's success that kept Brian O'Nolan from the bitter pain of exile, not Flann O'Brien's. *At Swim-Two-Birds* fared no better in Ireland than it did elsewhere, and by the time he published the second and third novels, he was in his fifties and permanently ensconced. *The Hard Life* and *The Dalkey Archive* are worthy of Myles and added to the reputation of the Dublin wit. It has often been charged against Joyce that he wrote for a limited coterie audience, but O'Nolan's catering to the tastes of his Dublin cronies, the public house intelligentsia, provided him with a much smaller and less cosmopolitan public. *At Swim-Two-Birds* was a major accomplishment for a writer in his twenties, but the two decades of literary silence following it almost proved fatal. *The Hard Life* and *The Dalkey Archive* indicate a potential talent, but potentiality for an artist in his fifties is cold comfort.[6] And even that comfort is cancelled by O'Nolan's death in April, 1966. His play (sic) *An Béal Bocht* is in Irish, and its substance depends so much on his clever handling of the language that no translation into English appears likely. A posthumous novel *The Third Policeman* was brought out last September by his British publisher, and a collection of journalistic pieces – presumably titled *The Best of Myles* – is much talked about as a possibility in Dublin, as is the publisher's promise of "a collection of other writings."

It seems assured that Flann O'Brien will have his place in Irish literary history because of *At Swim-Two-Birds*. It represents a milestone in the development of the imaginative, non-realistic novel in our century, a worthy companion of such early Beckett novels as *Watt*[7] (with which it shares a propensity for convoluted and ornate language, the sort of vocabulary that Beckett later replaced with a laconic use of basic French, but which O'Brien attempted to perpetuate without the same degree of facility). The novel examines the Irish landscape of both the past and the present, and in particular the use of the Celtic past, concentrating on the concern of the Irish writer with making literature out of a fusion of life and myth. This is approached through a multifaceted control of subject matter and a multilevel structure that allows a frame within a frame (the narrator is writing a book about Dermot Trellis who is writing a book about a handful of characters who assume a life of their own to write a book about Dermot Trellis). Life engenders life as literature engenders literature, until the literary art subsumes in its vastly imaginative world the prosaic and limited environs of "real" life – O'Brien not only puts Wilde's theory into practice, but carries it into absurdity. His narrator offers the reader three possible openings (about the Pooka, Finn, and Furriskey), each of which contains its own level of unreality (folklore, historic legend, and literary fiction) and its own style of language (colloquial narrative, bardic rendering, and contemporary forms of prose). To this O'Brien adds the frame of the life of the narrator himself, and the independence of those personages (his friends, his uncle, the uncle's friends) who come into contact with him. The result is a frame story in which the frames take possession of the stories and eclipse them, the method of narration triumphing over the narrative. That careful balance that Joyce achieved in *Ulysses* between the means of telling the story and the story itself (and which he may have lost in the composition of *Finnegans Wake)* O'Brien wilfully shatters. The language of literature triumphs over content, and the superstructure of the work of art is paramount.

Flann O'Brien's success in *At Swim-Two-Birds* is commendable, but a heavy price is paid for it. The absence of a precise link between the author and his characters has already been noted: O'Brien has difficulty in establishing proper distancing between himself and the author of the manuscript (Joyce's ability to maintain complex attitudes towards his characters, even with those of the *Wake*, again delineates a major strength). Nor do O'Brien's disparate pair of disclaimers alleviate his difficulty: In *At Swim-Two-Birds* is found the familiar "All the characters represented in this book, including the first person singular, are entirely fictitious and bear no relation to any person living or dead"; while *The Hard Life* offers a witty converse: "All the persons in this book are real and none is fictitious even in part." O'Brien's cleverness is well taken: The traditional disclaimer presumes that reality is superior to fiction, while O'Brien's "second thought" does not so much ally him with his creations as claim for them a reality of their own. Yet Brian O'Nolan's function in the guise of Flann O'Brien is not really literary but mythic. He shares with Joyce and Yeats a role as myth-maker, but in the process he loses sight of the writer's role in regard to the known world. Joyce and Yeats bridged the distance between myth and reality, between the fictive world as a reality and the mundane existence as a reality – although with varying proportions of emphasis. O'Nolan's difficulties are symptomatic of modern Ireland, where the imaginative artist so often prefers to render inoperative the inadequacies of ordinary life by means of a jest, concentrating on the elevation of both the myth and the myth-maker, the novel and the novelist, to a separate and superior position.[8] Sean O'Casey's critical lament for Cambridge undergraduates is equally applicable for Brian O'Nolan and much of his generation: The world is not enough with him.

The failure of Flann O'Brien to advance the potential of *At Swim-Two-Birds* parallels the failure of contemporary Ireland to fulfill the hopes engendered by political independence: Freedom from realism, like freedom from England, does not guarantee a superior product. The Ireland that spawned Flann O'Brien has never been content to see itself realistically depicted by its writers, and those who spurned the healthy paranoia that sent Joyce and O'Casey into self-exile have often had to avoid direct confrontaton with native reality, lest they suffer the fate of John McGahern. There is both mimetic appreciation and ironic deprecation in the treatment of Finn MacCool by Flann O'Brien, an envy of the heroic nature of the epic material of the past and a contemporary scorn for the outmoded. Joyce could translate the giant Finn into the hodcarrier Finnegan and pubkeeper Earwicker, into constables and postmen, savoring both the irony and the humanity of the transmigration, but O'Nolan could only reduce his Finn to literary depiction, keeping him safely unchallenged by a necessity to explain his human condition. In *At Swim-Two-Birds* the author himself began the process of confusing himself with his literary creation; his admirers in Ireland have abetted this transformation by evolving a mythos about the Brian O'Nolan-Myles na gCopaleen-Flann O'Brien triumvirate. The suggestion seems to be that in this setting myth is greater than either life or literature: It is never as unseemly and makes far fewer demands.

From *Éire-Ireland*, III, 3 (October 1968), pp. 51-65.

PROBABLY A MASTERPIECE

By Anthony Burgess

My third Irishman, Flann O'Brien, was an Irish journalist and Gaelic scholar whose real name was Brian O'Nolan. Of his very few books, *The Hard Life* and *The Dalkey Archive* are slight but funny (they have also been largely ignored by English critics), but *At Swim-Two-Birds* is probably a masterpiece. Of it, Philip Toynbee has said: 'If I were cultural dictator in England I would make *At Swim-Two-Birds* compulsory reading in all our universities.' The book was first published in 1939, which enabled James Joyce, with two years of life to go, to say: 'There's a real writer with the true comic spirit', but there is still no move to make *At Swim-Two-Birds* required reading anywhere. Still, its audience is growing, and university students in Dublin, its town of origin, quote from it as from a new Holy Writ.

It owes a great deal to Joyce, but it is not massive and its touch is light; it even approaches the whimsical. The narrator is an Irish student who, in the intervals of lying in bed and pub-crawling, is writing a novel about a man named Trellis who is writing a book about his enemies who, in revenge, are writing a book about a man named Trellis. In a way, then, the book is a book about writing a book about writing a book. The student-narrator is interested not merely in literature but in Irish mythology, which fact enables him to bring in Finn MacCool, legendary Irish giant, and indulge in comic-heroic language which sounds as though it is translated from the Erse:

'The knees and calves to him, swealed and swathed with soogawns and Thomond weed-ropes, were smutted with dungs and dirt-daubs of every hue and pigment, hardened by stainings of mead and trickles of metheglin and all the dribblings and drippings of his medher, for it was the custom of Finn to drink nightly with his people.'

Flann O'Brien did, in fact, discover a means of counter-pointing myth, fiction and actuality through the device of a sort of writer's commonplace-book. The technique is one of straight juxtaposition. The narrator has his first experience of drink and allows an extract from a Christian Brothers' literary reader to comment on its evils at clinical length. His typescript novel about Dermot Trellis, occupier of the Red Swan Hotel, is given in instalments and *in extenso*. There is no feeling of recession, of one order to reality (myth or novel or narration) lying behind another: all are presented on the same level. This is what gives the contrapuntal effect.

What O'Brien seems to be after in this very funny novel is an extension of the scope of the form but, at the same time, a limitation. All good novelists grow tired of plot with its wearisome manipulations, coincidences, simplifications. To keep narrative interest without having to impose overmuch action of the characters was Joyce's aim, it was also O'Brien's. It is best to push action either on to the margins (where it is merely heard about) or into passages of parody, extracts from heroic annals, newspaper reports and the like – all of which have a valid connection with the life of the hero, but only the life of his mind. Much of the action of *Ulysses* is relegated to dream, imagination or – most important – to parody of the literature of action. Action in *At Swim-Two-Birds* (other than pub-crawling) is reserved to the counterpoints of the main narration. This may be called a limitation, but it provides scope for the only kind of extension that means much to an Irish writer – extension in the use of language. Here again this novel comes close to *Ulysses* in calling on a huge vocabulary, a large variety of literary styles, including poetry, textbooks and newspaper reportage, and that world of myth which underlies actuality.

From Anthony Burgess, *The Novel Now. A Student's Guide to Contemporary Fiction* (London: Faber & Faber, 1971) pp. 78-80.

BRIAN, FLANN AND MYLES

By Niall Sheridan

We were constantly preoccupied with literary theories and with more mundane schemes designed to raise ready cash, a very scarce commodity in those days. Brian proclaimed that the principles of the Industrial Revolution must be applied to literature. The time had come when books should be made, not written – and a 'made' book had a better chance of becoming a best-seller.

If one thousand monkeys were chained to one thousand typewriters for a month, they would undoubtedly produce a steady stream of bestsellers and, probably, a few masterpieces. After further consideration, he announced that he had abandoned this project on purely economic grounds. What would be the cost of maintaining a thousand adult monkeys in good writing condition for a month? Where would we house his simian authors? Then there was the cost of hiring type-writers and purchasing several tons of flea powder.

His interest soon shifted to a suggestion of mine – the All-Purpose Opening Speech. This was to be one endless sentence, grammatically correct, and so devoid of meaning that it could be used on any conceivable occasion: inaugurating a President, consecrating a Cathedral, laying a foundation-stone, presenting an inscribed watch to a long-serving employee. This notion delighted him, and he decided that it must be given to the world, translated into every known language. If nation could speak fluently to nation, without any risk of communicating anything, international tension would decline. The Speech would be a major contribution to civilization, enabling any inarticulate lout who might lever himself into power to emerge (after a brief rehearsal) as a new Demosthenes.

I was to make the original draft in English. Denis Devlin was to undertake the translation into French and Brian himself would do the Irish and German versions.

I can remember only the opening portions of the Speech, which ran (still incomplete) to some 850 words:

> Unaccustomed as I am to public speaking, and reluctant as I am to parade my inability before such a critical and distinguished gathering, comprising – need I say – all that is best in the social, political, and intellectual life of our country, a country, may I add, which has played no inconsiderable part in the furtherance of learning and culture, not to speak of religion, throughout all the lands of the known globe, where, although the principles inculcated in that learning and that culture have now become temporarily obfuscated in the pursuit of values as meretricious in seeming as they must prove inadequate in realisation, nevertheless, having regard to the ethical and moral implications of the contemporary situation, etc., etc., etc.

When the translations had been completed we had a reading in Devlin's home. Any rubbish can be made to sound impressive in French, and Denis had produced a superb version, rhythmic, mellifluous and authoritative. It conveyed (to our delight and amazement) even less meaning than the original.

Brian (who delighted in the simplest sleight-of-hand), whipped a walrus moustache from his pocket, fixed it under his nose and read his Irish version, in a wickedly accurate impersonation of our Professor of Irish, Dr Douglas Hyde, later the first President of Ireland.

"What do you think of that?" he asked, looking from one to the other.

Denis told him that he admired his *brio* but deplored his occasional slurring of consonants. I told him that listening to his delivery was like wading through warm stirabout in one's bare feet.

Undeterred by this mixed reception, Brian quickly replaced the walrus moustache with a toothbrush affair and poured out his German translation in imitation of Hitler at a Nuremburg Rally. As he ground out the Teutonic gutturals, spitting and snarling in comic menace, he knew he had made the hit of the evening.

The most ambitious of all Brian's literary schemes for making money was probably quite feasible, though a little ahead of its time. He called us together in the "snug" of Grogan's pub in Leeson Street to announce that nobody had yet produced the Great Irish Novel. The time had come when it must be written or, rather, manufactured.

This great saga (working title: *Children of Destiny*) would deal with the fortunes of an Irish family over a period of almost a century, starting in 1840. It would illuminate a whole panorama of social and political history – the Famine Years, faction fights, evictions, lecherous landlords and modest maidens, emigration, the horrors of the coffin ships, etc., etc.

In America, a member of the family would rise through ward politics and Tammany Hall to the political heights, returning to Ireland to fight in the 1916 Rising, and dying gallantly (in full public view) – the last man to leave the burning ruins of the General Post Office. His son, graduating from politics to high finance, would become the first Irish-American Catholic President of the United States.

Brian proposed that he, Devlin, MacDonagh and I should write the book in sections and then stick the pieces together in committee. At least, we'd come cheaper than those monkeys.

A vast market was ready and waiting. Compulsory education had produced millions of semi-literates, who were partial to "a good read". So it must be a big book, weighing at least two-and-a-half pounds. We must give them length without depth, splendour without style. Existing works would be plundered wholesale for material, and the ingredients of the saga would be mainly violence, patriotism, sex, religion, politics and the pursuit of money and power.

Children of Destiny would be the precursor of a new literary movement, the first masterpiece of the Ready-Made or Reach-Me-Down School. There would be continuous action, a series of thrilling climaxes and great set-pieces and crowd scenes. In its power and scope, it would make the surge and thunder of the Odyssey seem like the belching and gurgling of a baby in swaddling clothes.

He himself would write the religious segment. This revolved around a scion of the family who (surviving a breach-of-promise action by a farmer's daughter) pursued his vocation with such dedication and cunning that he eventually broke the Italian stranglehold on the Papacy, to become Pope Patrick I.

While the Papal election is in progress, an immense throng (including a strong Irish contingent) fills St Peter's Square, tensely awaiting the plume of rising smoke which will indicate the result of the voting. Here, Brian had invented a very characteristic touch – an Irish Monsignor, in charge of the smoke-signals, smuggles in two sods of turf and, as the white smoke rises above the Sistine Chapel, the unmistakable tang of the bog, wafting out over the Bernini colonnades, tells his waiting countrymen that a decision (and the right one) has been reached.

For Pope Patrick I, Brian had planned a splendid apotheosis, which would bring the great work to its close. At the age of eighty-seven, he travels to his native land to perform the ceremony of throwing in the ball at the start of an All-Ireland Football Final between Cavan and Kildare, as the Tricolour and the Papal Flag (now incorporating a green harp) flutter proudly over Croke Park.

The description of the game would be couched in the florid sporting jargon so beloved of Irish provincial sportswriters: "In the closing minutes of the opening moiety, the Short Grass man – a tower of strength in attack as in defence – drove in a daisycutter which rattled the twines, to the consternation of the baffled Breffni custodian . . . .'

It's a ding-dong struggle and, with thirty seconds of play remaining, Cavan (leading by one point) appears to have the title in the bag. Suddenly, breaking clear of a mêlée, the redoubtable Short Grass man – 'a veritable Scarlet Pimpernel at midfield' – sends a high, dropping ball across the bar from forty yards out for the equalizing point. A DRAW! The vast crowd comes to its feet in a frenzy of excitement.

But the tension has been too much for the aged Pontiff. Stricken by a sudden seizure, he sinks back dying, literally, in the arms of his countrymen, while the sun descends flamboyantly behind the railway goal and 'Faith of our Fathers' thunders into the evening sky from eighty thousand Irish throats.

All this – and Heaven, too! Brian glared around him in triumph, as if challenging us to dissent. What more could any reader (or, indeed, any Pope) ask for at seven-and-sixpence a copy?

Work began at once on the great scheme. Brian ransacked *Hadrian VII* for ecclesiastical background material and Vatican colour stuff. MacDonagh discovered a history student who was doing a thesis on the Famine. Devlin bent his mind to the French scene, since one of the characters was to follow the trail of the Wild Geese and become, like the Hennessys, Garveys, O'Donnells and Lynchs, a world-renowned figure in the wine trade. My contribution, at that stage, was to write an account of the Football Final and also of the Grand National. It had been arranged that another member of this remarkable family was to win the famous Steeplechase against unbelievable odds.

There was a short period of hectic activity, but the Great Irish Novel never materialized.

One morning Brian told me that he had started to write a book on his own. The plot, he explained, was simple: it would concern an author, Dermot Trellis, who was writing a book about certain characters who, in turn, were revenging themselves by writing about him.

"That's not a plot," I told him. "It's a conspiracy."

The characters, he went on, would be drawn from legend, history, imagination and the works of past writers. Conventional notions of Time would be scorned. Past, present and future would be abolished, and the work would exist in a supra-Bergsonian continuum – communicating simultaneously on several planes of consciousness and also on various subliminal levels.

He could write quickly when a theme absorbed him and soon he began to show me sections of the book as it progressed, explaining the *rationale* behind each episode and its place in the overall design. Very soon, these sessions began to form part of the text, and I found myself (under the name Brinsley) living a sort of double life at the autobiographical core of a work which was in the process of creation.

In *At Swim-Two-Birds* he recreates the mood and atmosphere of our discussions with astonishing fidelity and an uncanny ear for the rhythms of ordinary speech:

A friend of mine, Brinsley, came in and looked about him at the door. He came forward at my invitation and asked me to give him a cigarette. I took out my "butt" and showed it to him in the hollow of my hand.

That is all I have, I said, affecting a pathos in my voice.

By God you're the queer bloody man, he said. Are you sitting on a newspaper?

I was talking to a friend of yours last night, I said drily. I mean Mr Trellis. He has bought a ream of ruled foolscap and is starting on his story. He is compelling all his characters to live with him in the Red Swan Hotel so that he can keep an eye on them and see that there is no boozing.

I see, said Brinsley.

Most of them are characters in other books, chiefly the works of another great writer called Tracy. There is a cowboy in Room 13 and Mr MacCool, a hero of old Ireland, is on the floor above. The cellar is full of leprechauns.

What are they all going to do? asked Brinsley.

Nature of his tone: Without intent, tired, formal.

Trellis, I answered steadily, is writing a book on sin and the wages attaching thereto. He is a philosopher and a moralist. He is appalled by the spate of sexual and other crimes recorded in recent times in the newspapers – particularly in those published on Saturday night.

Nobody will read the like of that, said Brinsley.

As the book progressed, Brian gleefully borrowed any material that came to hand. One day, I showed him a sales letter from a Newmarket tipster and it turned up *in toto* in the next wad of typescript that he produced. About the same time, I had done some translations from Catullus and he asked me for a copy of one of these. Later, it came out like this in *At Swim:*

That same afternoon I was sitting on a stool in an intoxicated condition in Grogan's licensed premises. Adjacent stools bore the forms of Brinsley and Kelly, my two true friends. The three of us were occupied in putting glasses of stout into the interior of our bodies and expressing by fine disputation the resulting sense of physical and mental well-being . . . .

Do not let us forget that I have to buy *Die Harzreise.*

Do not let us forget that.

Harzreise, said Brinsley. There is a house in Dalkey called Heartrise.

Brinsley then put his dark chin on the cup of a palm and leaned in thought on the counter, overlooking his drink, gazing beyond the frontier of the world.

What about another jar? said Kelly.

Ah, Lesbia, said Brinsley. The finest thing I ever wrote. How many kisses, Lesbia, you ask, would serve to sate this hungry love of mine? – As many as the Libyan sands that bask along Cyrene's shore where pine-trees wave, where burning Jupiter's untended shrine lies near to old King Battus' sacred grave:

Three stouts, called Kelly.

Let them be endless as the stars at night, that stare upon the lovers in a ditch – so often would love-crazed Catullus bite your burning lips, that prying eyes should not have power to count, nor evil tongues bewitch, the frenzied kisses that you gave and got.

Before we die of thirst, called Kelly, will you bring us *three more stouts.* God, he said to me, it's in the desert you'd think we were.

That's good stuff, you know, I said to Brinsley.

A picture came before my mind of the lovers at their hedge-pleasure in the pale starlight, no sound from them, his fierce mouth burying into hers.

Bloody good stuff, I said.

Kelly, invisible to my left, made a slapping noise.

The best I ever drank, he said.

The scene in the house of Michael Byrne, 'painter, poet, composer, pianist, master-printer, tactician, an authority on ballistics', recalls that remarkable man, Cecil ffrench Salkeld. At this period, it was Cecil's habit to rise about six in the evening and spend the entire night in reading, talk or the development of his many artistic projects:

You're a terrible man for the blankets, said Kerrigan.

I'm not ashamed to admit that I love my bed, said Byrne. She was my first friend, my foster-mother, my dearest comforter . . . .

He paused and drank.

Her warmth, he continued, kept me alive when my mother bore me. She still nurtures me, yielding without stint the parturition of her cosy womb. She will nurse me gently in my last hour and faithfully hold my cold body when I am dead. She will look bereaved when I am gone.

This speech did not please us, bringing to each of us our last personal end. We tittered in cynical fashion.

Glass tinkle at his teeth notified a sad concluding drink. Brinsley gave a loud question.

Wasn't Trellis another great bed-bug?

He was, I answered.

I'm afraid I never heard of Trellis, said Byrne. Who is Trellis?

A member of the author class, I said.

Did he write a book on Tactics? I fancy I met him in Berlin. A tall man with glasses.

He has been in bed for the last twenty years, I said.

You are writing a novel of course? said Byrne.

He is, said Brinsley, and the plot has him well in hand.

I remember that last remark of mine very clearly, and it gives one a curious *frisson* to find the whole scene and mood preserved with such a fusion of factual accuracy and imaginative truth.

When I got through the final draft of the book (there must have been over 800 pages of typescript), I told him it was too long. He had got such fun out of sending-up the Fenian cycle that he over-indulged himself and the weight of this material seriously unbalanced the latter half of the book

Like any writer with a big task just completed, Brian had no wish to return to it. Besides, he was already taken up with planning another novel.

'I am sick of the sight of it,' he told me. 'What about cutting it yourself?'

I took out about one-fifth of the text before the book went to Longmans, who published it on the strong recommendation of Graham Greene. Before the publication date, Brian gave me one of his six complimentary copies in which he had written:

Sheraton
To Mr Sheridan I unload
This celestial commode –

> Of that particular accessory
> It can be said that it is necessary.

About a month later (May 1939), he acted as best man at my wedding. We were honeymooning in Paris, and I had told him that I would be seeing James Joyce. At the foot of the gangway, as we boarded the boat at Dun Laoghaire, he handed me a copy of the book and asked me to bring it to Joyce (I hadn't seen it around during the ceremony or at the hurried breakfast afterwards). On the fly-leaf he had written the dedication:

> 'To James Joyce from the author,
> Brian O'Nolan, with plenty of
> what's on page 305'

On that page Brian had underlined the phrase *'diffidence of the author'*.

Joyce was then in the process of moving into a new flat at 34 rue des Vignes, which was to be his last home in Paris. He was alone in the flat when I called, and he said Sam Beckett had already praised *At Swim-Two-Birds* very highly to him and that he looked forward to reading it.

His sight was so precarious that he had long given up reading fiction; indeed, he rarely showed any interest in contemporary writers, apart from his great admiration for Yeats and Eliot and his friendship with Sam Beckett, Padraic Colum and James Stephens – born on the same day as himself, a significant coincidence for Joyce.

We spent most of the afternoon in his sunny living-room, as yet only partly furnished with two armchairs, a coffee-table on which lay a copy of *Finnegans Wake* and a large woven rug on the wooden floor. It had been given to him, he told me, by an admirer of *Finnegans Wake* and the design illustrated the course of the River Liffey from its source to its mouth. A few pictures hung on the walls, including the famous Tuohy portrait of his father, John Stanislaus.

Joyce greatly enjoyed *At Swim-Two-Birds*, which he considered a comic work of remarkable creative power. (He often complained that too many of the serious commentators on *Ulysses* failed to recognize that it was essentially 'a funny book'.) Although the War was less than three months away, he made every effort to have Brian's book brought to the notice of the most influential French critics. When he had left Paris for the South, and shortly before his last journey to Switzerland, he was still writing to me on this subject.

At Swim-Two-Birds was, I am certain, the last novel he read. Ten years later, in a catalogue of the small library left behind in his Paris flat, Brian's presentation copy is listed and described as: *Livre très aimé de Joyce....*

From Timothy O'Keeffe (ed.), *Myles: Portraits of Brian O'Nolan* (London: Martin, Brian & O'Keeffe, 1973), pp. 40-49.

LITERALIST OF THE IMAGINATION

By J. C. C. Mays

At Swim-Two-Birds was a long time in the making. It was begun during Brian O'Nolan's last year in College and during the year that followed it grew to many times the length of the book we have now. The original version was, according to Niall Sheridan,[1] less a book than a territory to which Brian O'Nolan retreated to develop as he would a multitude of themes that interested him. These origins account for the book's essential character, which is that of a compendium of anecdotes and competing voices. The way in which a degree of order was imposed on this marvellous but unwieldy thing was first of all not only by savage pruning, but by pruning which isolated a number of unifying structural motifs.

What remains in the book as we have it are three main plots – as the narrator remarks at the opening and close, he has a particular fondness for threes.[2] First there is the story of the narrator himself, his life at home with his uncle and as a student at University College; second, there are his occasional ventures into the legendary world of Finn MacCool and the Frenzy of Sweeny; and last there are his incursions into the fictional world of Dermot Trellis. All three plots move at speeds appropriate to the worlds they inhabit. The frame story moves carefully through the seasons of the narrator's final undergraduate year; by contrast the Finn story is timeless, recurring through the book as if at random and with minimal progression; the Trellis story moves between the two, and though there are gaps in its telling which are filled by synopses, only once is a scene presented out of sequence. None the less, if so much is clear, these matters are less clear actually in their working out. The effect of three narratives moving forward at an unsynchronized pace and at different removes of sympathy from the author who stands behind them, the movement from one world to another unprepared, the insertion of extracts drawn from such random sources as Falconer's *Shipwreck* and a forty-volume *Conspectus of the Arts and Natural Sciences,* in particular the complications and inversions of the Trellis plot, is of a swirling phantasmagoria in which a great deal of movement is accompanied by less advance.

The narrator's comment on his handling of the Trellis story is to be taken seriously, whatever reaction it provokes in Brinsley. He argues that 'a satisfactory novel should be a self-evident sham to which the reader could regulate at will the degree of his credulity' (*AS2B*, p. 33).[3] Characters are to be allowed 'a private life, self-determination and a decent standard of living' and should be 'interchangeable as between one book and another'. The argument describes the 'aestho-autogamy' or 'aestho-psycho-eugenics' on which the conflict between Trellis and his characters rests. However, it is not the idea in itself which makes up the character of the book, but how it is developed. Characters possess not only an independent existence which can be carried over from one book to another, but they move from one to another of the three plots of the same book. *At Swim-Two-Birds* is the 'work of reference' the narrator claims a modern novel should be, but in a more extended sense than is sometimes understood. There is an elusive but persistent relation established between the author-narrator so attracted to 'the tender trestle of [his] bed' (*AS2B*, p. 15), with his stye, and the flabby, pimply, bed-habiting author Trellis. An equally real if more elusive relation comes to be established between Trellis and Sweeny: in one version of Orlick's story towards the close of the book, the House-Moling who had before served Sweeny becomes the cleric Moling who clambers into Trellis's room (cf. *AS2B*, pp. 125, 238), in another Sweeny's initial crime is duplicated by Trellis (cf. *AS2B*, pp. 25, 118, 246), in another Sweeny the Kite of Cluain-Eo is reborn as the thorn-embedded tree-benighted Trellis – Sweeny is made to 'live in tree-tops and roost in the middle of a yew' as Trellis is set 'at his bird's roost on a thin branch surrounded by tufts of piercing thorns and tangles of bitter spiky brambles' (*AS2B*, p. 25, 265). Other characters and scenes are at the same time made curiously to echo one another, with a similar unsettling effect. Various details of the meeting over which the uncle presides and at which the narrator acts as secretary are picked up in the trial of Trellis, which again includes details from previous bar-scenes involving the narrator and his companions; Orlick's style inevitably recalls Finn's, Shanahan's recalls Kelly's, that of the Ringsend cowboys recalls faintly but unmistakably that of the College students (the oblique parallels extending here even to the matching of heating systems in the College and in an ideal ranch-house and to a penchant for pyromania).

This is the effect of the book as a whole and the point of its epigraph from the *Hercules furens*. If it is highly contrived, with plots set against counterplots, and styles against styles and parodies of styles, the balance so made up is not static. The counterpoint method is such that any connection between the parts of the book frustrates another at the same time that it establishes itself: "all things fleet and yield each other place". The effect of this method of counterpoint is in the end to communicate a fantastic imagination of a peculiar sort. The real subject of the book is vigorous ingenuity, wildness and sweetness, those qualities of the legendary Brother Barnabas and other *personae* which Brian O'Nolan's friends remember at their most unrestrained in his College years and in the years immediately following. Such satire, Niall Montgomery has written,[4] springs up "not out of bitterness but from helpless, disbelieving enjoyment of the perverse fantasy of conventional behaviour". Private jokes contribute to the mood, even when they are impenetrable. Cashel Byrne is the poetaster-painter Cecil ffrench Salkeld, for instance, but who is the small man Kelly covers with buff-coloured puke, whom Brendan Behan[5] claimed to have identified? It does not matter. Failure to assimilate totally the book's material is likewise paraded as attraction, and the relevance of the *Athenian Oracle* and other extracts to any of the plots is often remote.[6] An anonymous grammarian interjects the names of figures of speech; there are nonchalant lists, broken-off *resumés,* interrupted reminiscences, inadequately impersonal descriptions, detailed interpretations of motive and conduct which confuse more than they illuminate. Gratuity relished is the essence of this extra-ordinarily contrived book, and its variety is overwhelming. As the Good Fairy comments, "Counterpoint is an odd number ... and it is a great art that can evolve a fifth Excellence from four Futilities" (*AS2B,* p. 156).

There is of course a serious substrate to the humour of *At Swim-Two-Birds* which, without in any way giving the book a moral, prevents the whole fabric from collapsing upon itself in sheer facetiousness. A norm is asserted not only in the unerring openness and energy of the book's approach to its material but also in the shaping of the material. In the framing plot the narrator emerges from his involvement with Trellis to see his uncle and the ordinary world in the end not ungratefully; a certain pride and selfish indulgence gives way to an awareness of and generosity towards others. Again, as we grow in familiarity with the book and come to have a sense of it as a whole, we realize that the first extract from the narrator's Finn typescript is given where it is, out of sequence at the beginning and before the narrator's first experience of intoxicating beverages, because it stands as prologue. Finn, the weaver of a story-teller's book-web, prefigures both Trellis and Orlick, both the villain and also the person by whom the villain is ultimately vanquished. Who but a story-teller to introduce a story which concerns ill-usage at the hands of and eventual triumph over a story-teller by a story-teller for a story-teller? Finn is the least satirized of the three narrators of the three stories; his world of the out-of-bed outdoors is a parodied but still live and affectionately observed world. His songs – as a comparison with their middle Irish originals[7] will reveal – have little or no parody in them. Lamont's dismissal of them as "your fancy kiss my hand" and Shanahan's preference of "A Pint of Plain is Your Only Man" (*AS2B, pp. 110, 112-113*) are as overt a statement as Brian O'Nolan comes to make on the values they embody, but again it is significant that the longest of the Finn episodes in which they appear is the turning-point of the book.

The exact relevance of these matters is defined by the title *At Swim-Two-Birds.* On the one hand the title is suitably gratuitous, being merely one of the many places visited by

Sweeny ("on a Friday, to speak precisely"); on the other it is a place, at a church beside the Shannon opposite Clonmacnois, where cultural and religious values were for a spell coincident in a darkened Europe, "the clerics were engaged at the observation of their nones, flax was being beaten and here and there a woman was giving birth to a child" (*AS2B*, p. 95). Brian O'Nolan translates literally and without mockery from the *Buile Suibhne* here, and the lay that Sweeny sang there is at the centre of the positive values in the book. Quite properly he does not include it, but similar values are embodied in the following uncollected poem translated from the Irish:[8]

> Here's a song –
> stags give tongue
> winter snows
> summer goes.
>
> High cold blow
> sun is low
> brief his day
> seas give spray.
>
> Fern clumps redden
> shapes are hidden
> wildgeese raise
> wonted cries.
>
> Cold now girds
> wings of birds
> icy time –
> that's my rime.

At Swim-Two-Birds is Brian O'Nolan's Brother Barnabas book. His contributions to *Comhthrom Féinne* and to *Blather* are perforce more talked about than read, but the book writes out at large the same ever-renewing energy delighted in for itself that has passed into legend. This is where its centre lies and, though its construction is intricate, it gives little sense of shape. What shape it has was largely discovered in the process of bringing a semblance of order to the unorderable, as distinct from a shape either imposed or consciously built upon. The exercise of preparing *At Swim-Two-Birds* for publication was not without benefit, and Brian O'Nolan's next book was composed very much more quickly on the basis of what he learned.

From Timothy O'Keefe (ed.), *Myles: Portraits of Brian O'Nolan* (London: Martin, Brian and O'Keefe, 1973), pp. 85-90.

FORMS OF GLOOM

By Stephen Knight

The structure of *At Swim-Two-Birds* is both elaborate and elusive, but one does exist and the reader needs to have it clear in mind or he will tend to become lost. The narrator, who is never named, gives a series of ten separate "reminiscences" about his life, scattered throughout the book. He is a student, but most of his thinking is directed towards his "spare-time literary activities". The principal part of these is a novel he is writing about Dermot Trellis, eccentric landlord of the Red Swan. Trellis himself is writing a novel, and the structural mechanics of this latter work, though often given briefly and in asides, are important because they are the logical links between the narrator himself and the apparently errant narrative of *At Swim-Two-Birds* as a whole. Trellis's novel is to be a cautionary story of the process of evil in the world, and his purposes and his preparations are related at some length by the narrator. But it becomes clear soon enough that Trellis's novel-in-a-novel-in-a-novel is not going to work out: the narrator's own interest in it as planned seems to fade, for several of the characters are introduced in synopsis, when the narrator claims to have lost his manuscript, and on another occasion he explicitly abandons the effort to write a difficult part of his novel about Trellis. The actual function of Trellis's notional novel in *At Swim-Two-Birds* is as a flimsy structural device (a trellis-work?) upon which are arranged various characters who talk and act at large. Thus the narrator's life and Trellis's literary practices are the structural skeleton of *At Swim-Two-Birds*, but the wandering speeches and actions of Trellis's characters and the mental rambles of the narrator himself fill out the whole novel, and provide the greater part of its theme.

The characters themselves have a lot to do with the failure of Trellis's novel; to understand how this happens it is necessary to grasp the nature of these characters, based as it is on a premise crucial to both the comic nature of much in *At Swim-Two-Birds* and to the theoretical themes which the novel ultimately examines. The premise is that characters in a novel are as "real" as other people in every way: literature is a part of life, subject to the same conditions as "real" life. Consequently Trellis has to hire or otherwise assemble his cast, just as a theatrical producer would have to do. And, like theatricals, the cast of the novel have played before, on various stages. Finn MacCool, hero of Irish saga, is hired to play the part of father to Peggy, a domestic servant. Two plain men about Dublin are employed to be close friends of John Furriskey, the novel's villain: these two, Paul Shanahan and Antony Lamont are veterans of other novels, including some by William Tracy, author of *Flower o' the Prairie* and other cowboy novels. Two other minor characters, "Shorty" Andrews and "Slug" Willard are also from the Tracy stable. Furriskey himself has a different source: no suitable villain being available on the character market, Trellis is forced to conceive one himself. O'Brien is a great man for taking metaphors in a mercilessly literal way, and he describes in loving detail how Trellis gives birth to a villain who is already in early middle age: the theory and practice of authorial birth is analyzed, the basics of literary parthenogenesis, or "aestho-autogamy" as O'Brien has it, are investigated and a suitable cutting from the Dublin press is provided, announcing the birth. Other characters of note are the Pooka, Fergus MacPhellimey, "member of the devil class" and the Good Fairy. These two are borrowed from Irish fairy lore to represent the forces of good and evil in the novel.

When Trellis is asleep he is not employing these characters and so they are at liberty to lead their own lives. Furriskey falls in love with Peggy, whom Trellis had meant him to assault (the love of a good woman saves him from villainy), and they run a small sweet-shop together in Dublin, taking the precaution to drug Trellis so that their lives need have only minimal interruptions because of their literary employment.

Finn relates a number of long excerpts from Irish saga, the Pooka and the Good Fairy engage in discussions of various bizarre issues and the three plain men of Dublin give their confident views on an extensive range of topics.

The author insists on the "reality" of these characters; some of them discuss their earlier jobs:

> Mr Lamont recounted an adventure which once befell him in a book when teaching French and piano-playing to a young girl of delicate and refined nature. Mr Shanahan, who was an older man and who had appeared in many of the well-known tales of Mr Tracy, then entertained his hearers with a brief though racy account of his experiences as a cow-puncher in the Ringsend district of Dublin city.

One of Shanahan's reminiscences has a finely convoluted moment of literary "realism" when he and his friends are planning to attack a range in suburban Dublin but are short of numbers:

> Do you know what it is, says Slug, Tracy is writing another book too and has a crowd of Red Indians up in the Phoenix Park, squaws and wigwams an' warpaint an' all, the real stuff all right, believe me. A couple of bob to the right man there and the lot are ours for the asking, says he.

The *reality* of the characters and its logical consequences, lovingly pursued by O'Brien, is the principal oddity of *At Swim-Two-Birds*. Although the action of the novel is divided into segments, each segment is given a precise stage-direction and we are not faced with the structural difficulties that a novel like *Ulysses* offers the reader. There is only one instance of juggling with time in the novel, when, after discussing Trellis's practice of "aestho-autogamy", the narrator inserts a transcript from Trellis's trial, conducted by his "children" and employees, though this does not take place until the end of the story.

Structure and action are, in this way, relatively simple in terms of what really happens, though not in terms of why it happens. There is a little action in the narrator's own life, in that he passes his examinations at the end of the novel and his uncle turns out to be not the ogre the narrator thought him to be. In the novel within the novel there is little plotted action, and it is brought to an end when the narrator contrives that Trellis's servant should accidentally burn the manuscript, thus destroying all the characters who were so tormenting their employer. Action is not the essential part of *At Swim-Two-Birds:* the private activities of Trellis's characters and the wanderings of the narrator's mind provide most of the book: they encompass a whole world of literary and social reference and to grasp the flavour and to understand the themes of the novel it is necessary to look at the ground covered in this paper-chase through literature and Irish tradition.

＊

In the opening sequences of the novel O'Brien, through his narrator, clearly attempts to give a precise, logical tone. He uses formal signals sometimes to indicate this:

> I surveyed my uncle in a sullen manner. He speared a portion of cooked rasher against a crust on the prongs of his fork and poised the whole at the opening of his mouth in a token of continued interrogation.
>
> *Description of my uncle:* Red-faced, bead-eyed, ball-bellied. Fleshy about the shoulders with long swinging arms giving ape-like effect to gait. Large moustache. Holder of Guinness clerkship the third class.

At other times similarly minute description is built into the narrative:

> The mirror at which I shaved every second day was of the type supplied gratis by Messrs Watkins, Jameson and Pim and bore brief letterpress in reference to a proprietary brand of ale between the words of which I had acquired considerable skill in inserting the reflection of my countenance.

The effect is that of a painstakingly meticulous style – phrases like "of the type of", "in reference to", "in inserting the reflection of my countenance" give a slightly comic effect in this context by seeming over-meticulous, yet they do also assert a sort of exact realism; this is the means by which O'Brien leads us to his logical forms of fantasy. The precise tone makes the fantasy seem less fantastic, and this meticulously elegant style, often supported by a fussily exact diction, is constant through the novel.

A similar effect is derived from the use of direct quotation: documentary evidence is often used and this both helps to create the precise, logical tone and also supports the theoretical premise that the characters and actions of literature are as real as any of "real" life. The narrator often inserts documents into his reminiscences, like the tipster's letter he receives from "V. Wright, Wyvern Cottage, Newmarket, Suffolk". When he gives an account of his first bout of porter-drinking he includes an item from his earlier education about drink, an "Extract from Literary Reader, the Higher Class, by the Irish Christian Brothers." He also uses documentary material in a less direct way: when faced with the need to describe Trellis he inserts the description of a Dr Beatty, alleged to have come from *A Conspectus of the Arts and Natural Sciences,* forty calf-bound volumes of which stand on a shelf in his bedroom. Here it begins to look as if O'Brien is having fun with his technique, and this impression is even stronger when the narrator, speaking to his friend Kerrigan, uses the expression "That, I answered, would be the chiefest wisdom" and a page of quotation from Ecclesiasticus is provided to amplify the remark. This may say something about the narrator's consciousness, but its real function is to assert that the novel has a basic veracity that can be documented, and the strained manner indicates that the writer is aware that this notion, like all others, can become somewhat ludicrous when taken to a ruthlessly logical conclusion.

The pattern of these early passages of implanted material is continued and developed through the novel. The materials used in this way may not have, in themselves, any fantastic quality, but they are quoted in such a context that their use is fantastic, and generally there are internal references which insist on this fact as well as indicating that there is a larger purpose in bringing this material together.

The largest amount of transplanted material is that given about through Finn MacCool. Fionn Mac Umhaill, to give him his original Irish name, is the best-known hero of Irish saga and popular myth; there are many stories about him and he represents something like a combination of King Arthur and Robin Hood. His world is one of the many strands of traditional material O'Brien uses. In the old stories he is represented as a huge and beautiful warrior – "finn" means "white, fair, beautiful" in Irish. O'Brien presents him as an aged wreck – probably because of the antiquity of the legend, in a piece of O'Brienish literalism – who sits by the fire and rambles in mind. He is first mentioned in a passage of mock saga prose, one of the finest set-pieces in a novel notable for them:

> The mouth to his white wheyface had dimensions and measurements to the width of Ulster, bordered by a red lip-wall and inhabited unseen by the watchful host of his honey-yellow teeth to the size, each with each, of a cornstack; and in the dark hollow to each tooth was there home and fulness for the sitting there of a thorny dog or for the lying there of a spear-pierced badger. To each of the two eyes in his head was there eye-hair to the fashion of a young forest and the colour to each great eyeball was as the slaughter of a host in snow. The lid to each eye of them was limp and cheese-dun like ship-canvas in harbour at evening, enough eye-cloth to cover the whole of Erin.

This account of Finn and, as it goes on, of the qualities of the Fianna, Finn's warriors, is grandly hyperbolic. It is a fairly large distortion of the original accounts of Finn and his men; the basic hyperbole of the Irish saga has been allowed to flourish and by literally translating a whole series of Gaelicisms O'Brien has achieved the same distorting and parodic effect that Joyce produced in *Ulysses*. The fact that this is parody is signalled in the text, for the passage is headed: "Extract from my typescript descriptive of Finn MacCool and his people, being humorous or quasi-humorous incursion into ancient mythology." This is not part of Trellis's novel – it is another of the narrator's "spare-time literary activities". The passage is a delightful excursus, a statement of the novelist's dazzling verbal skill and an index of his real but ironically informed affection for Irish tradition.

When Finn begins to speak, as he does at a length disheartening to some of the other characters, he is different: no longer a parodic puppet manipulated by the narrator, he is presented as a "real" individual within Trellis's novel. Consistent with the ruthless logic of the novel, the material about him is no longer parodic: what he says is directly taken,

in excellent translation, from Irish saga. The distinction
between these two Finn sequences is crucial to an understanding of the novel – the Sweeney saga that Finn the
character in Trellis's novel relates may be wildly imaginative,
but it is not parody, it is the real thing, the legend of King
Sweeney, Suibhne Geilt ("Wild Sweeney"), the frenzy-ridden
royal poet-madman-bird-shaman of Irish myth (a close
relative, even doppelgänger, of Merlin, in the subtle world of
Celtic myth and legend). Through Finn, O'Brien gives us a
sharply written condensation of the saga of Sweeney as it is
found in Middle Irish.[1] He has selected the highlights of a
marvellously imaginative story and has retained many of the
best poems that are embedded in the original prose matrix.
O'Brien abbreviates a great deal, including the poems – the
first one, "My Curse on Sweeney" is in fact a skilful
condensation of two poems. The translation is masterly, for
O'Brien has the art of being close to the original while writing
a rich but lucid English. The best known of the poems from
this saga is a good example:

> A year to last night
> I have lodged there in branches
> from the flood-tide to the ebb-tide
> naked.

> Bereft of fine women-fold,
> the brooklime for a brother –
> our choice for a fresh meal
> is watercress always.

> Without accomplished musicians
> without generous women,
> no jewel-gift for bards –
> respected Christ, it has perished me.

> The thorntop that is not gentle
> has reduced me, has pierced me,
> it has brought me near death
> the brown thorn-bush.

> Once free, once gentle,
> I am banished for ever,
> wretch-wretched I have been
> a year to last night.

This is, in fact, stanzas 1, 3, 9, 13 and 15 of the fifteen stanza poem that appears in the original. The translation employs both imaginative selection and precise word-choice. In his article in *Encounter* on Flann O'Brien John Wain said of these poems that there were "a number of lyrics, some of which are mere comical parodies while others come across with genuine force as poems."[2] But none of the Sweeney poems is a parody and it is not really surprising that poems from this highly sophisticated early culture have what Wain, with an Englishman's condescending praise, calls "genuine force"; as Mr Shanahan succinctly puts it, these poems are the product of a culture that:

> brought scholars to our shore when your men on the other side were on the flat of their bellies before the calf of gold with a sheepskin around their man. It's the stuff that put our country where she is today, Mr Furriskey . . . .

The authorial irony visible at the end of Mr Shanahan's remark is typical of O'Brien's handling of his quoted material. Ireland's position in the world today is not the best testimony to the power of its early literature; like most Celts O'Brien has a firm devotion to his traditions and a very sceptical attitude to them at the same time. The plain men are not only, as here, acceptors of the value of tradition – they can also be the agents of a critique of its value, as when they frequently interrupt the rambling Finn because they find him boring. In this way O'Brien both controls this ancient material within the novel, preventing it from taking over, and also asserts the ironic distance so important to him: he implies that even this fine material may be seen as unimportant, depending on your point of view.

Several other traditions are invoked in the novel. In simply chronological terms the tradition closest to that of King Sweeney and Finn is that embodied in the Pooka MacPhellimey and the Good Fairy. The fairy-lore of Ireland is elaborate and of distinguished age . . . the Pooka, lordly master of the science of rat-flight, is more an agent in the novel than a figure who stands for anything. Although he is announced as the figure of evil, he is important as an initiator and manipulator of plot action and comic conversation, not as a vessel of meaning, and the same is true of the Good Fairy, though he (or she?) is less powerful in terms of the plot action than the Pooka. In general the Fairy is as evanescent and weak-minded a figure as are all the representatives of organized goodness in O'Brien novels – Father Fahrt in *The Hard Life*, St Augustine and Father Cobble in *The Dalkey Archive* are other notable examples.

Another tradition which appears is that of the cowboy novel, and this has nothing to do with plot mechanics. Shanahan recalls a rustling episode he took part in in one of Tracy's novels (Tracy seems to be an invention – I can find no trace of him). The scene is surely a modern version of the many cattle-raids in Celtic story:

> So when the moon had raised her lamp o'er the prairie grasses, out flies the bunch of us, Slug, Shorty and myself on a buckboard making like hell for Irishtown with our ears back and the butts of our six-guns streaming behind us in the wind ... Be damned to the lot of us, I roared, flaying the nags and bashing the buckboard across the prairie, passing out lorries and trams and sending poor so-and-so's on bicycles scuttling down lanes with nothing showing but the whites of their eyes.

This is a highly comic scene, and it seems fairly important for a critique of *At Swim-Two-Birds* to decide whether a longish sequence like this has any purpose other than sheer fun. If it were to be serious, I think we would have to see it as an alternative way of interpreting experience, an indication of the fact that the power of literature can be such that we can interpret normal life by its light. This reading is suggested by the end of the sequence, an excerpt from the press giving a description of the events in non-cowboys terms, terms which we are clearly meant to accept as being 'true':

> A number of men, stated to be labourers, were arraigned before Mr Lamphall in the District Court yesterday morning on charges of riotous assembly and malicious damage. Accused were described by Superintendent Clohessy as a gang of corner-boys whose horse-play in the streets was the curse of the Ringsend district...

I suggest that what we have in the cowboy sequence is a literary interpretation of city ruffians, basing itself, with a typical piece of O'Brien's mis-logic, on a literal reading of the metaphor in "horse-play". This seems to me consistent with the emphasis the novel keeps putting on the puzzling nature of reality: the Sweeney saga is in one view fine, in another boring; the uncle is in one view a dolt, in another a man of admirably simple good nature. The cowboy sequence is certainly extreme and certainly comic, but the end O'Brien gives to it links it into his theme of the nature of reality.

Another sequence in the novel goes further into this issue. The plain men of Dublin have a good deal to say about poetry in one comic and impressively written sequence. Arising from Finn's Sweeney poems, Shanahan speaks up for his own favourite poet, Jem Casey – "A hard-working well-made block of a working-man, Mr Lamont, with a handle of a pick in his hand like the rest of us." By the standards of this group of literary critics (and why should they not be called that?) the Yeatses and .Synges of the world score poorly:

> Give them a bloody pick, I mean, Mr Furriskey, give them the shaft of a shovel into their hand and tell them to dig a hole and have the length of a page of poetry off by heart in their heads before the five o'clock whistle. What will you get? By God you could take off your hat to what you'd get at five o'clock from that crowd and that's a sure sharkey.

Jem's masterpiece is a poem in praise of porter including the stanza:

> When food is scarce and your larder bare
> And no rashers grease your pan,
> When hunger grows as your meals are rare –
> A PINT OF PLAIN IS YOUR ONLY MAN.

The contrast with the fine art-poetry of the Sweeney saga is made even plainer when Shanahan offers a compendium of the two traditions:

> Listen man, Listen to this before it's lost. When
> stags appear on the mountain high, with flanks the
> colour of bran, when a badger bold can say good-bye,
> A PINT OF PLAIN IS YOUR ONLY MAN!

This plain man tradition, a literary tradition that Joyce in particular sanctified, in which men speak like real Dubliners rather than in Synge-like stage Irish, is here used to question our literary premises. Certainly the plain men are funny, but this does not vitiate their importance. They contrast with Finn, but they are also similar to him: Finn is himself fairly comic, and in one fine moment he agrees with them against writers:

> Finn is without honour in the breast of a sea-blue book, Finn that is twisted and trampled and tortured for the weaving of a story-teller's book-web. Who but a book-poet would dishonour the God-big Finn for the sake of a gap-worded story?

There are some other cultural traditions used in the novel. A version of the time-steeped courtroom scene is used at the end of the novel, and there is a comic phase when the Good Fairy speaks directly from a gangster film:

> All right, you win. But by God I'll get even with you yet, if it takes me a thousand years. I'll get my own back, if I have to swing for it, don't forget that!

These instances seem to me affectionate gestures to popular tradition, though in brief they have an effect like that of the lengthy cowboy sequence. O'Brien is a master parodist, and the selections from his newspaper column in *The Best Of Myles* provide dozens of instances of his precise ear for the characteristics of various styles. But the fact that the writer occasionally indulges himself in parody and convention for the sheer literary fun – or, better, love – of it cannot obscure the fact that in general he is doing more than amusing himself or showing off his abilities: he often poses questions about attitudes to "reality" and belief, questions that develop into serious, even urgent analyses of the bases of our knowledge. Unless we laugh off everything O'Brien has to say as the work of a witty and essentially unserious jester – and his sheer intelligence makes that hard to do – then passages like those I have discussed must make us wonder where we stand. Partly by the simple juxtaposing of literary traditions he asks the question, which tradition is real for you, which one do you accept as good? But further than that, he throws the traditions into conflict, even confusion: is the Sweeney tradition in any real way better than, or different from that of the cowboy novel? Having raised this problem he follows it up with the remorselessness that is one of his most marked features. He deliberately confuses and even merges characters from one tradition with others, and so implies that they do all merge into a mixed condition where our confident premises about value, even of difference, need to be abandoned.

Thus the Pooka, principal agent of Trellis's novel, assumes some of the most famous attributes of Finn, principal agent in his own sagas. The Pooka has a magic thumb, like Finn's and the seat of his trousers, like Finn's hempen drawers, are preternaturally capacious:

> By the sorcery of his thumbs the Pooka produced a canvas tent from the seat of his trousers of seaman's serge and erected it swiftly upon the carpet of the soft daisy-studded sward, hammering clean pegs in the fresh-smelling earth by means of an odorous pinewood mallet. When he had accomplished this he produced another wonder from the storehouse of his pants, videlicet, a good -quality folding bed with a hickory framework complete with intimate bed-clothes of French manufacture.

Trellis, in the agony inflicted on him by his characters, especially by the Pooka, takes on many of the attributes of King Sweeney, who also suffered royally for his pretensions:

> Trellis was beleaguered by an anger and a darkness and he was filled with a restless tottering unquiet and with a disgust for the places that he knew and with a desire to go where he never was, so that he was palsied of hand and foot and eye-mad and heart-quick so that he went bird-quick in craze and madness into the upper air, the Pooka at his rat-flight beside him and his shirt, red and blood-lank, fluttering heavily behind him.

The relationship between Sweeney and Jem Casey, poets both, is embodied not only in Shanahan's Sweeneyesque Casey-imitation (quoted above), nor only in Casey's expressed sense of fraternity with Sweeney, but also in a deliberately confusing passage when the style itself implies that Sweeney is about to appear:

There was a prolonged snappling of stiffened rods and stubborn roots and the sharp agonies of fractured branches, the pitiless flogging against each other of green life-laden leaves, the thrashing and the scourging of a clump in torment, a jaggle of briar-braced tangly-brambled thorniness, incensed, with a demon in its breast.
Crack crack crack.
A small man came out of the foliage, a small man elderly and dark with a cloth cap and a muffler round his wind-pipe.
Jem by God Casey! said Slug Willard. Two emblems of amazement, his limp hands sank down to his waist until the thumbs found fastening in the bullet-studded belt.

The whole short sequence is a pastiche of the Sweeney saga, right through to the locutions "Two emblems of amazement" and "found fastening" in the otherwise modern style of the final paragraph. Distinctions that have previously seemed clear are here being blurred by the verbal surface of the novel itself. A minor effect of the same confusing nature occurs when the leaps of Sweeney and the hag are mixed up with the tall Irish story of Sergeant Craddock, the leaping policeman, who could jump twenty four feet six in his police boots.

This merging of traditions and of characters is created in action in the two major set-pieces of the last part of the novel. First we have the traditional chase across Ireland, where most of the characters in the story join in a cheery rout through the country. This is a basic motif of Celtic story, well illustrated in two of the semi-comic masterpieces of the Celts, the Irish *The Story of Mac Datho's Pig* and the Welsh *Culhwch and Olwen*. This piece of action brings most of the strands in *At Swim-Two-Birds* together, presenting in the action of the novel the interweaving that has been implicitly stated in the passages just discussed. The same is true of the trial scene, where the twelve jurors represent many cultural traditions and several centuries. It is no doubt a deliberate gesture on O'Brien's part that these last two pieces of action come one from Celtic antiquity and one from Hollywood contemporaneity. It is an exact emblem of the scope of the novel and it indicates surely the way in which O'Brien yokes together seemingly disparate materials and challenges us to be confident that they are truly disparate.

*

Throughout these pages I have been putting forward the view that O'Brien questions our ideas of reality, probes the reader's notions of what are absolute standards of goodness and even what are absolute standards of knowledge. The method is often implicit and the attack on the reader's epistemological certainties has been made through the implications of both the style of the novel and its structure. Towards the end of the novel O'Brien makes the assault more overt, though it is never absolutely so. For a fairly long sequence the characteristics of Shanahan, Lamont and Furriskey are expanded by Orlick Trellis, who has here taken over Trellis's novel and the three men merely bowl facts at each other for some time:

> Everyday or colloquial names for chemical substances, observed Mr Shanahan, cream of tartar – bitartrate of potassium, plaster of Paris – sulphate of calcium, water – oxide of hydrogen. Bells and watches on board ship: first dog – 4 p.m. to 6 p.m., second dog – 6 p.m. to 8 p.m., afternoon – noon to 4 p.m. Paris, son of Priam, King of Troy, carried off the wife of Menelaus, King of Sparta and thus caused the Trojan War.
> The name of the wife, said Lamont, was Helen. A camel is unable to swim owing to the curious anatomical distribution of its weight, which would cause its head to be immersed if the animal were placed in deep water. Capacity in electricity is measured by the farad; one microfarad is equal to one millionth of a farad. A carbuncle is a fleshy excresence resembling the wattles of a turkey-cock. Sphragistics is the study of engraved seals.

This disconnected discourse (it goes on for a long time) is a satire of fact; fact can be quite worthless. Nothing, in a sense, could be more real than the facts the three plain men bandy about but nothing, in this context and in this form, could be more worthless. Again, and here very clearly, the lack of absolute standards of knowledge and judgment is being asserted.

Throughout the novel the topic is pursued. When a novel has a narrator who occupies a good deal of the action, this normally gives a viewpoint. It is not so here: the narrator is as

helpless before the contents of his novel as Trellis is before his –
there are strong similarities between the two figures, of course,
both spending so much time in bed. (Not that this either is
necessarily a bad thing, as the epigraph to *The Hard Life*
reminds us: "Tout le trouble du monde vient de ce qu'on ne
sait pas rester seul dans sa chambre." – Pascal) The narrator's
powers of judgment within his own reminiscences are fairly
clearly faulty, but even in structural terms the narrator's
viewpoint is relative. The book, we recall, has three variant
openings and three variant conclusions. The narrator has no
place to stand as organizer of the novel's thoughts – O'Brien,
with a wholly admirable dedication to his craft, avoids that
simplicity as well .In this context the book's epigraph demands
to be quoted:

$$\text{'Εξίσταται γὰρ πάντ' ἀπ' ἀλλήλων δίχα}$$

Meaning "All things stand apart from each other," this is good
evidence that the tendencies I have been seeing in the novel
are neither accidental nor illusory, that O'Brien knows what
he is doing. Things stand apart, cannot be subjugated to a
system of order and are therefore of equal value.

Being outside the novel this epigraph is the voice of the
author; at one other place in the novel O'Brien – one might
almost now say O'Nolan as the man emerges from behind the
novelist – sums up the relativity of truth and reality. In the
"ultimate" conclusion, neither in the voice of Trellis nor the
narrator, though still maintaining the comic tone that has
been present throughout the novel, he says:

> But which of us can hope to probe with questioning finger
> the dim thoughts that flit in a fool's head? One man will
> think he has a glass bottom and will fear to sit in case of
> breakage. In other respects he will be a man of great
> intellectual force and will accompany one in a mental
> ramble throughout the labyrinths of mathematics or
> philosophy so long as he is allowed to remain standing
> throughout the disputations.

If the conclusion that O'Brien comes to is that lines cannot be
drawn, that an order cannot be established between sanity and
madness, relevance and irrelevance, truth and untruth, then
this must be in many ways a disturbing conclusion, offering

little comfort of any sort apart from a sense of clear-sightedness. O'Brien's great strength here is that he can follow through a line of argument: the last words of the novel set out the desperate gloom that his comic explorations have arrived at, and with a stylistic consistenty that is truly impressive he states this in grimly comic form:

> Well known, alas, is the case of the poor German who was very fond of three and who made each apsect of his life a thing of triads. He went home one evening and drank three cups of tea with three lumps of sugar in each, cut his jugular with a razor three times and scrawled out with a dying hand on a picture of his wife good-bye, good-bye, good-bye.

From "Forms of Gloom: The Novels of Flann O'Brien", in Don Anderson & Stephen Knight (eds.), *Cunning Exiles: Studies of Modern Prose Writers* (Sydney: Angus & Robertson, 1974), pp. 105-20.

ENTIRELY FICTITIOUS

By Miles Orvell

Throughout Flann O'Brien's writings one senses a playing at the edge of things – of conventions, of cultural traditions, of madness – as if the pervading question in his career were, What kind of literature can an Irishman write today? Writing in the *Irish Times* as Myles na gCopaleen, he scorned what he considered the cozy realism of O'Faolain and O'Connor – "wee Annie going to her first confession, stuff about country funerals." In another Myles column one detects, beneath the joking and posturing, a kind of nostalgia for the great grand themes of Irish poetry, the "five things and five things only that can be written about"; "Friendship ... treachery ... destruction of good by good. Passion which over-rides reason. VIOLENT AND PROUD DEATH!" Just these themes may be found in the medieval Irish poem, *The Madness of Sweeney*, which of course is retold in *At Swim-Two-Birds*. But the heroic Golden Age has clearly given away, for O'Brien, to the Ironic

Age: the old poem is parodied in *Swim,* and the hero Sweeney
straying into O'Brien's novel is far more hapless as an exile in
the modern world than he was as a blasphemer in his own
world.

   If O'Brien laid aside the traditional grand themes of
literature, he by no means discarded the sublime conception.
In a mock formulation of the creative ecstasy, Myles describes
writing "a 'novel' so vast in scope, so perfect in execution, so
overwhelming in conception, so sited in unheard-of dimensions
that ... no responsible publisher could risk bringing it before
the world." We may suspect a not very oblique reference to
Swim here, also perhaps to *The Third Policeman,* which in fact
did go unpublished until after O'Brien's death. But we may
also read into Myles' reasoning the axiom of modern art that
when traditional forms and rules wear out the artist must
invent his own. Several of Myles' columns were devoted to
educating the public to the demands imposed by recent art,
and one column especially offers considerable insight into
O'Brien's own fiction, in stressing that art is not an imitation of
reality but an independent form: "If I paint you a still life ...
this canvas can be placed *beside* any similar "natural" object, a
flower, a shell, a leaf, in *competition,* not in imitation." At first
this may seem merely a positive restatement of Coleridge's
negatively phrased point that "if the artist copies the mere
nature, the *natura naturata,* what idle rivalry." But Myles
chooses by way of illustration not the flower or leaf –
traditionally vegetable images of the artist's imitation of
"organic" form – but rather the shell; and pointedly missing
from his elaboration is precisely the usual metaphor of vital
growth. "A shell, in its accidents, is the phenomenal expression
of a design ... which is rigid, logical, coordinated ... In the
human scale, my paintings must inevitably exhibit the same
characteristics." Except in suggesting regularity and
symmetry, the non-mimetic attributes of the shell as Myles
describes it – rigid, logical, coordinated – well fit O'Brien's
novels. And to these we might add: convuluted and, at best,
reverberating with uncanny effect.

   Each of O'Brien's novels has its own "world", its own
physical characteristics, laws of space and time, its own formal
properties. In *At Swim-Two-Birds* it is a world of fiction, a
conventional or generic world, its laws the laws of reading.

Our tendency as readers to enter into an orderly world, to connect with the characters and events, is defeated at every page. To begin with there is a nest of plots – the student-narrator writing about his life with his uncle, about his school chums, and about the book he is writing – which itself forms a major thread, with its own inner tangles of sub-authors; then there are the various extracts of alien printed material incorporated into the text, from encyclopedias, dictionaries, and from *The Madness of Sweeney;* in addition there are fabricated "press" extracts, poems, multi-clause colloquies between a Good Fairy and a Pooka, and a slapstick episode involving rival gangs of cowboys – an updating, one assumes, of the traditional Irish tales of cattle raids.

On first reading, the whole is anything but "rigid, logical, coordinated." But certainly much great literature involves disordering as well as ordering, and Walter Slatoff's observation that when we reread fiction very often the "same structures which had served to fragment experience now serve to pull it together," is eminently true in the present case. For one, the "three openings entirely dissimilar and inter-related only in the prescience of the author" – with which *Swim* begins – in fact do come together, the different casts intermixing; and we come to realize that the initial separation is a device for arousing expectation by withholding information. Other binding forces are the several parodies that run throughout the book – the parodies of the heroic description of Finn MacCool and of *The Madness of Sweeney,* to name just two. Still other passages seem part of a web of associations, cross-references, and parallels: Sweeney's leaps prompt a celebration of Sergeant Craddock's athletic long jumps; the use of the phrase "chiefest wisdom" sprouts an extract from *Ecclesiasticus,* the source of the "distinctive adjective," and so on. It would be bizarre to claim any sort of traditional unity for *Swim,* but it is by no means without design. One might liken it to the newt Lord Edward Tantamount manufactures in Huxley's *Point Counter Point:* a tail attached where a leg should be. Ungainly, but alive.

Like *Tristram Shandy, Swim* derives its primary impulse from the author's delight in controlling the reader's response. Writing as Myles, O'Brien scorned the passive aesthetic experience, which assumes that the artist is "strictly a turkish bath attendant." Thus in *Swim* O'Brien repeatedly interrupts the narrative flow by a variety of devices. When, for example, the narrator's uncle inquires after his nephew's health – "And how is our friend?" – we are not given the reply itself, but a description of it: "Nature of my reply: Civil, perfunctory, uninformative." And throughout the novel material is introduced – or concluded – with a label of some sort, as if drolly solicitous of the kind of sentiment expressed by one of the characters (a philistine): "I like to know where I am, do you know." The contrary device, of *not* telling us when some transition has occurred is also used to comic effect, as in this passage from the "third opening":

> Three fifties of fosterlings could engage
> with handball against the wideness of
> [Finn MacCool's] backside, which was large
> enough to halt the march of men through a
> mountain-pass.
>   I hurt a tooth in the corner of my jaw
> with a lump of the crust I was eating.

The latter sentence, we realize after a moment of confusion, is the student-narrator's resumption of the narrative. Both of these devices – interrupting reflections on the material and lack of usual transition between passages – distance us from the "content" of the story, to make us attend to the telling of it. Yet curiously the interruptions, by engaging the reader in a game with rules of attention, may also create a more intense involvement and come to seem an integral part of the whole.

A further aspect of O'Brien's control of the reader's response is his playing with our normal empathy for fictional characters, especially our sense of their physical being. Thus the characters in the employ of Dermot Trellis, the student-narrator's author-hero, discuss preferred ways of dying ("Do you know what it is, said Furriskey, you can drown me three times before you roast me") and move on to the minute particulars of home medical treatments: "They tell me if you steam the face, said Shanahan, the pores will – you know – open. That's the man for blackheads, plenty of steam." Such dialogue would be laughable under any circumstances, but our heightened awareness of the speakers' status as characters in Trellis' fiction lends it a poetry all its own – if we take

Marianne Moore's definition of poetry as "imaginary gardens with real toads in them."

If the question of control is central to the author-reader relationship in *Swim,* it is equally the key to the various author-character relationships that shape the action of the novel. Several theories are floated by the student-narrator and by Dermot Trellis, his novelist-hero, and each is subjected to a somewhat ironic development. The student-narrator's thesis is that "it was undemocratic to compel characters to be uniformly good or bad or poor or rich. Each should be allowed a private life, self-determination and a decent standard of living." The thesis is illustrated, in a fashion, by Trellis, who is writing just such a despotic book as the narrator condemns – despotic in its control of the reader's response and despotic in the author's control of his characters, each of whom is given a fixed role to play in a moral drama designed to illustrate Trellis' contention that "all children were born clean and innocent .... They grew up to be polluted by their foul environment and transformed ... into bawds and criminals and harpies." What actually happens in Trellis' novel demonstrates the dangers of novelistic despotism. Two contrary theories of character invention govern Trellis' book, and both lead to chaos. One, affirmed by the student-narrator and apparently bequeathed by him to Trellis, states that "characters should be interchangeable as between one book and another." Thus the student-narrator recirculates Sweeney and Finn MacCool, while Trellis borrows, among others, Antony Lamont (from an undisclosed author) and Paul Shanahan (from William Tracy, the fictitious author of numerous popular Dublin cowboy stories). The second theory of character invention, called "aestho-autogamy," exploits the fact that most characters spring full grown from their author's brow, their age and identity part of the novel's donnée. The supposed villain of Trellis' fiction, John Furriskey, is a creature of this process and is called upon by the plot to seduce and corrupt two women – Peggy, a domestic, and Sheila Lamont, "a very beautiful and refined girl." But in the working out of his despotic plot, the author loses control: Furriskey and Peggy fall in love and decide to lead virtuous lives in defiance of Trellis' orders. And the author is so taken with Sheila Lamont that he assaults her himself. The product of this union is a third, and unexpected, type of literary creation – the novelist's son Orlick Trellis, himself a writer.

When the characters, unhappy in their assigned roles, become determined in their rebellion against Trellis, they propel *Swim* to its chaotic climax. If characters "keep on being good, according to pattern, or bad, according to pattern, or even volatile, according to pattern, they cease to live, and the novel falls dead," D. H. Lawrence wrote. "A character in a novel has got to live, or it is nothing." It is precisely by their struggle to break out of Trellis's pattern that his own characters live, though it remains at least debatable whether their rebellious lives were assigned to them, according to pattern, by the student-narrator. But we hardly notice this involution of *Swim's* irony: O'Brien's novel lives in the comic vibrations between our belief in the characters and our knowledge of their fictional status. And for all its contrivance, the novel, ballasted by the sentient corporeality of the characters, escapes being overly artificial.

The last section of *Swim,* labelled *"Conclusion of the book, ultimate,"* is climaxed by an anecdote of a "poor German who was very fond of three and who made each aspect of his life of thing of triads. He went home one evening and drank three cups of tea with three lumps of sugar in each cup, cut his jugular with a razor three times and scrawled with a dying hand on a picture of his wife good-bye, good-bye, good-bye." It is not, perhaps, as gratuitously grim a conclusion as may seem at first, for the novel has balanced uneasily between order and chaos, between control and impulse, and this last image suggests that even self-destruction can be encompassed by controlling structures and made an orderly and in some way satisfying act – for a madman.

From "Entirely Fictitious: The Fiction of Flann O'Brien", in *The Journal of Irish Literature*, III, 1 (January 1974), pp. 93-98.

AN EXTRAORDINARY ACHIEVEMENT

By Anthony Cronin

The works which Brian O'Nolan published as Flann O'Brien are four in number and the brief list is headed by an indubitable masterpiece, *At Swim-Two-Birds,* the reputation of which continued to dog its author for the rest of his days, certainly affecting his judgment of the book to such an extent that the mere mention of it, in latter years at least, appeared to cause him pain, and probably, which is more important, inhibiting the production of a fitting successor.

There is an initial irony here in that it was not to begin with, in the ordinary sense indicated by reviews and sales, much of a success; and although Flann O'Brien's first novel achieved a quite genuine place in the affections of a considerable number of people, there were confusions and misconceptions attending its partial and localised reception which in the absence of any very perceptive criticism tended to attract attention to certain superficial aspects of it as well as to conceal (perhaps even from its author) the true nature of what had been achieved. It is discouraging to be underestimated and even more so to receive no praise at all; but to have the accidental and secondary characteristics of what has in fact been done elevated above the important ones makes continuance in the true vein difficult, as Flann O'Brien (who was oddly suggestible and anxious for reassurance about anything he wrote) was to find. Criticism where *At Swim-Two-Birds* was concerned tended to lag woefully behind mere enjoyment; and while that situation has its charms it cannot (to the extent that criticism is ever of any help to an author) have been of much assistance to him. More important for us now perhaps is the fact that ten years after his death much of the nature of his achievement and much of its greatness remain unrecognised.

Foremost among the confusions surrounding *At Swim-Two-Birds* have been the related ideas of the prodigiously clever literary jape and the brilliantly opportunistic commentary on or pastiche of the works of James Joyce by a member of a younger literary generation. That *At Swim-Two-Birds* is in part a sort of comic coda to all the previous utterances of humanity is indeed true; but then so is most of the great literature of the twentieth century. That it is in any subservient sense a commentary on, or, in any sense at all, mere parody of Joyce's works is a woeful misconception.

But the Joycean idea quickly took root, in Dublin and elsewhere. It was known that the book had been praised by James Joyce. Perhaps by a sort of corollary, it was assumed to be Joycean. Through a curious set of chances there were more copies of *At Swim-Two-Birds* available in Dublin of the nineteen-forties and early fifties than there were of *Ulysses,* and since what could be taken as the Joycean characteristics in Flann O'Brien's book were indeed evident, some quite intelligent people were prepared to take the Joycean domination of it for granted, without any very close examination of the differences between, or even of the properly complementary aspects of, the two.

*

There was, for one thing, the syncretic and eclectic method, known to be Joyce's, whereby a great deal of earlier literature and heroic myth had been included and exploited for some reason pertaining to the contemporary characters and their situation. The purposes of this procedure even in Joyce's case were not yet clear; but in each instance the effect was, whatever else it might be, comic; and so the intention was presumed to be identical. And although both are mentioned in Flann O'Brien's text it was overlooked that the American poets T. S. Eliot and Ezra Pound had been up to precisely the same game.

Allied to this there was in the case of both Joyce and Flann O'Brien the devouring, almost all consuming interest in the way words exposed their users and frequently mocked them, revealed the false and ridiculous aspects of a culture and an era and allowed individuals and civilisations generally to make fools out of themselves. That within the narrower and less discursive limits of poetry, this had been one of the pre-occupations of Pound and Eliot also was likewise overlooked.

There was too the substitution of an apparent incon-sequentiality for the machinery of a dramatic causation and the exploration of the merely banal and the undeniably sordid in place of what had been regarded hitherto as the dramatically interesting or the poetically significant. *Ulysses* has also resembled *The Waste Land* and other works in that it had done both. The difference was that it had done so in prose, where, if the banal was more allowable, and its rewarding aspects perhaps easier to demonstrate (the matter is debatable) the achievement of a certain sort of lifelike inconsequentiality was more difficult, precisely because up to that point all prose utterance had been more firmly bound than poetry in the apparent laws of consequential logic; and the novel in particular had been compelled to obey the rigid command-ments of plot.

What was perhaps less often noticed in the case of *Ulysses* then (both because the book itself was hard to come by and because the debate on the future of the novel which it initiated had hardly begun) was the effect that work had had on the future of the form. In abandoning dramatic interest and significance, Joyce had done almost everything to abolish the novel as a form except finally to expose the merely wilful and autocratic relationship between the creator and his fictions. Whatever the relationship between the book and Stephen Dedalus, the final step had not been taken. That somewhat ambiguous young man was not declared to be the writer of the fiction in which he appeared. The novel as a form was spared the ultimate indignity of being exhibited as the product of one of its characters.

Flann O'Brien went one better. It was a brilliantly conceived step; but unfortunately for him it was also a brilliantly and deliberately nihilistic one; and partly because of his peculiar relationship with his audience it put him in a position which he found it difficult to develop and from which he found it almost impossible to withdraw.

And that in the meantime in all these things Flann O'Brien was in the central stream not just of Irish post-Joycean literature but of the modern movement in general was the more easily overlooked because to add to the Joycean confusions there was the identity of subject matter. Irish Catholic students and members of the Dublin Catholic lower middle classes were the principal characters in both Joyce and Flann O'Brien, while in each also the main protagonist was a Catholic student would-be writer with an interest in the fundamentals of Catholic teaching.

*

This was an accident. There was no way out of it unless to write a fiction of an entirely different sort and in fact Flann O'Brien made the more sensible decision and occasionally adverted to it obliquely in his text. In doing this he was in part, of course, properly calling attention to the fact that he and Joyce were both sharers in and would ultimately be seen as early founders of a tradition. Irish literature in English was in its infancy. He doubtless intended to make his position clear; and in any case a degree of incestuousness is certainly no harm in the case of a threatened and ambiguously positioned literature such as our own.

But he can scarcely have been in any doubt that what he was doing was of significance not only for Irish, but for modern literature in general. It was not only James Joyce, but modern literature and poetry which had been concerned since Baudelaire with what appeared to be the sordid, unfruitful, desultory and boring aspects of modern life. To these it had juxtaposed fragments of mythology or of archaic splendour which suggested that the dimensions of that life were narrower and its conditions meaner than those of any previous era. The *Waste Lane, Ulysses* and even the Cantos and *Hugh Selwyn Mauberley* had continually shocked and surprised by opening up vistas beyond the contemporary in humanity's store of mythology or exhibiting evidence of other values than the contemporary in fragments of its heroic past. Although their purpose in doing this was, as has been said, debated, it was generally agreed that the net effect on the contemporary was diminishment. Bloom was seen as a comic, sordid and unworthy Odysseus. The seduction by the Thames in *The Waste Land* was in the poem deliberately contrasted for dignity and significance with the love of Elizabeth and Leicester; the abandonment seen as shabby and degrading when the story of Dido and Aeneas was hinted at. So far as the present writer is aware, until he said so in the nineteen sixties there had been no-one to suggest that the use of myth in *Ulysses* "cuts both ways", and that if it cast a peculiar light on Bloom and his contemporaries it also shed an odd one on the pretences of epic and heroic poetry. (See *Twentieth Century Views: Joyce* edited by William M. Chace. Prentice-Hall, 1974). Joyce had, it was recognised, indulged himself in some rather heavy humour at the expense of the gigantism of Irish saga; but it is not at all unlikely that it must have seemed to the author of *At Swim-Two-Birds* in the 1930s that a humanisation of myth, a reduction of it to humanity's scale and an exploration of the revivifying as well as the comic possibilities of myth-juxtaposition was long overdue.

All of these things in any case he has brilliantly achieved in *At Swim.* The devices by which he does so are beyond number and include comic realignments and subsumations of all descriptions. But intricately planned and structured as the book was and although these devices were all the time comic ones, the triumph is, as it should be, more a matter of feeling than of thought; and in the end it is the extraordinary extension of feeling that counts: to Finn as an old bore who yet has dignity sharing the firelight in the digs with Shanahan and Lamont; to Sweeny as a representative of all bare, forked humanity in its ultimate distress.

And along with this tender diminishment and humanisation of myth goes a positive elevation of the banal and the inconsequential. Joyce had managed this of course; indeed it had from *Dubliners* onward been one of his principal concerns and ambitions to do so. But there had always, from the story called "Grace" to the scene in Holles Street, been a shadow of impatience and of near-Swiftian disgust in Joyce's dealings with the banal; and his delight in it had never been so freed from the shackles of his own kind of consequence and plot as the story of the jumping Irishman or the discussion of the fiddle as an instrument was freed.

Nor is there in Joyce, to suit these processes of reduction and elevation, such a necessary and again feelingful reduction of the creator himself. Joyce's loyalty to the artificer had always remained absolute. He had insisted time and time again on the godlike characteristics of the writer. Not so Flann O'Brien. Prodigously talented though the author of all the sub-plots in *At Swim-Two-Birds* may be showing himself to be, he is simultaneously revealing himself as a dependant stripling whose literary activities are merely part-time. "Great man" and rival of Joyce's "God of creation" though Trellis may be, he is yet at the mercy of his own creations and exposed as a frequent victim of the haphazard and the accidental in a way that contrasts strangely and refreshingly with the claim to be the unerring master of extraordinarily deep-laid strategies which had been central to the method and the pretensions of James Joyce (or Stephen Dedalus or whatever god-like creator lurked behind *Ulysses*). That Flann O'Brien was at the same time proving himself the master of quite fantastic strategic turns and coups only added to the irony of his own young author's abdication of the claim.

At Swim-Two-Birds was in all these respects an extraordinary achievement; and it might – indeed it ought – to have been seen as at least as central of the whole nascent modern tradition as it was in any way merely relative to the work of James Joyce. Since it is also unfailingly interesting, hilariously funny and a marvellously controlled display of as much as he intended to reveal of its author's personality, its perculiar brilliance would in any case and in ordinary circumstances have been difficult to surpass. But there were special circumstances pertaining to Flann O'Brien's case which made the process of development more difficult than it otherwise might have been....

From the *Irish Times* (5 December 1975).

AFTER *AT SWIM*

By Anthony Cronin

When *At Swim-Two-Birds* was published in 1939 the chief masterpieces of modern, avant-garde writing in English were not quite 20 years old; and the main elements of Flann O'Brien's book were those of its celebrated predecessors. There was the juxtaposition of ancient myth and contemporary reality in order to reveal something about humanity's past imaginings and present condition. There was the contrast between the banalties of everyday communication and the now suspect but still powerful resources of poetry. And there was the achievement of a form which rejected the old laws of sequence and consequence in favour of a consequentiality which had its own links and tensions.

Twentieth century literature was in part a comment on a perhaps irrelevant past and in part a confrontation with a present which the past would have found unimaginable. Flann O'Brien had placed himself unerringly in the central tradition of that literature and he had done so with a single book.

Like all books, it posed the problem of what its author should do next. This was a problem which both the inclusive and the nihilistic strains in the archetypal masterpieces of modern literature had already created for their authors. Joyce's mistake of direction after *Ulysses* is notorious: Eliot's difficulty about finding one after *The Waste Land* almost equally apparent: in the eight years that followed he wrote only one short poem. And in Flann O'Brien's book the nihilistic elements – those which tended to break down if not to abolish altogether the form in which he wrote – had been particularly strong.

SPECIAL FACTORS

At Swim-Two-Birds had been a genuine anti-novel and its author's delight in flouting the restraints and mocking the conventions of the genre had been extreme. What he had done would in any case have rendered either advance or retreat within the boundaries of prose fiction exceptionally difficult (and a retreat into the plotted and mapped placidities of the ordinary novel might even have been the best thing for him) but there were special factors obtaining in his case which must have made it more so.

In U.C.D. he had acquired a reputation for extraordinary cleverness and virtuosity. However and wherever acquired such reputations tend to turn men of true originality and capacity into mere wits and measurers of effect, dinner-table virtuosos and creatures of unfulfilled promise; and in Dublin, although there are no dinner-tables to speak of, they are especially deleterious because the conditions and atmosphere of U.C.D. are reproduced almost exactly among the more or less literate in the town at large.

In any other society an artist such as Brian O'Nolan had now (as Flann O'Brien) shown himself to be would have had a better chance of escaping such an initial disadvantage as having great things expected of him before he had properly begun represented. Even here a man of his resources might have dismayed his admirers in unexpected ways, but much now conspired against him.

At Swim-Two-Birds had attracted no worthwile published criticism to speak of; and although, according to Miss Clissmann, "for one glorious week in April (1939) *At Swim* replaced *Gone With The Wind* as top of the best-selling list in Dublin", it turns out that it sold in fact 244 copies in the first six months after publication (a fact which may stand as a comment on all Irish success stories whatever, then or now). When its immediate successor, *The Third Policeman,* was rejected by one or more London publishers in the following year the attractions of other modes of expression for an energetic and ambitious man whose attitude to literary form was, to say the least, provisional and experimental must have been increased.

IN SEARCH OF MEANING

But even *The Third Policeman,* highly praised though it was on its posthumous appearance 27 years later, shows what a trap his masterpiece and his U.C.D. reputation may have conjoined to create for him. Flann O'Brien's first novel had been on the surface at least, a brilliantly resourceful and quick-witted book. To some (even among its author's admirers) it may have seemed little more. Alternatively however, it was the sort of work which could be interpreted as having a "meaning", which is something that criticism is always inclined to search for: indeed in the case of *Ulysses* academic criticism has not abandoned the search yet. If a book as intricately constructed but apparently as pointless as *At Swim-Two-Birds* is to be more than clever, the argument runs, it must be profound. And whether indeed he was influenced by the desire to show that he had a great deal more to offer than the presumed virtuosity of *At Swim-Two-Birds* or not, *The Third Policeman* seems to betray at the very least an anxiety on its author's part to show that he could write a work which contained an important inner meaning, which was in fact "profound". The usual device of those who wish to do that is allegory, *The Third Policeman* is allegorical.

It suffers, therefore, from the usual fault of allegory in that the world of its author's imagining lacks substance, texture and, even, detail. The book is full of oddly generalised and amorphous description, that of landscape, which occupies such a large part of it, being composed in the most laborious way out of mere landscape elements, like a child's picture; while the people seem to be constructed in the manner of photo-fit pictures with feature added to feature in a painstaking way until the whole is complete. And if the mere anxiety to describe is disquieting enough, apart from its visual aspects the prose in which it is done would have seemed to somebody who had an ear for such matters and was given an opportunity of reading the book in sequence after *At Swim-Two-Birds* to be something of a give-away. Now that the covers were off was the manipulator of so many modes to be seen to have none of his own?

Nor does the allegory appear, to this reader at least, to be consistent with itself, which all allegory must be or else fail utterly. There is a Faustian theme, within which is included admittedly one brilliant joke: the ambition of Faust in the modern world being to write the definitive book about somebody else, in this case the ineffably tiresome De Selby; but if the narrator is Faust there is too much left hanging and too much contradiction; while if it is all an allegory about man and the machine it is a highly simplistic one. If on the other hand the book is an exploration of guilt and retribution, the variations of mood within such a short compass would seem to vitiate it, for guilt is the most pervasive and unremitting of emotions. Though its pressures may vary, it remains a constant, a fact which Kafka's *The Trial* wonderfully exemplifies; but in *The Third Policeman* it is as if the author's natural bent and zest are pulling him all the time towards the comically inconsequential and the banal but he is refusing to give way, so that in the net result he has substituted an equally false consequentiality for the consequentialities of plot which he had already learned to do without.

MYLES NA gCOPALEEN

Not long after the rejection of *The Third Policeman* Brian O'Nolan began, as Myles na gCopaleen, to write a column for this newspaper and he continued to do so on and off for the next 26 years. About the merits of this column there can be no dispute, for apart from anything else the prose in which it was written would have made it remarkable, while as an exercise in what he called the "compartmentation of personality for the purposes of literary utterance" it was even more so; and in the best years of the column the ingenuity, humour and intelligence as well as the selected compartments of his total personality thus displayed were a constant joy. Such were its merits in fact that "Cruiskeen Lawn" may well have been the best piece of sustained journalism that the last 30 or 40 years have produced in any language, but one thing which many of its admirers have claimed it to be it was not. As satire the column (which in any case never struck this reader at least as having a true satirical intent) was too closely in tune with its audience, too fanciful and too quirky to be more than occasionally worthy of note; and when in its later years it became sometimes querulous and bed-tempered the purposes of satire were not served either.

About the other productions of Myles na gCopaleen opinions may differ. *An Béal Bocht* is true satire, right enough, and although much of the joke may be lost on those whose Irish is not sufficient to grasp it, even in translation it seems to the present reader at least to be a considerable work, about the human condition as well as the Irish, while the first act at least of *Faustus Kelly* is true satire and is hilarious.

After these works, though, for a very long time, nearly twenty years in fact, there was to all intents and purposes only the column. One sort of promise remained unfulfilled, while another, perhaps that which some of his contemporaries had in their heart of hearts forecast for him, became in its fulfillment a feature of the Dublin scene. For if the man of promise everywhere holds out to his admirers the possibility of brilliant failure, in Ireland's and Dublin's mode of response up to now the man of genius is always a man of flawed achievement, the prisoner rather than the triumphant possessor of his own talent, the victim of his gift. Besides the difficulty of choosing between the expedients with which he was now confronted, and apart altogether from his own temperament and the choices it imposed, Brian O'Nolan had now like others a part to play out which was the result of a curious collaboration between himself and the race. In these circumstances it is remarkable enough that he should have produced two more novels in the years remaining to him, and still more remarkable perhaps that one of these, *The Hard Life* should be such an astounding little success.

THE LAST NOVELS

Not least because to do so would be some sort of an affront to the essentially modest nature of the work itself, one does not wish to make too large a claim for it, so suffice it to say here that all Flann O'Brien's original discoveries about the inconsequential and the banal, all his mastery of Dublin speech and delight in the pointless dialectics of its citizens are again on display. For those who will have the Joycean element there is the marvellous inspiration he quite evidently derived from the relationship between Stanislaus and Stephen (and how he managed that one does not know, for *My Brother's Keeper* was a practically simultaneous publication). If this is a universalisation there is a great deal that is particularly Irish in the book too, not least in the exegesis of a particular mode of squalor of which the sub-title gives promise; but even on the level of the day to day it is amazing how much ground is covered and how topical the book (set as it is at the turn of the century) is proving to be: women's rights, the relaxation and liberalisation of religious dogma, the relationship of nationalism to practical reform and violence as an instrument of change being among the many topics that are touched on. It is no use growing solemn about it, but those who do not recognise it for the gem it is, are, I suggest, lacking in a particular faculty of recognition.

THE ACHIEVEMENT

About *The Dalkey Archive*, though, perhaps the least said the better. If the revelations of personality in *At Swim-Two-Birds* and *The Hard Life* are superbly judged and controlled, in this there appears to be the sort of failure even to notice when they occur which is almost always disastrous in a novel. The elements of *The Third Policeman* which have been taken over are spoiled, such as they are, in the taking; and there is again a lamentable attempt at profundity. Catholicism is treated as a shared joke in the manner of clerics being daring. Only James Joyce and the underwear do something to redeem things.

The impression of course remains that in spite of all the hard work and the effort of one kind or another, the achievement of Brian O'Nolan could have been greater than it is; but although since we live in a particular society and a particular country it is important to discuss, for the future's sake at least, the societal factors in what went wrong, it is nevertheless important that criticism should see the total achievement for what it is, leaving out the wastage and the element of flawed promise. How much of the column and the miscellaneous writings will survive the years is dubious. Probably not much, but they were alive in our time and we in theirs, and a journalist with his eye on eternity is in any case a contradiction in terms. Among the novels (leaving out *An Beal Bocht)* there are two which will survive: one masterpiece which is, or should be, central to Irish literature and increasingly seen as important to the world's; and, whatever about *The Third Policeman,* one little gem which in the opinion of the present writer at least will prove very durable. Considering we live in a poor country, not bad.

From the *Irish Times* (12 December 1975).

THE STORY-TELLER'S BOOK-WEB

By Anne Clissmann

At Swim-Two-Birds by "Flann O'Brien" (the name by which O'Nolan became known to thousands of readers and by which he will be referred to throughout the rest of this study) was published in 1939, having occupied its author some five years. It was written during the latter part of his time at UCD (while he was completing his MA thesis) and his early years in the civil service. The book is first mentioned in *Comhthrom Féinne* in June 1935. In an article entitled "Literary Antecedents" Niall Sheridan informed his readers that 'Ó Nulláin is now engaged on a novel so ingeniously constructed that the plot is keeping him well in hand.'[1] Later Sheridan was to realise that, as Brinsley, he "shared with Finn MacCool the honour of being one of the characters"[2] in the book. O'Brien showed him the various sections as they were written and when the book was completed gave him a free hand to prune its excessive length.

None of O'Brien's other novels was to take such a time to complete. In general, once he had the idea for its plot, each book was written very quickly. The delay in completing *At Swim* was due partly to the fact that it was started at a time when O'Brien was engaged in many other activities. The basic plot of *At Swim* was developed as early as 1934 when O'Brien was still writing for *Comhthrom Féinne*. From that he went on to write, illustrate and edit *Blather*, to complete his MA thesis, and to pass the civil service exams and begin a new career. In his job he worked a five-and-a-half-day week and can have had little time to devote to the progress of the book. It was, however, finished early in 1938, when O'Brien claimed that it was suffering from hypertrophy, particularly in the Finn MacCool sections, and reduced it in length by approximately one-third.

O'Brien began to make the rounds of publishers and agents. On 31 January 1938 he wrote to C. H. Brooks at the office of A. M. Heath & Co., the literary agents, and told him about the book.

> It is called *At Swim-Two-Birds* and is a very queer affair, unbearably queer, perhaps. For all its defects, I feel it has the ingredients that make the work of writers from this beautiful little island so acceptable.[3]

O'Brien probably wrote this tongue-in-cheek, but however insincere it might have been, the letter had the desired effect. Brooks asked to see the book. He liked it, and A. M. Heath became, and remained, O'Brien's literary agent. Longmans in England were secured as publishers. At this time Graham Greene was with Longmans, and he was most enthusiastic about the book. O'Brien later showed his appreciation for this support when he dedicated *The Hard Life* to Graham Greene. Greene was not, however, the only person at Longmans who felt such enthusiasm. A. M. Heath reported to O'Brien that Longmans had written to them saying "We are all rather excited over his MS and would like to meet him."[4]

The publication did not proceed without some difficulties, most of them of O'Brien's own making. He was discontented with the title, which he described as "defective from the commercial viewpoint" and suitable only as the "title for a slim book of poems".[5] He suggested *Sweeny in the Trees* as an alternative. But by this time, the people at Longmans had grown accustomed to *At Swim-Two-Birds* and were reluctant to change it, though it is possible that O'Brien's suggestion might have been a better choice. Swim-Two-Birds (or Snámh-dá-én) is only one of the places visited by Sweeny in his flight through Erin, and the lay which he recited in that place was not included in O'Brien's translation. *Sweeny in the Trees* is a title derived from a line in the "Conclusion of the book, ultimate": "Sweeny in the trees hears the sad baying as he sits listening on the branch, a huddle between the earth and heaven" (p. 314). The line is an important one for it highlights the importance of the Sweeny section in the book's overall plan. The change of the title would have pointed even more strongly to the central importance of Sweeny in the structure and vision of *At Swim*. The title *At Swim-Two-Birds* leads the reader to expect some special significance from the section where Sweeny visits Snámh-dá-én but this expectations are baffled by the exclusion of the lay spoken there.

At one stage O'Brien decided to change his pseudonym from Flann O'Brien to John Hackett. He had first used "Flann O'Brien" in the O'Connor-Ó Faoláin controversy and did not wish his book to be associated with that somewhat acrimonious dispute. He wrote to Longmans and told them that he did not want his "real name" to be linked with anything that was not entirely orthodox.[6] But by that time it was (fortunately) too late to change it. "John Hackett" would have been an unfortunate choice, whereas "Flann O'Brien" carries with it the right sort of associations for this book. As O'Brien himself had pointed out to Longmans on 10 November 1938, it "has the advantage that it contains an unusual name and one that is quite ordinary. 'Flann' is an old Irish name now rarely heard." The name "Flann" means "blood-red"[7] and was probably thought suitable for the angry opponent of O'Connor and Ó Faoláin, but it was also borne by the ninth-century scholar-poet Flann mac Lonán and by the seventeenth-century historical scholar Flann Mac Aodhagáin, while O'Brien was the family name of a number of kings of Ireland. The complete name therefore associates the author with the Gaelic royal families and with the early Irish literary and scholastic tradition.

The book, when it appeared on 13 March 1939, was called *At Swim-Two-Birds* and it was by "Flann O'Brien". Perhaps the date of publication was an inauspicious one, for the book was to prove a financial failure. Six months later only 244 copies had been sold. The outbreak of war may have made bookselling more difficult, or was O'Brien's own explanation correct?

In the year 1939, a book curiously named *At Swim-Two-Birds* appeared. Adolf Hitler took serious exception to it and in fact loathed it so much that he started World War II in order to torpedo it. In a grim irony that is not without charm, the book survived the war while Hitler did not.

The book survived the war due to the fact that, although it was not widely read, it was received with intense enjoyment by a small but influential group of discriminating critics and writers. It became, and remained until its reissue in 1960, a coterie taste, a book which its small number of owners were reluctant to let out of their hands – even to friends – because they knew it would not be returned. It came to have a reputation as a "difficult", "intellectual" book, its patterns of parody and literary cross-reference only clear to the highly educated.

Those enthusiasts who had greeted the book in 1939 did not share this view. It was praised by Graham Greene and William Saroyan, and Niall Sheridan's story of Joyce's reception of it is well known. In a letter to MacGibbon & Kee he said:

In the spring of 1939 I brought a copy of the novel (inscribed by the author) to Joyce in Paris. His eyesight was then so bad that he could read very little. I was amazed to find that he had already read, and greatly enjoyed, *At Swim-Two-Birds*.

He took very little interest in contemporary writing, but his verdict on Flann O'Brien's book was emphatic and brief: "That's a real writer, with the true comic spirit. A really funny book." It was significant tribute, for he later went on to speak of the pomposity and solemnity of many critics of *Ulysses*. He felt they had missed the point, and he wished that more of them realised that *Ulysses* was essentially a *funny* book.

Joyce's interest in the book took a practical form. He went to considerable trouble to have it noticed in French literary circles and wrote to tell mc of his efforts. He persuaded the well-known critic Maurice Denhof to write an article for the *Mercure de France,* but Denhof died suddenly and the project came to nothing.

Although the war was now on and Joyce had moved to the South, he kept on trying to interest various literary friends of his in the book and was still writing from Vichy on the matter only nine months before his death.

There's an interesting postscript to the story. Before moving to his last Paris residence (34 rue de Vignes) Joyce pruned his library drastically. After his death this reduced remnant of the library was sold by his Paris landlord. Paul Leon and some other friends managed to buy in about two-thirds of the books and among them was the copy of *At Swim* which I had delivered in 1939.

It is included in a catalogue of the salvaged books which was published by the Librarie la Hune (170 Blvd. Saint-Germaine) in 1949. The entry relating to *At Swim-Two-Birds* is followed by a notice in italics which reads "Livre tres aimé de Joyce...[8]

For one glorious week in April *At Swim* replaced *Gone With the Wind* as top of the best-seller list in Dublin. It was favourably reviewed in the Dublin newspapers and sold well until the middle of April, and again for a week in June, after which it disappeared and was not again available until 1960, more than twenty years later.

It was not published in America until 1951. The American branch of Longmans had decided in 1939 that "it was a little too odd for the market",[9] and they rejected it. O'Brien wanted an American edition, so when William Saroyan offered to find a publisher, he accepted eagerly. Saroyan's efforts met with no success and it was not until 1951 that Pantheon decided to publish *At Swim.* There is some confusion about this publication. O'Brien made some visits to the USA in 1948 and 1949, but when he wrote to Tim O'Keeffe in 1959 he said that he had no knowledge of how the American publication had come about. O'Keeffe made enquiries and wrote to tell O'Brien that the book had been recommended to Pantheon by James Johnson Sweeney of the Guggenheim Museum. Seamus Kelly of the *Irish Times*, however, was under the impression that the publication was a result of the enthusiastic advocacy of Richard Watts, Jnr of the *New York Herald Tribune*. Richard Watts has himself confirmed this in a letter to the present writer. He said that when he was press attaché in Ireland in 1942 he had been introduced to O'Brien by Seamus Kelly. He was impressed by O'Brien's work and wrote a number of articles about him. He continued:

> I finally persuaded an American publisher to bring out *At Swim-Two-Birds* here. But the wonderful novel was ahead of its time here, and it sold virtually no copies. In fact, it drove the somewhat obscure publishing firm out of business.[10]

This letter adds to the confusion, as Richard Watts cannot here be referring to Pantheon. Were there two American editions of *At Swim?* The Pantheon edition of 3,000 copies appeared in March 1951. American reviewers were, simultaneously, both enthusiastic and puzzled. The book sold only moderately well and its popular acceptance had to wait a further ten years. There is no mention of an American edition in *Cruiskeen Lawn.*

By this time O'Brien's dislike of his book was quite well established. Indeed, his aversion to it may have begun as soon as it appeared in print. In the earliest letter to A. M. Heath, O'Brien had described it as "queer", but he ordered two special copies to be sent, one to Donagh MacDonagh and the other to Denis Devlin in Rome. At the same time he sent a copy to Ethel Mannin with a covering note explaining that *At Swim* was

> a belly-laugh or high-class literary pretentious slush, depending on how you look at it. Some people say it is harder on the head than the worst whiskey, so do not hesitate to burn the book if you think that's the right thing to do.

Miss Mannin did not understand or like *At Swim*. She replied on 17 July 1939 saying that it was "altogether too latter day James-Joycean." She added: "Perhaps I am over-simple.

Leave it at that." But O'Brien was never really allowed to leave it at that. The critics were often confused by *At Swim* but they were unanimous in noticing the influence of Joyce on it. The constant mention of Joyce in connection with his own work infuriated O'Brien. In 1961 he wrote to Tim O'Keeffe and told him: "If I hear that word 'Joyce' again, I will surely froth at the gob!"[11] By that time, ironically, *At Swim* was at last a success. Its reissue in England by MacGibbon & Kee had brought O'Brien the recognition he had long deserved, but at a time when he felt the object was unworthy of the attention it was receiving. O'Brien decided to do whatever he could "in the promotional sphere" even while protesting that he had, by then, no faith in the book. He decided that "at least 2,000 copies will be sold in this little island alone" because the "true worth" of the book was "quite irrelevant".[12] In spite of the great popularity of *At Swim*, the translations, reissues, and paperback editions, O'Brien's opinion of it never changed. In 1965 he told Tim O'Keeffe:

> I am so sick of this *At Swim-Two-Birds* juvenile scrivenry that I just can't take it seriously on any level and absolutely loathe the mere mention.[13]

Later, in December of the same year, he added:

> If I get sufficiently drunk over Christmas I'm going to read that damned book for the first time. Those birds must have some unsuspected stuffing in them.[14]

By then it did not really matter what O'Brien thought of it. Graham Greene remembered it vividly and his comments, with those of Dylan Thomas and James Joyce, were included on the jacket of the new edition. Review copies were sent out in July 1960. Reviews were numerous and, on the whole, favourable. On 17 August O'Brien wrote to Brian Inglis and told him: "The book is, of course, juvenile nonsense but I understand that the sales are enormous and that it is 'going like a bomb'." It continued to sell well and to attract increasing critical attention over the years. John Wain, in an article in *Encounter*, described it as "a gargantuan comic novel which makes a simultaneous exploration on four or five levels of Irish civilisation".[15] Richard Harrity of the *New York Herald Tribune* stated emphatically: "This is a comic masterpiece of modern Irish literature that is as dazzling as the aurora borealis and twice as difficult to describe,"[16] and Vivian Mercier writing in *Commonweal* asked "How is an addict [of O'Brien], lacking the powers of a Baudelaire or a De Quincey, to convey to the as yet unensnared anything of the true nature of his artificial paradise?"[17]

A number of critics, whilst expressing enthusiasm for the book, speak also of the difficulty of categorising, or even describing it. Their difficulty is quite understandable as a quick "synopsis of the plot" will make clear . . . *At Swim* as a whole can be seen . . . to be a sustained questioning of many of Joyce's assumptions. References to Joyce are pervasive in the book and the wish to parody or question Joyce's writing to a great extent determined the structure of the book.

The impulse to parody Joyce had begun as early as *Comhthrom Féinne*. The anonymous skit "Op. $\frac{1}{8}$" connected a parody of Joyce with one of serialised novels and contained a "synopsis of the plot" such as is found in *At Swim*. O'Brien could have found in "Op. $\frac{1}{8}$", then, an already established association between Joyce and the form of the novel, and he was to extend this in *At Swim*.

The parody of Joyce is, perhaps, most obvious in the figure of the student narrator. Equally obviously the student is semi-autobiographical. It is, therefore, productive to look at those details of the narrator's life and character which are similar to O'Brien's so as to make it clear when the autobiographical elements end and the parody of Joyce begins.

The narrator is a student at UCD. He lives with his uncle, who constantly complains of his inattention and laziness. The student, on the whole, does not like his uncle very much, his descriptions of him are most unflattering and are usually provided at moments of irritation. The uncle's charges against him are, however, largely justified. He spends more time in bed and in idleness than in studying and his personal appearance suffers in consequence.

> Whether in or out, I always kept the door of my bedroom locked. This made my movements a matter of some secrecy and enabled me to spend an inclement day in bed without disturbing my uncle's assumption that I had gone to the College to attend to my studies. A contemplative life has

always been suitable to my disposition. I was accustomed to stretch myself for many hours upon my bed, thinking and smoking there. I rarely undressed and my inexpensive suit was not the better for the use I gave it, but I found that a brisk application with a coarse brush before going out would redeem it somewhat without quite dispelling the curious bedroom smell which clung to my person and which was frequently the subject of humorous or other comment on the part of my friends and acquaintances (p. 11).

The narrator is forgetful and careless and resents his uncle's attempts to shake him out of his lassitude. The uncle is always ready with a homily, a proverb or a piece of "Christian" advice for his nephew, who is much more interested in backing horses, drinking in Grogan's pub and pursuing women in company with his friend Kelly. Kelly is a countryman, a failed medical student and a man who

was addicted to unclean expressions in ordinary conversation and spat continually always fouling the flowerbeds on his way through the Green with a mucous deposit dislodged with a low grunting from the interior of his windpipe. In some respects he was a coarse man but he was lacking in malice or ill-humour (p. 26).

It was Kelly who first introduced the narrator to the joys of alcohol. He began with pints but soon changed "to brown stout in bottle", and was prepared to accept the "painful and blinding fits of vomiting which a plurality of bottles has often induced in me" (p. 29). The after-effects of alcoholic indulgences are often so severe that the narrator is forced to stay in bed, hiding his ill-used suit under the mattress to disguise its sight and smell. On one occasion, pretending to have a chill, he lies in bed, exhausted and noisome, discussing art and literature with his friend Brinsley – a conversation which is quite at odds with the sordid state of his life and person.

My dim room rang with the iron of fine words and the names of great Russian masters were articulated with fastidious intonation. Witticisms were canvassed, depending for their utility on a knowledge of the French language as spoken in the medieval times. Psycho-analysis was mentioned – with, however, a somewhat light touch (p. 32).

Brinsley, the narrator's closest friend, chief audience and major critic is described as "Thin, dark-haired, hesitant; an intellectual Meath-man given to close-knit epigrammatic talk; weak-chested, pale" (p. 30). He, too, is a student at the college, a poet and a billiards player.

The narrator obligingly provides a description of the college.

Description of College: The College is outwardly a rectangular plain building with a fine porch where the midday sun pours down in summer from the Donnybrook direction, heating the steps for the comfort of the students. The Hallway inside is composed of large black and white squares arranged in the orthodox chessboard pattern, and the surrounding walls, done in an unpretentious cream wash, bear three rough smudges caused by the heels, buttocks and shoulders of the students (p. 45).

The student narrator describes the bell which announces the beginning of lectures, the hasty extinguishing of cigarettes, the bravado of some of the students. He spends much of his time in the old, ruined part of the college, in the "Gentlemen's Smokeroom", which was usually occupied by "card-players, hooligans and rough persons". Here, he remains quite isolated from the general mass of the students, watching them in a cold and detached manner. "I sat alone in a retired corner in the cold, closely wrapping the feeble citadel of my body with my grey coat. Through the two apertures of my eyes I gazed out in a hostile manner" (p. 46).

In cold weather even these infrequent visits to the college cease and the student spends all his time in his room concerned with his "pulmonary well-being" (p. 60). This results in his discovering, in February, that his person has become "verminous", and the discovery shames him into a resolution to reform of his lifestyle. He draws up a timetable for a régime of "physical regeneration which included bending exercises" (p. 61), attends college every day and begins to walk about Dublin talking to friends and casual acquaintances. On these long walks he discusses poetry with Brinsley and pursues virgins with Kelly, with whom he also discusses "dog-racing, betting and offences against chastity" (p. 65). He attends meetings of the L & H Society and describes the gathering in vivid detail: the horse-play in the lobby, the extinguishing of the single gas jet, and the jokes played on various auditors. His stance during these "diabolic" proceedings was to maintain "a position where I was not personally identified, standing quietly without a word in the darkness" (p. 67).

Yet another friend is a Mr Kerrigan "a slim young man of moustached features usually attired in inexpensive clothing" (p. 70). With Kerrigan he visits the house of Michael Byrne "a man of diverse intellectual attainments [whose] house was frequently the scene of scholarly and other disputations" (p. 134).

At home, the narrator's relations with his uncle deteriorate as he is forced to listen to frequent lectures on the subject of his slothfulness. It is only when the uncle interests himself in the local musical society and in organising a céilí that he is left to his own devices. He then leads a life of "dull but not uncomfortable character" which he itemises thus:

Nature of daily regime or curriculum: Nine thirty a.m. rise, wash, shave and proceed to breakfast; this on the insistence of my uncle, who was accustomed to regard himself as the sun of his household, recalling all things to wakefulness on his own rising.

10.30. Return to bedroom.

12.00. Go, weather permitting, to College, there conducting light conversation on diverse topics with friends or with acquaintances of a casual character.

2.00 p.m. Go home for lunch.

3.00. Return to bedroom. Engage in spare-time literary activities or read.

6.00. Have tea in company with my uncle, attending in a perfunctory manner to the replies required by his talk.

7.00. Return to bedroom, and rest in darkness.

8.00. Continue resting or meet acquaintances in open thoroughfare or places of public resort.

11.00. Return to bedroom (p. 212).

The narrator allots himself an average of 1.4 hours of study per day, but, despite this meagre allowance, passes his "final examination with a creditable margin of honour" (p. 301), thus exceeding the achievement of most of his companions. As a reward his uncle presents him with an antique watch, the gift of which effects a reconciliation between them and causes the narrator to see his uncle's character in a new light. *"Description of my uncle:* Simple well-intentioned; pathetic in humility; responsible member of large commercial concern" (p. 312).

It is clear, then, that a number of the events in the student narrator's life are paralleled by happenings in the life of his creator. They both attended UCD in the 1930s, though the narrator's dead-pan, peripatetic prose occasionally produces a deliberately archaic sentence like "We went eventually to the moving pictures, the three of us, travelling to the centre of the city in the interior of a tramcar" (p. 65). In spite of his frequent use of this archaic descriptive style, the college which the narrator portrays is essentially the same place vividly described by O'Brien in his article on the L & H in James Meenan's book.

> I entered the big Main Hall at an odd hour on the second day of Michaelmas term 1929, looked about me and vividly remember the scene. The hall was quite empty. The plain white walls bore three dark parallel smudgy lines at elevations of about three, five and five-and-a-half feet from the tiled chessboard floor. Late I was to know this triptych had been achieved by the buttocks, shoulders, and hair-oil of lounging students. They had, in fact, nowhere else to lounge, though in good weather many went out and sat on the steps.[18]

In this article O'Brien went on to describe the smoking-room, the card-playing and billiards and the general chaos of L & H meetings in terms very similar to those found in *At Swim*. It is also clear that O'Brien's friends at college provided the models for the narrator's friends in *At Swim*. Brinsley is Niall Sheridan, his name in the novel being derived from that of Richard Brinsley Sheridan. When Niall Montgomery read the book he wrote in delight to O'Brien: "You've got Sheridan so well it makes me nervous." Niall Montgomery himself believes that he figures in the story as Kerrigan and complains that his clothing was never of "inferior quality". Kelly was a student called O'Rourke who came from Roscommon. He afterwards became a teacher. Donaghy, the poet which whom Brinsley and the student discuss "the primacy of America and Ireland in contemporary letters" (p. 62) was the writer Donagh MacDonagh and Michael Byrne was the painter Cecil Francis Salkeld who was, Niall Sheridan asserts, "an expert on everything".

Not only were these characters identified at once when the book was published, but some of the events of the story were recognised as having a basis in fact. On conferring night in 1934 O'Brien, O'Rourke and Sheridan drank in Grogan's pub on the corner of Stephen's Green and Leeson Street. Later on, near Lad Lane police station, they were accosted by one of the regular inhabitants of Stephen's Green, a man who usually wore a black coat with velvet reveres and a bowler hat. He made a practice of stopping students but this time he made a bad choice. In a state of extreme intoxication O'Rourke vomited all over him as he tried to interest them in the ideas of Émile Rousseau. The incident is reported in *At Swim* (p. 53). The racing tipster's letter which the student reads to Brinsley was, in fact, given to O'Brien by Sheridan himself, who thought he would be amused by its stylistic extravagances. Brinsley's "Lesbia" poem, which he recites to the student in Grogan's is a translation of a poem by Catullus and can be found under Sheridan's name in the *Oxford Book of Irish Verse*.

There are, however, as many differences as there are similarities between O'Brien's life and that of his student. In *At Swim* the narrator lives with his uncle; O'Brien lived with his parents during his time in UCD. The narrator does not play billiards and remains aloof from college life, particularly from the proceedings of the L & H; O'Brien was a leader and brilliant performer at the L & H and a keen billiards player. The narrator spends most of his day in bed, lying in an odour of stale stout with an unwashed, verminous body; O'Brien was a most active attender at college, a very hard worker, and not in the least verminous.

Why did O'Brien make these changes? Niall Sheridan thinks that the uncle may be a portrait of O'Brien's father, devised in that form because of O'Brien's wish to distance and protect his family affairs. This may be true, but it fails to account for the persistent emphasis on the squalor of the narrator's life, his cold and aloof bearing, his pose of hostility and general degeneracy.

The answer is, surely, that these aspects of the narrator's life are intended to be a mockery of the overstatements, conscious posturings and squalid habits of James Joyce's Stephen Dedalus. Joyce's presence in *At Swim* is pervasive both in style and content inasmuch as O'Brien mocks, albeit gently, aspects of *Dubliners, A Portrait of the Artist and Ulysses*. This mockery of Joyce is an important feature of the book; it is one of the strands which bind together many of its diverse elements, and it provides an important clue to O'Brien's own conception of the purpose and function of literature.

Like O'Brien's narrator, Stephen Dedalus was a student at what was to become UCD. He was lazy, inattentive, addicted to alcohol, verminous, given to pursuing women in the streets of Dublin. He takes long walks about the city, propounds an "aesthetic" to his friend Lynch and is in rebellion against his family (particularly his father), his country and his church. He is aloof, self-consciously superior, pedantic and given to imagining himself as various literary stereotypes. He takes as his omen his namesake Daedalus, whose son Icarus flew too near the sun while escaping on waxen wings from the labryinth and fell to his death.

These aspects of Stephen are parodied in *At Swim* primarily in the person and habits of the narrator (though O'Brien uses Orlick Trellis and Sweeny as other Stephen-figures in the book). We know immediately that he is at odds with his uncle[19] who is the "holder of a Guinness clerkship the third class" (p. 11). Simon Dedalus used to be "something in Guinnesses" so there is an association between the uncle, who irritates the student, and Simon, against whom Stephen rebelled. The uncle is a devout but naïve Catholic. At one point he tries to persuade Brinsley to join a religious order. He is, then, connected with the church which tried to claim Stephen but which he rejected. The uncle is a member of the Gaelic League, a patriot, interested in the Irish language and Irish dancing. (He opposes the old-time waltz on the grounds that it might be regarded as "foreign".)[20] In this aspect he stands for the third force against which Stephen rebelled. In his quarrels with the uncle the narrator is, therefore, associated with Stephen.

The first lines of *At Swim*, self-consciously pedantic as they are, call Stephen's characteristic modes of expression to mind at once. Both characters conceive of themselves in terms of literary models, and the lives of both present a comic disparity between the squalor of their daily activities and the richness of their imaginations. Both characters are fascinated by language, both are lazy, drunken, dirty and aloof. Joyce tells us that Stephen "chronicled with patience what he saw, detaching himself from it and tasting its mortifying flavour in secret".[21] O'Brien's narrator describes his imaginative detachment: "I closed my eyes, hurting slightly my right stye, and retired into the kingdom of my mind." (p. 15) this aloofness and detachment in the student is depicted as something silly and self-conscious. "It was my custom to go into the main hall of the College and stand with my back to one of the steam-heating devices, my faded overcoat open and my cold hostile eyes flitting about the faces that passed before me" (p. 61).

Stephen partially identifies himself with Lucifer, Prince of Light who became the Prince of Darkness; O'Brien's narrator has a habit of always sitting "in the dark". Stephen discusses the nature of faith with Cranly; O'Brien's narrator spends some of his time sitting in a pub with the Shader Ward, "talking about God and one thing and another" (p. 31). He is, indeed, as learned and intellectual as Stephen and has an equal tendency to blaspheme. "We talked together in a polished manner, utilising with frequency words from the French language .... The Holy Name was often taken, I do not recollect with what advertence" (p. 62). Stephen's long walks around Dublin and his encounters with prostitutes, his desire to sin with "another of his kind"[22] are paralleled by the perambulations of O'Brien's narrator with Kelly.

> Purporting to be an immoral character, I accompanied him on a long walk through the environs of Irishtown, Sandymount and Sydney Parade, returning by Haddington Road and the banks of the canal.
> *Purpose of walk:* Discovery and embracing of virgins (p. 65).

Stephen's friends in *A Portrait* are paralleled by the narrator's friends in *At Swim*. Brinsley shares some of the characteristics of Cranly and Lynch. Stephen discusses his religious views with the former and his aesthetic theories with the latter. The student discusses his aesthetic theories with Brinsley, and Brinsley is also seen to be the more concerned with religion of the pair, since it is he who is approached on the subject of joining the Christian Brothers. The narrator, however, has no inclination towards the religious life, as his uncle recognises, neither does he show any evidence of religious doubt. Kelly corresponds to Lynch in his foul habits and to Davin in his rural origins. On one occasion in *A Portrait*, Stephen meets Temple who talks to him about Rousseau. O'Brien's narrator remembers a man in black who addressed him on the same subject.

In the parallels drawn between the two characters it is difficult to establish O'Brien's intentions. He may have been simply presenting a more obviously comic version of Stephen while being aware of the ironic undercutting which that character had received at Joyce's hands. Or O'Brien may, in fact, have been unaware that there was a real separation between Joyce himself and his creations. In later writings, when he speaks of Joyce as a "heretic", O'Brien does seem to imply that Stephen's arguments are Joyce's. On balance it would seem that O'Brien's intention in presenting his narrator as a Stephen-figure was to mock Stephen and to imply that the events and circumstances which drove him to voluntary exile were no longer valid there. If this is so, then it might indicate a serious misunderstanding of Joyce's aims on O'Brien's part, or at least a failure to think out his own theories about artistic creation and apply them to Joyce.

In any case, it is quite clear that things have changed in Ireland. At least the brutality of the Prefect of Studies which Stephen experienced is a thing of the past. The uncle asks Brinsley if the masters are hard to please. When Brinsley replies that, on the contrary, they do not seem to care very much, the uncle comments that it was very different in his days for "the old schoolmasters believed in the big stick" (p. 36). Equally, Stephen's real experience with the prostitute is debunked by the "purported immorality" of the narrator and Kelly.

We walked many miles together on other nights on similar missions – following matrons, accosting strangers, representing to married ladies that we were their friends, and gratuitously molesting members of the public. One night we were followed in our turn by a member of the police force attired in civilian clothing. On the advice of Kelly we hid ourselves in the interior of a church until he had gone. I found that the walking was beneficial to my health (p. 66).

The student's "aesthetic" is a parody of Stephen's. Stephen saw drama as the most important of the literary arts because it was the most impersonal. "The esthetic image in the dramatic form is life purified in and re-projected from the human imagination".[23] O'Brien's narrator, too, places drama at the highest point of literary achievement, but for slightly different reasons.

It was stated that while the novel and the play were both pleasing intellectual exercises, the novel was inferior to the play inasmuch as it lacked the outward accidents of illusion, frequently inducing the reader to be outwitted in a shabby fashion and caused to experience a real concern for the fortunes of illusory characters (p. 33).

The narrator goes on to explain that "the novel, in the hands of an unscrupulous writer, could be despotic". It could, that is, impose the writer's vision of reality as the *only* reality. To counteract this he suggests that

a satisfactory novel should be a self-evident sham to which the reader could regulate at will the degree of his credulity (p. 33).

Joyce's creator is an autocrat, a god, bending all the elements of his novel to his artistic will; O'Brien's narrator wants a democracy. "It was undemocratic to compel characters to be uniformly good or bad or poor or rich. Each should be allowed a private life, self-determination and a decent standard of living" (p. 33).

In mockery of Joyce's levels of consciousness and the substratum of classical, biblical and historical reference on which his novels are based, the narrator prescribes that

Characters should be interchangeable as between one book and another. The entire corpus of existing literature should be regarded as a limbo from which discerning authors could draw their characters as required, creating only when they failed to find a suitable existing puppet. The modern novel should be largely a work of reference (p. 33).

This prescription would, he predicted, preclude "persons of inferior education from an understanding of contemporary literature" (p. 33).

As Stephen explains his aesthetic to Lynch, an aesthetic which is based on ideas from Aristotle and Aquinas, Lynch listens inattentively and protests: "Stop! I won't listen! I am sick. I was out last night on a yellow drunk with Horan and Goggins."[24] Brinsley replies in similar vein at the end of the narrator's explanation. "That is all my bum, said Brinsley" (p. 33).

The parallels between *At Swim* and *A Portrait* are by no means limited to the principal characters. In the Trellis section of the book the scope of the references is extended. If the student is O'Brien's Stephen Dedalus, Trellis is, in some aspects, his parallel for Leopold Bloom.

The references to *Ulysses* are introduced initially in the description of the Red Swan Hotel, where the mock legal language is a parody of the legalistic manner of the "Ithaca" section of *Ulysses*.[25] Trellis's bed, "a timber article of great age in which many of his forefathers had died and been born", draws the reader's mind to a memory of Shakespeare's second-best bed and thus to the sub-theme of Shakespeare and Stephen's theory about him in *Ulysses*. Joyce, who drank quite heavily, created an *alter ego* in Bloom who was relatively abstemious in that respect. Trellis is reportedly very like Dr Beatty, of whom it is reported "that towards the close of his life he indulged to excess in the use of wine" (p. 41); nevertheless, like Joyce who created an abstemious hero, Trellis as author forces his characters to refrain from the use of alcohol. Dr Beatty, on whose description in *The Conspectus of Arts and Natural Sciences* Trellis's character is modelled, has lost a beloved son. Bloom too had lost a son, but he finds in Stephen a spiritual son, rescues him and brings him to his house. There is a suggestion that Stephen might teach Italian to Bloom's wife Molly, though the idea that Stephen would be left alone with his wife worries the jealous Bloom. This is paralleled in *At*

Swim, where Orlick Trellis is Trellis's literary-spiritual son, born according to the principles of aestho-autogamy. This process was developed by Tracy who managed to have his own wife delivered of a "middle-aged Spaniard". Although the Spaniard was Tracy's offspring, a sort of spiritual son, he refused to allow him to be close to his wife, in a kind of comic inversion of the Stephen-Bloom-Molly association.

In the Nighttown sequence of *Ulysses* Bloom undergoes a strange nightmare trial and punishment at the hands of Bella, the whorehouse madam. He is, metaphorically, turned into a pig. Trellis also suffers a nightmarish trial sequence when his characters put him on trial in a bar-room, where an orchestra plays and the drunken judges, jury and witnesses are all interchangeable. In the course of his punishment, Trellis is changed into a rat. His defence lawyers are two dumb Greek sailors, Timothy Danaos and Dona Ferentes, their names being a pun on Homer's (sic) lines which mean "I fear the Greeks when they bring gifts." This may be a parody of Joyce's classical substructure in *Ulysses*. To it could be added the Greek quotation which adorns the frontispiece of *At Swim* and the references to the world of the Odyssey contained in the extract of the argument of Falconer's poem "The Shipwreck" which the student reads from *The Conspectus of the Arts and Natural Sciences:* "Ithaca, Ulysses and Penelope, Argos and Mycenae. Agamemnon. Macronisi. Lemnos. Vulcan. Delos. Apollo and Diana. Troy. Sestos. Leander and Hero. Delphos. Temple of Apollo. Parnassus. The muses" (p. 306).

Trellis's character Finn MacCool is yet another story-teller, and he too has his connections with Joyce. The first "Description of Finn" is given in an exaggerated manner which is itself a parody of the giantism of Joyce's description of the Citizen in the "Cyclops" episode of *Ulysses*. Later Finn announces in phrases which unite him to some of the themes of Ulysses:

> I am an Ulsterman, a Connachtman, a Greek said Finn...
> I am my own father and my son,
> I am every hero from the crack of time.

Finn's story is the tale of the madness of King Sweeny, who was cursed by St Ronan and caused to believe that he was a bird. The version of *Buile Shuibhne* as given by O'Brien in *At*

Swim is very nearly a literal translation of the original Middle Irish romance. In certain places, however, he departs from the original and gives a variant version which is usually chosen because it draws a parallel between Sweeny and Stephen, or rather between Sweeny as bird-man and Stephen as Icarus falling to his death because his wings have melted. All the images of flight and falling in the Sweeny tale correspond with those implied by the Icarus-Daedalus theme in *A Portrait*. Stephen, in fleeing the "nets" that are thrown to hold him down, is associated with Icarus fleeing the labyrinth. Sweeny too takes flight after a battle with the Church and has to strive to escape nets. "But being besieged with nets and hog-harried by the caretaker of the church and his false wife" (p. 97). Sweeny falls from his tree and is captured and the version in *At Swim* emphasises all the different ways he is imprisoned. "He fell with a crap from the middle of the yew to the ground and Linchehaun hastened to his thorn-packed flank with fetters and handcuffs and manacles and locks and black-iron chains" (p. 98).

The fourth story-teller in the book is Orlick Trellis, who is yet another Stephen figure, the artist of the 1890s, posing, concerned with art for art's sake. He is also a rebel in whom the Pooka has sown the seeds of rebellion and "non serviam". Orlick's literary style resembles the conversation of the student and Brinsley. A few pages of his are found to contain portions of a high-class story in which the "names of painters and French wines are used with knowledge and authority" (p. 236). This reminds us of the student whose "dim room rang with the iron of fine words and the names of great Russian masters" which "were articulated with fastidious intonation" (p. 32).

As a story-teller, Orlick is very particular about his art, which is, however, derivative. His story about Trellis is a pastiche of Finn's story about Sweeny. He is, therefore, using past literature as "a work of reference". When urged by Shanahan, Lamont and Furriskey to get on with the violent punishment of Trellis he rebukes them. "You overlook my artistry, he said. You cannot drop a man unless you first lift him" (p. 240).

Trellis's fate is apparently to be similar to Sweeny's. He is to be lifted, then dropped. Indeed, the style of the telling renders

Trellis almost indistinguishable from Sweeny. So Trellis becomes, by identification, Stephen as well as Bloom. He too has flown too near the sun in his aim for a "great book". As his story proceeds, Orlick accuses Trellis of sins which are more properly associated with Stephen.

> He corrupted schoolgirls away from their piety by telling impure stories and reciting impious poems in their hearing (p. 242).

> *DRUNKENNESS,* was addicted to. *CHASTITY,* lacked . . . *DIRTINESS,* all manner of spiritual, mental and physical, gloried in (p. 245).

Orlick is dwelling on Trellis-Sweeny's battle with the Church when his readers recall him to a proper sense of values. "You won't get very far by attacking the church, said Furriskey" (p. 247). The hell to which Orlick sends Trellis is remarkably like the hell which is so vividly evoked in the retreat sermon in *A Portrait.* It has the same physical qualities, noisome stenches and impenetrable darkness being among its chief characteristics.

References to Joyce can thus be found in all the various levels of *At Swim.* There are far more than have been mentioned here. Niall Montgomery, writing to O'Brien before the publication of *At Swim,* told him: "Your uncle is better than anything in *Dubliners*", and there may be a conscious reference to *Dubliners* during the tea-party at this Furriskey household when Lamont remarks: "Paralysis is certainly a nice cup of tea". (p. 228)[26] Bloom's inadvertent tip about the horse Throwaway may find an echo in the casual mention of Grandchild by Brinsley, which reminds the student of the tipster's letter he had received. The juxtaposition between Brinsley reciting his "Lesbia" poem and Kelly calling for "three stouts" is stylistically similar to the scene in Barney Kiernan's pub, where the Citizen is described in mock-heroic manner and there is an abrupt transition to Dublin dialect. There are many other such stylistic similarities, but it would be tedious to enumerate them. It is certain that the parody of Joyce was conscious and widespread in *At Swim,* and the "conclusion of the book, ultimate" provides the final comment, which draws many of the strands together.

Was Hamlet mad? Was Trellis mad? It is extremely hard to say. Was he a victim of hard-to-explain hallucinations? Nobody knows. Even experts do not agree on these vital points. Professor Unternehmer, the eminent German neurologist, points to Claudius as a lunatic but allows Trellis an inverted sow neurosis wherein the farrow eat their dam (pp. 314-15).

The farrow are Trellis's characters who turn on him to destroy him. Joyce had said: "Ireland is the old sow that eats her farrow".[27] O'Brien presents a situation in *At Swim* where Joyce's remark is inverted, and in this inversion lies the reason for his mockery of Joyce. Trellis, Orlick, Sweeny and the student are all Joycean figures. Orlick's art is stylised and destructive and he is swept out of existence at the end of the book. Trellis's art is moral and committed to Ireland. He is forgiven and saved. Sweeny, through madness, is reconciled with the church he had attacked and dies honoured and befriended by St Moling. The student who translated his anger at his uncle into the treatment of his fictive counterpart, Trellis, is reconciled with his uncle at the end of the book. The uncle had, it is clear, represented the three forces which Stephen Dedalus rejected: church, country and family. Joyce's character rejected his Irish background, choosing exile rather than involvement. O'Brien's character consciously chose reconciliation and acceptance instead of exile and anger. O'Brien's parody of Joyce springs, then, from his mockery of Stephen's character and from his conviction that Joyce himself was wrong to accept exile, to reject his Irish heritage (here seen in terms of Gaelic literature)[28] and to accept a classical rather than an Irish model for the mythological basis of his book. O'Brien takes Finn MacCool rather than Ulysses for his hero and Finn himself tells us that he is "every hero from the crack of time ... an Ulsterman, a Connachtman, a Greek".

In the reconciliation of hitherto opposed forces which occurs at the end of the Sweeny and "biographical reminiscence" sections, and in the destruction by fire of Orlick who had been taught to declare "non serviam" O'Brien was acknowledging his own allegiances.

To the generation writing after him it must have sometimes seemed that Joyce had said everything. Flann O'Brien was not prepared to accept this. His attack on Joyce may have been partly motivated by envy of the other man's great achievement but it was almost certainly inspired as well by the conviction that there were still other ways, equally valid ways, of looking at the world, other sources of myth, and other possible balances between reality and imagination than were to be found in the pages of Joyce's novels.

O'Brien himself held Joyce's greatest attributes to be his enormous humour and his ear for Dublin dialogue.[29] Like Joyce, O'Brien excelled in the presentation of the Dubliner; and some critics, such as Niall Montgomery, have even declared that he surpassed Joyce in his portrayal of particular characters. There are two types of Dubliner in *At Swim*. The uncle and his friends hover on the verges of the middle class, while Shanahan, Lamont and Furriskey represent the working class. The presentation of these two groups, together with that of the narrator's life, constitute the element of formal realism in *At Swim* and are those sections in which O'Brien's style and concerns seem closest to Joyce's.

From Anne Clissmann, *Flann O'Brien. A Critical Introduction to His Writings* (Dublin: Gill & Macmillan, 1975), pp. 76-115.

AESTHO-AUTOGAMY AND THE ANARCHY OF IMAGINATION: FLANN O'BRIEN'S THEORY OF FICTION IN *AT SWIM-TWO-BIRDS*

By Ninian Mellamphy

Philip Toynbee once mused that were he cultural dictator among the English he would make *At Swim-Two-Birds* required reading in all their universities.[1] Unfortunately, perhaps because this gentleman was never offered his desired preferment, the book is not yet required reading in all the universities of England or elsewhere, much to the regret of the initiates who share Toynbee's would-be tyrannical enthusiasm, who admire, with Joyce, the work of "a real writer with the true comic spirit,"[2] and who agree with such commentators as John Wain, Vivian Mercier, V. S. Pritchett and Anthony Burgess that this rather whimsical, quite provocative and very disconcerting story is, beyond question, a work of genius.[3] *At Swim-Two-Birds* is a *rara avis* in the world of fiction. It shares with *Finnegans Wake* the distinction of being an acclaimed masterpiece that is as often praised as read and more often read than understood. If the measure of critical acclaim is, in this one respect at least, similar, the measure of popular awareness is not. Anyone who informs his fellows that he intends to engage "in sapient dialectics with the bag-eyed Brehons" on the art of Mr. Joyce can expect nods of approval and queries of interest. Anyone who confesses to the denizens of forest or campus, especially in Canada, his intention of saying or hearing words on the art of *At Swim-Two-Birds* may feel suspected of dabbling in the exotica of some unknown Oriental yclept "Flann Who?" The necessary business of explaining both the identity of the author and the oddity of the title might be avoidable if only some cultural dictator or someone with the appropriate missionary zeal could persuade those of us who teach courses in fiction or in Anglo-Irish literature that to deprive our students of the chance of grappling with this Protean comic *tour-de-force* is to preclude the pleasure of their coming to grips with an elusive but significant aesthetic document.

If, since its publication in 1939 and its re-publication twenty-one years later,[4] *At Swim-Two-Birds* has persistently remained a trouvée of the *cognoscenti* and has, even in Brian O'Nolan's own Dublin, failed until recently to win a wider audience, it may be that it so challenges the reader with the task of coping with the virtuosity of its very complex form, and so dazzles him with an inventiveness that is as confusing as it is brilliant, that it teases him with its facetiousness while blinding him to its seriousness. One finds it easier to respond to the playfulness of its discrete parts than to seek out a key to the whole – easier because to recognize the narrative as a cruiskeen lawn of the farcical and the satiric is to discover, with readers of *The Anatomy of Melancholy, Tristram Shandy* and *Ulysses*, not to mention *Finnegans Wake*, that one needs, perhaps, a cork rather than a key.

If, however, one is to persist in the effort to provide a key for what is an aesthetic Pandora's box (and still a cruiskeen lawn, of course), it seems both necessary and dangerous to attempt a brief description of this, the first, and surely the best, of the novels of Flann O'Brien – necessary, because there must be a bird or two among us who may not yet have swum in this choppy stream of the author's fantasy, and one or two others who may need a refreshing splash before preening the feathers of memory. Dangerous, because any description, good or bad, obscures what is essential, the *life* of the design, and proves as poor a thing as a print that makes the golden bird of Byzantium look for all the world like the croaking raven of Inverness.

At Swim-Two-Birds is an experimental novel in the form of an autobiography covering a nine-month span in the life of a humble, opinionated, intelligent, verminous and nameless undergraduate at University College, Dublin. This lad resides at the home of an inquisitive, well-meaning, annoying and smug *petit-bourgeois* uncle. His energies are absorbed by the limited intellectual demands of a full-time commitment to university life and by the limitless imaginative demands of what he likes to call his "spare-time literary activities" (p. 9, *et passim*).[5] These activities involve him in the composition of a *magnum opus* which is an experimental novel that has as its subject the agonies of an artist involved in writing an experimental novel in which one of the characters is overwhelmed by an impulse to write an experimental novel. The problems of each author in turn are minutely analysed, discursively and dramatically, with the exception of those of the unacknowledged primary author, the real Brian O'Nolan, the pseudonymous Flann O'Brien, who never intrudes in the narrative but who broods over the whole as an unseen presence, like a god of creation biting his fingernails. It is in the mysterious prescience of this god that the controlling principle of organisation must lie, for the student autobiographer, whatever his pretentions to aesthetic control, seems at the mercy of the grim world of circumstance as he transmutes its phenomena into the stuff of fiction. He does this through the alchemical process of imaginative recollection, once he has retreated to the contemplative and slummy Arcadia of his bedroom, there to become a Gregor Samsa of isolation and a Wordsworth of productivity. It should be already evident that to the observation that we have here a Pandora's box there must be an addendum: it is one of the Chinese sort, rather than the Greek, containing an infinite number of images of itself, all of them bothersome to the prying reader.

The primary story is a kind of journal of the soul, a confessional record of the life of a B.A.(Hons.) candidate that is, in his own most engaging way, the model of the young person intelligent and presumptuous who takes all knowledge to be his province. It is a record of the action of a mind which perceives and captures the poor here-and-now of the Dublin of the thirties and, recoiling therefrom, radiates out into time past and into timelessness to evaluate actuality from the more attractive perspectives provided by history in the guise of fiction and myth. It is organized into ten labeled (and one unlabeled) biographical reminiscences[6] of the rather humdrum domestic, social and intellectual activities of the chronicler. These serve as bases from which he provides us with extensive extracts from the fictional manuscript he is writing, with accounts of his formulations of the theory which informs it, and with the history of his cronies' evaluations of the theory and the tale. The fictional extracts include numerous and varied excerpts from oral and literary narratives, from discursive literature of bygone times, from what looks like newspaper articles of the moment and from poems of many kinds and ages. Many of these borrowings are directly transcribed. Most of them are purloined and plagiaristically transformed as models for the varieties of story and style that, abruptly juxtaposed, constitute the tesserae of the autobiographical mosaic.

The autobiographer owes no allegiance, *qua* autobiographer, to Flaubertian, Jamesian or Joycean principles; hence, *qua* novelist, he can flout the ideal of the unobtrusive author who should so contrive his fiction that it seems to render itself dramatically. Paying outrageous homage to Fielding, Sterne, and Thackary, he persistently and insistently treats his readers as intimates: *ars est non celare artem.* He addresses us as discerning, though somewhat lazy, confidants, as people who know our artistic conventions, who recognize modal and generic distinctions (and mélanges!) and who, therefore, can never be expected to be (like some Dublin cowboys in a true story within the novel within the autobiography) "a pack of lousers that can be taken in by any fly-by-night with a good story" (p. 54).

Hence, we are expected to distinguish between *oratio recta* and *oratio obliqua;* to recognize incidental exploitations of such rhetorical figures as *litotes (meiosis), synecdoche (autonomasia), anaphora (epibole)* and *anadiplosis (epanastrophe),* and to be pleased that he telegraphically signals to us his own recognition of these very aspects of his craft. Hence, too, his expectation that we discern, as he does, "constructional and argumentative difficulties," understand his shock at discovering lacunae in pagination, and approve his judgment, when, in the interests of structural cohesion, he deletes no less than forty pages of his manuscript and replaces them with a synopsis, thus transcending the demands of both telling and showing and providing a short-cut demanded by his limitations in artistry and, presumably, by ours in patience (pp. 60-61, 144-45). But, however intimate the autobiographer becomes, however confidential about his characters and the universe, however destructive of illusion, "his bar-parlour chattiness" is never "devastating" in its effects, as E. M. Forster thinks this sort of thing must be.[7] This is so because the narrator never really shows the real author's hand. Our position is like that of the narrator himself when, one day at U.C.D., he watched practitioners of the craft of billiards, observed the quick darting of the balls, and endeavoured "to deduce from the results of a stroke the intentions which preceded it" (p. 51). We are left alone to observe O'Brien's formal craft and are offered no confessional directives to enable us to pluck out the heart of its mystery.

The first few dozen pages of *At Swim-Two-Birds* provide an example of the book's method in its least complex manifestation. First we find the narrator in his bedroom, withdrawn into the privacy of his own mind, contemplating the inadequacy of the conventional single opening and single ending of literary works, essaying three entirely dissimilar openings, one romantic-folkloric, one realistic-scientific, one heroic-mythic, all ideally leading to three hundred times as many endings; all, again ideally, interrelated in the (as yet unrealized) prescience of the writer. Then his vacant, pensive mood is shattered by toothache and by the intrusion of his uncle, who, ignorant of the young man's authorial proclivities and worried about his scholastic duties, recalls him to the perception of his surroundings with the ironically ill-timed demand, "Tell me this, do you ever open a book at all?" There follows the drama of an unsatisfactory dialogue; the reading of a letter from an English punter; a long extract in the style of the Irish oral epic; a reminiscence about the chronicler's introduction, some months earlier, to the excessive pleasures and after-effects of porter-drinking. In this last we find gobbets of a moral essay transcribed from a school reader and a passage of self-interrogation pilfered from Keats and Milton, the first associating drink with adder's hiss and physical degeneration, the other with-what else? - pipes and timbrels and wild ecstasy. Next there is a bedroom-scene in which the narrator, with his friend Brinsley, discusses modern European fiction (drawing, perhaps, more on E. M. Forster's reading than their own), tenders "an explanation spontaneous and unsolicited" concerning his literary activities and their informing aesthetic, and reads from his manuscript passages in various styles – passages which reveal the identity of Dermot Trellis, the novelist-hero of this novel, and describe the public-house-of-fiction that is his abode. The remaining segments show the protagonist perusing another letter from the English tipster, discussing gambling and art with Brinsley, and observing the efforts of his uncle to inculcate in his friend a vocation for the noble life of the Christian Brothers.

The reader must play Theseus in the labyrinth if he is to discover the meaning of all this, even to prevent the time-sequence from becoming a destructive minotaur. If he is to come to terms with the book's technique, these basic perceptions must not escape him. First, the heroic manuscript excerpt and the unheroic drinking-scene represent in counter-point two possibilities of transcending the dungy earth of every-day, on the one hand through the self-affirmation of the mythic warrior, Finn MacCool, on the other through the intoxicated self-oblivion of the vulgar soldier, Kelly. (Indeed, though this is far from apparent in the sequence of the narrative, it is as an intuitive reaction against the drabness of Kelly as companion that Finn emerges from his shadow and invades the kingdom of the narrator's mind, thus providing a mode of transcendence through art.) Second, the uncle, who is spanceled by Jansenistic morality, and Finn, who most certainly is not, define in terms of their different realities contrasting visions of the nobleness of life. Third, the English letter-writer, with his trite tipster information, and the Irish lad of letters, with his curious work in progress, are both involved in a quest for significance through "book-making."[8] Fourth, Trellis is endowed with the uncle's moral earnestness and with the nephew's own susceptibility to somnolence, intoxication and literary creativity: thus, in creating him the student-author gains a subliminal form of revenge on life, while transmuting leaden normalcy into something rich and strange. He creates a golden world in which Grogan's pub in Leeson St., the scene of pretentious student discussions and of other, duller confabulations, becomes the Red Swan Inn, where the author-Trellis can lodge the personae of his timeless (anachronistic!) world of story and have them tell their tales. Thereby he spins a web of narrative which is a curiously-wrought analysis of the problems of civilization and the nature of art.

The reader who, in the light of perceptions such as these, begins to get the drift of *At Swim-Two-Birds* must next come to terms with the student-narrator's theory of fiction, whose four main tenets are as follows: (i) A satisfactory novel must have multiple openings and endings; (ii) A satisfactory novel must not exploit the credulity of its reader, but must be a self-evident sham; (iii) "The entire corpus of existing literature must be regarded as a limbo from which discerning authors could draw their characters as required, creating only when they failed to find a suitable existing puppet;" (iv) "The modern novel should be largely a work of reference," for the good reason that the majority of writers spend their time inditing what oft was thought and oft was better said (p. 25). It is obvious that these tenets are not a manifesto but a mere acknowledgement of the characteristic limitations of the novel genre and a description of the informed reader's awareness of the tricks of the narrative trade and his appreciation of the relationship between the individual novel and the tradition on which it feeds voraciously and cannibalistically. If there is anything in the book which may be seen as critical manifesto it is implicit in O'Brien's practice. For example, my description of the opening movement of the "autobiography" suggests a fifth tenet: the modern novelist should reject the traditional *mythos,* or plot, in favour of an Eisensteinian principle of montage. Another is buried in the account of that intriguingly-named process, "aestho-autogamy" (of which more anon): the novelist should dramatize the tensions between chaos and control essential to the dilemma of the artist as creator and to the experience of the reader as interpretative co-creator. To this we might add a seventh tenet – really an extension of the sixth (which implies that reading should in some way be as different as writing) – the principle of polyphonic composition farcically exemplified by the Pooka McPhellimey and the Good Fairy when, in "multi-clause colloquy," they microcosmically encapsulate O'Brien's own narrative method as they discuss, with control unflawed, two distinct and apparently unrelated subjects:

> The fugal and contrapuntal character of Bach's work, said the Pooka, that is a delight. The orthodox fugue has four figures and such a number is in itself admirable. Be careful of that pot. It is a present from my grandmother.
>
> Counterpoint is an odd number, said the Good Fairy, and it is a great art that can evolve a fifth Excellency from the four Futilities (p. 110).

Since, according to the Pooka's mystic arithmetic, "truth is an odd number" (p. 106) and since seven is an odd number, I'll stop right here and pretend, with some truth, that *that* is the whole of the theory. In these seven principles and their implications O'Brien's own theory of fiction can be found and, with it, his views of the relation between art and life – that problem so central to the concerns of his narrator.

At Swim-Two-Birds anticipates the post-war preoccupations of Robbe-Grillet and the craftsmen of *le nouveau roman* in its irreverence for Aristotelian categories and in its attack upon the sacred-cow conventions of mimetic fiction. Yet, while it exposes the inadequacy or adolescence of the shams of plot, plausibility, temporality and causality, the sham verisimilitude of realism and naturalism, it does not question to the slightest degree the truth of Henry James's assertion that the only reason for the existence of the novel is its attempt to imitate life, to show that humanity is immense and that reality has a myriad forms.[9] No, this is its very purpose. But it shows that human reality involves, and that the novel must imitate, more than watches and mirrors and chewing of crusts; more than the stagnation and spiritual blindness that too often in the mimetic tradition replace the peripeties and discoveries of high art; more than the too-neat logic suggested by the clarity of plot and structure and by the thematic and modal consistency of the traditional novel, which enables the passive reader to understand all. It shows that reality involves the whole range of human perception, observation, cogitation, memory and, above all, desire; that man, *rationis capax* is also *irrationis capax*, in that he longs and strives for a perfection which he knows to be unattainable. In fine, it attests to the reality of the unrealizable by attempting to crystallize in its form the interplay of man's poor actualities and his poor dreams, the worlds of facts and wonder – those two birds that are forever at swim on the stream of his consciousness.

The characteristic technique of the book is that of juxtaposition, by means of which O'Brien contrives not just a mosaic but a geodesic dome, whose facets of mythic, folkloric, romantic and realistic imitations of reality are all arranged with equal immediacy and with equal prominence, all equidistant from the ideal nucleus of truth at the centre of the artifact. One effect of this is to put realism in its place – to assert, as it were, that Malory's art mirrors life as truly as Defoe's. Another effect is to downplay Aristotle's primacy of action, because "action" in the simplest sense is to be found in the autobiographer's fiction rather than in his life. We may find, however, that "action" is not so much downplayed as reinterpreted and, hence, may be said to retain its classical primacy. It is transferred from the story to the reader of the story; to the reader in the throes of creative participation; to the reader as he, no longer duped into conventional expectations, no longer needing to suspend his disbelief, casts a cold eye on every word, line and passage, recognizes influences, archetypes, parallels, plagiarizings and, thus, perceives the love-hate relationship between the narrative and the tradition which inspires and sustains it as it modifies and for the moment completes that tradition; to the reader whose efforts to discover, and whose recognition of, the meaning of the design constitutes the fifth Excellency that evolves from the four Futilities, the odd number which symbolizes the truth represented by the "self-evident sham."

The compositional principle of parallax perspectives by which he redefines "action" is not a *creatio ex nihilo* of O'Brien.

Gide's diarist, Edouard, had, one might say, outlined the whole method of *At Swim-Two-Birds* in *Les-Faux Monnayeurs;* and the passage in which Edouard does so had been paraphrased in Forster's *Aspects of the Novel*[10] – a book which must have taught O'Brien a great deal about the craft of fiction, especially about the technique of "bouncing" as something of more central importance than narrative point of view, Percy Lubbock's prime concern. The idea of "the musicalization of fiction" was theoretically outlined in Philip Quarles' notes in Huxley's *Point Counter Point*;[11] the Pooka on Bach is but one subtle "footnote" to the influence of this work. And the Chinese-box novel was an onion peeled not only by Gide and Huxley but also by Padraic Colum's friend James Branch Cabell, whose *The Cream of the Jest* was admired by O'Brien, as Anne Clissmann tells us.[12] Furthermore, reference to Joyce, Pound and Eliot is frequent and obvious enough to provide us with hints that these writers are a source of inspiration and of models. What is new, then, is O'Brien's forging of his materials, his success in implementing what others had discussed and, above all, his achievement of an unique formal embodiment of the twentieth-century vision.

The form of *At Swim-Two Bords* does not merely picture what we might call modern reality. It evaluates it too. This evaluation is effected by the juxtaposing and counterpointing of the sordid here-and-now with versions of the past. This past is embodied not so much in history as in the history of art. It is not really a past at all but, rather, a symbol of the timeless ideals that recede from us as we try to hear their echoes in the world of time. It is notable that when the narrator in this novel opts for self-realization through writing rather than self-evasion through alcohol the first passage he attempts is in the mock-epic style, a passage in which Finn MacCool enchants with the magic of words men whose names-in-progress reflect the evolution of Irish society (or its devolution from Irishness):

Who is it? said Finn.

It is Diarmuid Donn, said Conán, even Diarmuid O'Diveney of Ui bhFáilghe and Cruachna Conalath in the West of Erin, it is Dermot Brown of Galway.

Who is it? said Finn.

It is Caolcrodha MacMorna from Sliabh Riabhach, said Conán, it is Caelcroe McMorney from Baltinglass.

Comic devices such as this abound. They suggest that this novel, and, because of its subject, *the novel,* is essentially a monument to human failure, especially to this "failure" in terms of man's awareness of his alienation from the wholeness of life celebrated in epic literature. The epic poet sings of a universe in which man, heroic and self-sufficient, recognizes no necessary gap between transcendent ideal and immanent real, and should recognize none; in which man, like Finn or Odysseus, can realize himself by struggling against and gaining control over forces outside of and antagonistic to the self, and can act as if truth were nothing if not the intuitive certainty of his own significance. The novelist cannot imitate the epic poet's song, or at best he can only parody it, for the world in which he lives and which he mirrors in his art is one of incompleteness, uncertainty and alienation, a world in which the quest for significance is, as Eliot showed, typically a search for shards of meaning discoverable in an absolete past. O'Brien shows that the epic vision, or what it symbolizes, is to modern man as grotesquely improbable as it is nostalgically attractive; this we see in his "humorous or quasi-humorous" treatment of Finn, the Gargantuan non-thinker who gets wisdom from the sucking of his thumb. Prompted into narrative by the ubiquitous and timeless "hidden Conan" (the mythic voice that prompts story-telling) Finn can so extensively celebrate the "musics" sweetest to his ear that his responsive epic catalogue becomes a celebratory hymn of acceptance of nature in its entirety, its pain and joys equally:

> I like the surf roar at Tralee, the songs of the three sons of Meadhra and the whistle of Mac Lughaid. These also please me, man-shouts at a parting, cuckoo-call in May. I incline to like pig-grunting in Magh Eithne, the bellowing of the stag of Ceara, the whinging of fauns in Derrynish. . . .
> A satisfying ululation is the contending of a river with the sea. Good to hear is the chirping of little red-breasted men in bare winter and distant hounds giving tongue in the secrecy of fog. The lamenting of a wounded otter in a black hole, sweeter than harpstrings that (pp. 12-13).

He describes the trials of aspirants who, before being inducted into the Fianna, must be accomplished poets, warriors, sorcerers and ascetics, and must so transcend the limitations of nature as to be Brobdingnagians in grossness and elves in delicacy. He does this in such a way that, in the absurd comedy of his narration, we discover an affirmation both of man's identification with, and control over, nature:

> For five days he [i.e. the Fenian novice] must sit on the brow of a cold hill with twelve-pointed stag-antlers hidden in his seat, without food or music or chessmen. If he cry out or eat grass-stalks or desist from the constant recital of sweet poetry and melodious Irish, he is not taken but is wounded. When pursued by a host, he must stick a spear in the world and hide behind it and vanish in its narrow shelter or he is not taken for want of sorcery. Likewise he must hide beneath a twig, or behind a dried leaf, or under a red stone (p. 17).

Finn can refuse to recount a tale which casts doubts on his integrity, choosing, instead, to assert the primacy of his own unquestionable reality:

> Who has seen the like of Finn or seen the living semblance of him standing in the world, Finn that could best God at ball-throw or wrestling or pig-trailing or at the honeyed discourse of sweet Irish with jewels and gold for bards, or at the listening of distant harpers in a black hole at evening?
> I am an Ulsterman, a Connachtman, a Greek, said Finn,
> I am Cuchulainn, I am Patrick.
> I am Carbery-Gathead, I am Goll.
> I am my own father and my son.
> I am every hero from the crack of time (p. 19).

He can launch then in to a tirade against the artistic necessities of story-tellers who, incapable of uncompromised apprehension of the marvellous, must denigrate what is too lofty and too strange for their base fancies:

> Small wonder, said Finn, that Finn is without honour in the breast of a sea-blue book, Finn that is twisted and trampled and tortured for the weaving of a story-teller's book-web. Who but a book-poet would dishonour the God-big Finn for the sake of gap-worded story? (p. 19).

The kind of coherence of vision typical of Finn is necessarily comic for the modern reader. But the comedy is a two-edged sword wielded by the satirist in O'Brien, for whom the "past" of which Finn is part is a metaphor of human nostalgia for a lost security. He shows how feeble and vague is this nostalgia in the Dubliner of his day and, thereby, mocks the delimiting *weltanschauung* of the old sow that suckles her farrow in smugness and narrowness. He achieves this through the interrelationships of various levels of story, especially in the changing role of Finn throughout the book.

In the heroic passages of the student's manuscript, the God-big Finn, raging giant and plaintive bard, lover and rummager of generous women, non-thinker and chess-champion, is free to define himself and to create his world in his own image. In anti-heroic passages of Trellis's novel we find Finn the anachronism; Finn sharing digs with wild-west heroes from the south-east of Dublin; Finn by Trellis's unique form of intentional fallacy recreated as father and protector of a new-coined maiden – the muscular rummager reduced to the role of *custos virginitatis* in a story which, if the author could write it, would get the seal of approval from the Catholic Truth Society. Yet this is a Finn who, as Trellis's imagination dictates (or, at least, that part of it not wholly dissociated from the mythic vision), utters a testament to the sad reduction of the possibilities of life when he (again in response to promptings of "hidden Conán") recites the Middle-Irish romance, "The Adventure of Suibhne Geilt."[13]

This is the saga of Sweeny, a Finn-like hero, whose martial destructiveness following the battle of Magh Rath broke the truce engineered by a monk named Rónán. Reproached by the man of God, he demonstrates his penury of humility by tossing the saint's psalter in a brook and, for this, is transformed into a madman and metamorphosed into a bird. The mad bird spends years in flight from yew-tree to yew-tree throughout Erin and beyond until, at last, mortally wounded by a small-minded inhabitant of a drab domestic world, he, a mangled Prometheus, is reclaimed to humility and to sanity by St Moling, a poet who is no puritan.

Sweeny is the central symbol of the novel. In the painful isolation enforced on him by his madness and his metamorphosis, he "never ceases from the recital of sweet poetry and melodious Irish". His is the poetry of the heart, poetry that blends elegiac lamentation of his lost freedom and wholeness with ecstatic eulogizing of nature's bounteousness and bitter railing against her harshness. He sings of his unavailing struggle to recapture what we recognize as the condition of the mythic Finn. Thus he expresses and embodies the plight of Everyman, aspiring but limited, as he attempts to concretize within the bounds of form the boundlessness of his imaginative vision. Furthermore, the story of Sweeny presents the romance as a kind of middle ground between the realms of the epic and the novel, placing side by side the reality of the epic vision (as Sweeny nostalgically recreates his past) and the reality of the fragmented vision of non-heroic man (as Sweeny confesses his feelings of limitation and cyniscism). Sweeny in the trees, "a huddle between earth and heaven," his mind a shell, empty and receptive, lunatic and visionary (p. 208), mediating between the two realities of desire and conscience, is the very heart of the matter.

To make claims about a book which is above all a comic tour-de-force might seem extravagant, were it not that O'Brien himself subtly suggests that the laugh that is *At Swim-Two-Birds* is really a disguised cry, a light-hearted treatment of the stuff of tragedy. Though he fails to reveal the meaning of his title and hides behind the mask of his narrator, he does allow us to find one clear fingerprint of the real artist on the surface of the artifact he has given us – and this is the epigraph:

’Εξίσταται γὰρ πάντ’ ἀπ’ ἀλλήλων δίχα

This line (which for some reason the critics have overlooked) may be translated as follows: "All things are separated from themselves." It is a line that strangely, or perhaps not so strangely, foreshadows Yeats's "Things fall apart; the centre cannot hold." It is taken from Euripides's *Heracles* (better known to us by its Latin title *Hercules Furens*), a line uttered by Amphitryon when, during his son's heroic mission in the underworld (to bring to light monstrous Cerberus), he discovers that the Theban king, Lycus, plots the destruction of Heracles's wife and children. He tries to comfort these doomed souls with what is the first (and last) speech of hope in the play, but in his role of comforter voices this dark thought. That O'Brien chose to remind us of the fate of Finn's classical counterpart should hardly surprise us, especially if we have come to terms with the serious implications of Finn's role. That he chose to quote Euripides, the most sceptical of Greek makers of tragedies, should not surprise us either, because here is the model for his own treatment of the relationship between the grand past and the puny present. This tragic poet has as his constant theme the idea that the grand and terrible passions of men are more terrible than grand, because the possessors of those passions mired in the slough of reduced life, are cut off from visions of significance that once were available but are no longer. In his plays – and *Heracles* is typical – he reveals how tragically unfair is the contest between human ideals and human limitations, and teaches us to say with Gloucester, "As flies to wanton boys are we to the gods."

Something very like a Euripidian concern with the lost vision and the lost or dimly-seen ideal informs the hilarious interplay between Finn's Sweeny recitation and Shanahan's account of the attack on the Circle N ranch in Ringsend. Finn on the battle of Magh Rath stirs Shanahan into song: the sublime elicits the ridiculous. Shanahan, whose source of mythology is the Hollywood dawn rather than the Celtic twilight, tells a tale in which he seems unconsciously (as must be the case) to anticipate Seamus Heaney's "We have no prairies" and, in doing so, to become a proleptic counter-Heaney, choosing to super-impose the scope and excitement of the Wild West upon Dublin's tame city: for him no delving into the revelatory and pertinent mysteries of the bog of his own psychic past. Still, he is not totally deaf to echoes of the past, though somewhat hard of hearing. His story has something in it of the *Táin Bó Cúailnge* and *The Pirates of Penzance,* something of the Battle of Clontarf and of the Irish Civil War, but a great deal more of Hamlet's failure to kill Claudius. In fact, it has more to do with failure than success, though he does not see this. Through his story, all breadth and no depth, O'Brien limns a parodic map of the modern Irish mind, full of fancy, empty of imagination, in its pursuit of that which would transform and in its attainment of that which merely distorts.

Of course, here as elsewhere, O'Brien is not content to leave us without feelings of ambivalence.[14] He shows at the same time how the real artist transforms the water of cliché into the stout of story: *omnis fabula fundatur in historia.* He produces a very probable newspaper-cutting (p. 59) on the arraignment of some Ringsend rowdies arrested for hooliganism (for horse-play!), tacitly revealing the source of the student-author's inspiration: Shanahan's horses have much in them of Myles na gCopaleen's shaggydogs. Similarly, he shows a pub aphorism (p. 22) to be the inspiration for the scenes in which Finn's recital prompts the interruptive and irrepressible Shanahan into praise of Sweeny's poetry – too arcane though it be for the man in the street! – and into ecstasies of still greater approval of the balladic verse of the seer Jem Casey, "poet of the pick," oracle of escapist earthiness, who, as we hear Sweeny's eulogies of aspiration (in Finn's voice) makes affirmations (in Shanahan's) to convince us that "A pint of plain is your only man" (p. 121f). Thus we are shown visions of reality as they arise *de profundis* – the banal commonplace being imaginatively recreated and comically heightened.

For all the contrast in their outpourings, modern Casey, balladeer of Booterstown, and medieval Sweeny, seer of Snámh-dhá-én, symbolize the struggle of the poet to forge in words the stuff of inspiration. Casey, when we first see him, is tangled in a clump of briars where, he later explains, he is "reciting a pome to a selection of my friends" (p. 120). Evidently, the poetaster's task is no more comfortable than that of his betters. But why, we may ask, must the modern "maker" be trite, and what explains this instance of the dislocation in vision between past and present? The answer, as we might expect, is to be found where we might least expect it – in O'Brien's device of providing amusing, disparaging echoes of an intervening culture. These are not echoes of Swift or Burke but an English middle-class culture as it reveals itself in the copious and compendious writings of the Smithfield Muses – men such as John Dunton and Rev. Samuel Wesley (father of a famous son), men of urbanity, approved judgement and conventional morality, who expounded their theology of smugness and their philosophy of non-daring in *The Athenian Oracle*.[15] These were the men whose good sense would prevent all potential Sweenys from being borne along on the wings of madness or ecstasy and from being prickled by the thorns of poetic *Angst*. O'Brien, engaging in wryness, not *saeva indignatio*, debunks their wisdom – the wisdom of the forbears of Yeats's gentry – by the simple trick of leaving his average reader in the position of misreading the long s as f:

Extract from the book referred to: I: Whether it be poffible for a woman fo carnally to know a Man in her fleep as to conceive, for I am fure that this and no other way was I got with child.

When we consider that the wisdom of the *Athenian Oracle* and of the more frequently quoted *Conspectus of the Arts and Natural Sciences*[16] is not unlike the wisdom of the uncle, which is not unlike that of the Christian Brothers (the wisdom of approved taste and disapproved aspiration), we should see these excerpts as an "ancient" example of what cuts off Casey, the representative citizen of the hiberno-anglo Free State, from the grandeur of his high past – as an instance of one of the major problems crystalized in the narrative mode of this novel.

The problem most extensively dealt with in *At Swim-Two-Birds* is that of the artist as he shapes his artifact and, specifically, that of the novelist as he attempts to effect a consonance between centripetal intention (for instance, theme) and the centrifugal forces of the unreined, because free, imagination (as exemplified, let's say, in character). Here we have to do with "the persistence of the past" in the purely figurative sense – with demands of an aesthetic ideal which, alack, belongs more to the reality of desire than of accomplishment. Characteristically, the matter is treated with such facetious discursiveness and in such a frenetic narrative romp that we may fail to notice it at all – and all the more so because the discussion is based on a curious phenomenon given the still more curious label of "aestho-autogamy".

"Aestho-autogamy" is the art of "producing a living mammal from an operation involving neither fertilization nor conception" (p. 40). This art is perfected by the hero of the student-narrator's *magnum opus*, Mr Dermot Trellis of Red Swan fame, whom we discover in the process of creating the non-plagiarized Furriskey. This character has the distinction of being born at the age of twenty-five, and of entering the world *with* a memory but *without* a personal experience to account either for the memory, the fillings in his tobacco-stained choppers, the inscrutable status of his virginity, or the knowledge of physics which extends no further than to Boyle's Law and the Parallelogram of Forces (pp. 1, 40). The daily press reports the event and quotes Trellis's acknowledgment of his researcher's debt to Mr William Tracy, writer of western romances, famous not only for bivouacking his Redskins near the obelisk in Phoenix Park but for his "efforts to change the monotonous and unimaginative process by which all children are born young" and his "success, after six disconcerting miscarriages, in having his wife delivered of a middle-aged Spaniard, who lived only six weeks" (p. 41):

> Our Medical Correspondent writes . . . Aestho-autogamy with one unknown quantity on the male side, Mr. Trellis told me in conversation, has long been a commonplace. For fully five centuries in all parts of the world epileptic slavies have been pleading it in extenuation of uncalled-for fecundity. It is a very familiar phenomenon in literature (p. 40).

Is this merely an authorial practical joke and our amused victimhood the point of it all? Or is there some sense underlying the nonsense, as Claudius discovered at the end of "The Mousetrap"? That there is a hidden Hamlet somewhere becomes apparent when we notice that the label and definition of "aestho-autogamy," however outlandish they seem, are really only outlandishly fresh. We have all read Henry James's preface to *The Portrait of a Lady,* so we remember, but hardly remember being shocked by, that aesthetic celibate's account of his waking up one fine morning to find that he had come into possession of Mme Merle, Gilbert Osmond, and the rest in all of their adulthood and their adultery.[17] What O'Brien does is to take the Jamesian metaphor and, with Kafkaesque humour and Pirandellian inspiration, render it as fact. He makes it a scientific process by which characters literally come to life. He goes a few steps further than James, who (without mixing his metaphors) spoke of *ficelles* that got too big for their boots, and Pirandello, who dramatized in a revolutionary manner the implications of our ability to imagine characters in situations never thought of by the playwright.[18] He shows that characters, once born (who can speak of "conception" when there's nothing new under the novelist's sun?) are not only independent but anarchic, and that, *especially while the work is in progress,* they make of the author a *creator agonistes.*

In the *Swim-Two-Birds* catechism there are many questions, all of which ask, "What kind of creator is the novelist?" There are many answers, and in many of them O'Brien, with tricks such as his reference to a tradition of maculate conceptions such as that which surprised the *Athenian Oracle* lady, steps so facetiously on the Galilean waters of orthodoxy as to disconcert less than broad-minded theologians of the Big Endian variety. As the student-diarist's novel about Trellis's novel-writing shows, "the novelist" is, not unexpectedly, much more a Sweeny than a god; or if he is a god, he is not so much the Father, Creative Principle in timeless Procession of the Son, as the Father-Maker of Adam, whose reproduction of the Ideal Creature in the recalcitrant world of time and matter was too soon to issue in an unideal *non-serviam*. But, perhaps this is to protest too much, for Trellis is no God; he is at best Frankenstein – and a debased Frankenstein at that. Witness the fate of Trellis the moralist! For the purposes of his *chef d'oeuvre* on the nature and wages of sin, he borrows Finn and Sweeny from Irish epic and romance; Shanahan, Lamont and others from Irish cowboybooks; the courteous, dark, mystic devil-figure of the Pooka from Irish folklore, and the Good Fairy (a Puck who thinks he's Ariel) from God knows where; then, because his hortatory intention necessitates concretization of the vileness it decries (p. 35), he invents, for lack of prototype, the intended-lecher Furriskey and a virgin named Peggy, the intended-lecher's intended-victim. Failure to control this motley cast would be a novelist's (and landlord's) nightmare, and Trellis, we remember, has Pandora's gift of somnolence. Failure in control is Trellis's fate, for his characters are living beings. The borrowed ones perform the unheroic equivalent of spicing his metheglin; they drug his Guinness. Thus they gain the freedom to act and speak according to their own art-for-art's sake impulses. His new creations rebel too. Furriskey's heart is set on the family rosary rather than on rape: he secretly courts and marries his virgin, upright lad that he is. Such is the moralist's nightmare – the real life of these "puppets" is the analogue of nightmare – that Evil perniciously insists on being Good.

The portrait of the novelist as Frankenstein is only part of the answer. Just as Ireland produced her Oscar Wilde as well as her Canon Sheehan, our scholar-author produces a Trellis who is aesthete by inclination as well as moralist by choice. Since every author's work, however much it fails to reflect his ideal design, pleases, nay delights him, his role is not only that of Frankenstein but Pygmalion too, the creator of an antithetical type of monster. This is only too apparent when Trellis, again for lack of prototype, creates Sheila Lamont, the epitome of beauty and innocence, a victim for Furriskey, a daughter for Finn. Such is his attraction to his Galatea (and such the risks of practising aestho-autogamy in bed) that he rapes her forthwith. The results of this abuse of his artifact are drastic: Sheila dies giving birth to an adult son. This is Orlick, an avenger of his mother's honour, a *novelist*-avenger, who makes of his pater a fiction and sets about destroying him (in a novel, within the novel, within the novel, within the diary). This brings us full circle to Frankenstein and his destructive monster. The energy of O'Brien's creativity here is such that even the most alert reader may forget the parabolic design. If he does, then he experiences his own version of the novelist's problem – the too-great delight in the thing *per se*, the failure to maintain critical distance, the inability to recognize the structure as mousetrap. Even the alert reader, were he willing to describe the Homeric preparations for Orlick's birth, the Borgesian ingenuity of Orlick's craftsmanship, and the Mylesian effrontery of the book's multiple resolutions and conclusions, would share the fate of Trellis in the marvellous nightmare sequences composed by his vindictive son: the reader, like the writer, is no transcendent and indifferent god; he is Claudius – the limed soul that, struggling to be free, is more engaged.

Now it is proper that this should be so, because a book that speaks of the interplay of the worlds of fact and wonder, showing the inescapability of both but measuring the dimensions of things in the grander scale of marvellings, should leave us with the humility to be silent about the ineffable; it should leave us with the conviction that the artistic imagination however risible its tendency towards the fantastic and grotesque, speaks to the dreamer and idealist in us when mere reason must be mute.

It is such a view of the role of the imagination that informs O'Brien's implicit idea and explicit model of the novel as hybrid. It is such a view that informs his critique of the traditional novel, which does not reflect our awareness of life's actualities as well as it pretends to do and which does not reflect our dreams of a grander and simpler life as well as the epic and the romance have done. O'Brien demonstrates how the novel might embody in its form our experience of life as a condition of becoming, a condition in which "to be" is simply "to be finding out." To do so he transfers the action from the story to the reader and makes the art of reading a reminder of our normal consciousness of the tensions between the self and all that is outside of the self. At the same time, he demonstrates how the novelist, whose perfectionism about the problem of form itself mirrors the human search for the ideal, can create a world which, while it reflects life's incoherence and incompleteness, has its own discoverable homogeneity. In his consistent concern with the ideal, with perfection, with the "past," he poses for us the question, "Whither is fled the visionary gleam?" His formal achievement in *At Swim-Two-Birds* reveals to us that the answer is not unlike one offered by that cold-voiced philosopher, the not-so-Good Fairy, during the trial of the failed novelist Trellis just before the endings of all the novels within this novel:

> Answers do not matter so much as questions. . . . A good question is very hard to answer. The better the question the better the answer. There is no answer at all to a very good question (p. 201).

It is surely no accident, by the way, that the Good Fairy is speaking "from a key-hole."

From *The Canadian Journal of Irish Studies*, IV, 1 (June 1978), pp. 8-25.

TWO META-NOVELISTS: STERNESQUE ELEMENTS IN NOVELS BY FLANN O'BRIEN

By Rüdiger Imhof

One of the salient issues of O'Brien criticism has been the influence of other writers on O'Brien or the affinities of his work to those by other authors. The name most frequently

mentioned in this respect is James Joyce.[1] Even the early
reviewers recognised that *At Swim-Two-Birds* owes much in
compositional and thematic regards to Joyce's *Portrait* and
Ulysses. And for his "exegesis of squalor", as he subtitled *The
Hard Life*, O'Brien was influenced by Joyce's exegesis of
squalor: *Dubliners*. The frequent mention of Joyce finally
annoyed O'Brien; he wrote to Timothy O'Keeffe: "If I hear
that word 'Joyce' again, I will surely froth at the gob."[2]
Probably out of admiration, he adopted Joycean devices and
themes; out of detest and hatred, stemming – so it seems – from
envy for the other's achievement, he parodied the man Joyce –
most evidentally in *The Dalkey Archive*, which has Joyce, in a
typical O'Brien joke, wash the Jesuits' dirty linen – and his
work. Another author to which O'Brien is sometimes brought
into relation is Beckett; although so far no convincing
demonstration has been offered of the similarities in the two
men's writings.[3] Des Esseintes, hero of Joris-Karl Huysman's
A Rebours, has been cited as an unquestionable source for de
Selby in *The Third Policeman,*[4] and many of de Selby's weird
ideas and theories have been traced to J. W. Dunne's *An
Experiment in Time* and *The Serial Universe.*[5] Further, Miss
Clissman has found surprising parallels, both structural and
verbal, between *The Cream of the Jest* by James Branch Cabell
and *At Swim.*[6] Such parallels could also be drawn to Tieck's
Der gestiefelte Kater, Brentano's novel *Godwi,* and Immermann's
Epigonen. It would, however, seem difficult to prove a direct
influence of these German authors on O'Brien. Laurence
Sterne is another writer whose name is occasionally evoked in
discussions of O'Brien's novels,[7] but in most cases, the points of
reference are the apparent compositional chaos in *At Swim* and
the "learned wit" passages in *The Third Policeman*. It is the
purpose of the present study to provide a close comparison
between *Tristram Shandy* and O'Brien's novels, which, beyond
such superficial similarities, shows an enormous amount of
compositional and thematic correspondences. In order to point
out these correspondences, it will be necessary to introduce
frequent quotations without which the article would be
incomplete.

It is not intended to demonstrate that O'Brien imitated
Sterne, consciously and deliberately, as, for instance, Henry
MacKenzie did by his *Man of Feeling* (1771). Nor is the

intention to prove a direct influence of Sterne on O'Brien. For both these matters, it is difficult to arrive at conclusive evidence. The purpose is rather to show that O'Brien belongs to the tradition of comic-experimental, or, preferably, meta-novelists, which ranges from the anticipants of the Sternesque novel[8] to B. S. Johnson and other contemporary practitioners. The term "Sternesque" is meant to denote narrative devices as well as subject matters employed and exploited by Sterne in *Tristram Shandy*. This is not to argue that Sterne was the first to utilise these. Sterne is seen as a point of reference because in *Tristram Shandy* most of the devices and subject matters previously employed were utilised collectively to form a new type of novel. Of O'Brien's *oeuvre*, it is primarily *At Swim* and *The Third Policeman* with which the article will be concerned. *The Dalkey Archive* is negligible as the Sternesque elements there are cooked-up versions of parts from *The Third Policeman*. *The Hard Life*, O'Brien's most "realistic" novel, falls largely outside the range of the present investigation, except for the "hobby-horsical" character drawing. The parallels between Sterne and O'Brien are grouped into four categories: (I) explicit and implicit commentary on the nature of the novel as well as on the possibilities of writing fiction; (II) devices to lay bare the methods and conventions of novelistic writing; (III) narrative strategies and stylistic idiosyncracies; (IV) subject matter.

I

The most obvious common characteristics of *At Swim, The Third Policeman,* and *Tristram* is that all three are extremely witty, comic novels. It was because of their wit and their comic nature that they were initially appreciated. And for a consider-able period, this was the only critical response to them. Such a reception obstructs the critic's view for their other merits. The three novels are much more than the creative offspring of eccentric minds, much more than "a belly laugh or high-class literary pretentious slush".[9] The latter epithet was often at the tip of the tongue of those who in the early years of the books' existence spoke and wrote about them.[10]

Tristram Shandy and *At Swim* are meta-novels. This term may best be defined against the term "anti-novel", which, although controversial has come to acquire some kind of definitional meaning. Novels falling under the label "meta-novel" consciously and explicitly reflect on the stipulations for the possibilities of writing novels; they may be "constructed in a negative fashion, relying for [their] effects on omitting or annihilating traditional elements of the novel, and on playing against the expectations established in the reader by the novelistic methods and conventions of the past", as M. H. Abrams has maintained for anti-novels.[11] Their primary concern, however, is not the mere debunking of established modes in fictional writing; rather these novels strive against the background of accepted norms and codes to overcome their deficiencies and to lay out new methods in novelistic writing. An anti-novel complies largely with the demands of M. H. Abrams in that "it is deliberately constructed in the negative fashion ...". Its main goal is to debunk established novelistic methods. In doing so, the author of an anti-novel produces another novel, which, by virtue of its anti-character, points to a new way of conceiving a novel, but he undertakes this task implicitly. The difference between a meta- and an anti-novel, then, lies in the fact that the former reflects the conditions for writing novels consciously and explicitly, whereas the latter treats these matters implicitly.

Tristram contains numerous explicit statements and ideas on the nature of the novel, on problems asking to be solved by a novelist as well as on particular narrative techniques and devices. It may be argued that Sterne was dissatisfied with the way novels were being written at his time to form picaresque quasi-biographical "history" books. In the course of the narrator's reflection on the business of writing such "history" books, Sterne has him put the question:

> Shall we for ever make new books, as apothecaries make new mixtures, by pouring only out of one vessel into another?
> Are we for ever to be twisting, and untwisting the same rope? for ever in the same track – for ever at the same pace? (TS, V, p. 339)[12]

The dissatisfaction with the state of the novel led Sterne to parody, even pervert, established novelistic conventions, advance his own views, and, utilising these, produce a new, curious type of "history" book, which for lack of structural coherence, owing to the apparent incompetence of its narrator, seems to fall apart and force its pronounced hero into the role of a minor character. Narrative devices and techniques together with specific problems of novel writing are continuously discussed throughout the nine books. There is, for instance, a chapter on writing a chapter (TS, IV, x). Or Tristram reflects on the narrative progress of his preceding volumes and demonstrates their digressive nature by meandering graphic lines. Comparing the lines, he finds that in the fifth volume he was "quite good ... till John de la Casse's devil led me the round ... marked D" (TS, VI, p. 454). And since in the sixth volume he has "done better still", he expresses the hope:

> If I mend at this rate, it is not impossible ... but I may arrive hereafter at the excellence of going on even thus;
> _____
> which is a line as straight as I could draw it ... (TS, VI, p. 454)

And Tristram voices his opinion on the problem of time, which poses itself in various aspects to every novelist. He considers himself a "biographical writer" (TS, IV, p. 286), planning to give an account of his life and opinions as minutely and accurately as possible. But, to his dismay, he realises that his efforts are thwarted by the impracticability of reconciling the rate in which he is able to write this account down to the rate in which he grows older: "... write as I will, and rush as I may into the middle of things, as Horace advises, – I shall never overtake myself ..." (TS, IV, p. 286).

Whereas Sterne did not advance a complete theory of his type of novel, but instead chose a piecemeal method, distributing his theoretical views over the whole of his book, O'Brien has the UCD-student narrator of *At Swim* pronounce a clear-cut theory quite early in the book, which explains its nature and intentions. The student, like Tristram, is a writer. He is working on a novel-within-the-novel about one Dermot Trellis, himself also a writer, who is conceiving a novel "on sin and the wages attaching thereto" (ASTB, p. 35).[13] The student holds that a satisfactory novel should be a self-evident sham to which the reader could regulate at will the degree of his credulity. It was undemocratic to compel characters to be uniformly good or bad or poor or rich. Each should be allowed a private life, self-determination and a decent standard of living ... Characters should be interchangeable as between one book and another. The entire corpus of existing literature should be regarded as a limbo from which discerning authors could draw their characters as required, creating only when they failed to find a suitable existing puppet. The modern novel should be largely a work of reference. Most authors spend their time saying what has been said before – usually said much better ... (ASTB, p. 25)

This theory has its origin in one of O'Brien's fantastic plans with which his head was buzzing when he was at UCD and which, in later years, he was to exploit in his *Cruiskeen Lawn* column. Niall Sheridan, O'Brien's life-time friend and the co-initiator of the bogus controversies in the *Irish Times*, remembers:

He called us together in the 'snug' of Grogan's pub in Leeson Street to announce that nobody had yet produced the Great Irish Novel. The time had come when it must be written or, rather, manufactured. This great saga (working title: *Children of Destiny*) would deal with the fortunes of an Irish family over a period of almost a century, starting in 1840 ... Brian proposed that he, Devlin, MacDonagh and I should write the book in sections and then stick the pieces in committee. Existing works would be plundered wholesale for material, and the ingredients of the saga would be mainly violence, patriotism, sex, religion, politics and the pursuit of money and power. *Children of Destiny* would be the precursor of a new literary movement, the first masterpiece of the Ready-Made or Reach-Me-Down-School ... Work began at once on the great scheme ... There was a short period of hectic activity, but the Great Irish Novel never materialised.[14]

Instead O'Brien created *At Swim*; in a way, this is his Great Irish Novel, uniting, as it does, almost the whole gamut of the

different types of Irish writing to a remarkable symposium,
from mythological and folk tales as well as medieval lays to
contemporary cowboy romances, working-class ballads and
"straight realistic" novels. Weird though the UCD student's
theory may appear at first sight, O'Brien demonstrates by *At
Swim* that such a novel is possible. A considerable part of the
student's "spare-time literary activities" (ASTB, p. 9) consists
of stealing and borrowing from existing literature. He adapts
the Finn MacCool legend and the mythological romance of
Mad King Sweeny (Buile Shuibhne). For the description of the
main characters of his novel, Dermot Trellis, he takes the
characterisation of one "Doctor Beatty" from "A Conspectus
of the Arts and Natural Science" (ASTB, p. 30f.). To define
the different meanings of the word 'kiss', he includes an
"Extract from the Concise Oxford Dictionary" (ASTB, p. 51).
Dermot Trellis, like his creator, writes his *opus* with reference
to "existing" literature. Most of his characters, he has stolen
from the works of one William James Tracy, author of Western
romances. "There is a cowboy in Room 13 [of the Red Swan
Hotel where Trellis lives] and Mr. McCool [sic], a hero of Old
Ireland, is on the floor above. The cellar is full of leprechauns'
(ASTB, p. 35). In the trial, near the end of the novel-within-
the-novel, Trellis is accused by Tracy of plagiarism. Paul
Shanahan, one of Tracy's cowboys, "borrowed" by Trellis,
gives an account of the gun-fight at the Circle N Ranch in
Dublin (!), in which he and two other "cow-punchers" were
involved. Sensing that they would be defeated by their
opponent Red Kiersay unless someone came to their rescue,
they called in "a crowd of Red Indians" (ASTB, p. 57) Tracy
was writing about at that time in another book. The rule that
every author should be democratic, allowing his characters a
private life, is observed insofar as Trellis betrays himself to be a
despotic, God-like author who "is compelling all his characters
to live with him in the Red Swan Hotel so that he can keep an
eye on them and see that there is no boozing" (ASTB, p. 35).
This "undemocratic" behaviour gives rise to the open revolt of
the characters in the novel. They drug their creator into sleep
to "maintain a decent standard of living" (ASTB, p. 35),
because he has control over them only when he is awake
(ASTB, p. 35).

   The demand that a novel should borrow from existing

literature is, interestingly, also realised in *Tristram Shandy*. Tristram describes Slawkenbergius's way of writing a book as being of a model character for "all writers, of voluminous works at least" (TS, III, p. 237). The method is one of "begging, borrowing, and stealing as he [goes] along" (TS, III, p. 237). And that is also the method Tristram himself frequently adopts, when he makes use, for instance, of the "MÉMOIRE présenté à Messiers les Docteurs de SORBONNE" (TS, I, pp. 84ff.), or "the ninth tale of [the] tenth decade" of Slawkenbergius's *opus* on noses (TS, IV, pp. 249-73).

Implicit commentary on the possibilities of writing a novel, in addition to the explicit theorising, bulks large in *Tristram Shandy* and makes the book into one of the first anti-novels. Naturally, every anti-novel depends upon some type of the novel, the conventions of which it debunks. In the case of Sterne's book, it is the quasi-biographical "history-book", proliferating in the eighteenth century. Generally, these novels are concerned, in a Cervantesque manner, with the life and adventures of their central hero as related by a narrator who usually lays great emphasis on the objectivity of his account. About Tristram's life, however, the reader learns comparatively little. Tristram's conception, birth, christening, circumcision and journey to France are briefly sketched into an otherwise long-winded narration about other people's affairs. It is on his opinions that the book is centred. The diffuse parts of the narration are held together by being projections of Tristram's consciousness. Sterne's novel is still a "history-book", but, owing to the idiosyncratic way Tristram tells his story, it is a "history book ... of what passes in a man's mind" (TS, II, p. 107). His skipping thoughts permanently lead him off into unintended directions; structurally, his work gives the impression of a disastrous chaos. The technical difficulties he encounters in composing his "vile work" (TS, I, p. 95) are often insurmountable to him. In short, his efforts fail to produce the conventional novel of the time, with its focus on outer events strung to form a clear-cut, linear plot, each particle of which is made to click into place at the precise moment. Instead, Tristram brings forth the first stream-of-consciousness novel, with a narrative process governed by "two contrary motions ... thought to be at variance with each other" (TS, I, p. 95). In accordance with the workings of the human mind, which – so the prevalent theory of the time by John Locke asserted – associates one idea with another and, in doing so, wanders in every possible direction, Tristram's account of his life and opinions is "digressive, and ... progressive too, – and at the same time" (TS, I, p. 95). It progresses from Tristram's conception to his journey to France; it digresses into a "history-book" of, predominantly, Uncle Toby's adventures.

"Digressive" and "progressive" are the very adjectives to characterise the narrative process of *At Swim*. Part of the novel is, like *Tristram*, a history of a period in the UCD student's life. In ten "biographical reminiscences", the narrator relates some of the events that took place during his last year at UCD. In the first of these, he gives the time, when he first experienced intoxicating beverages, as summer (ASTB, p. 20). In the third, he discovers, after spending a lengthy period in bed in February, that "[his] person [is] verminous" (ASTB, p. 44). And through the subsequent recollections, he steadily progresses to the moment when he comes home to receive the congratulations of his uncle and Mr Corcoran for having passed his examination "with a creditable margin of honour" (ASTB, p. 208). *At Swim* becomes digressive every time the student retires "into the privacy of [his] mind" (ASTB, p. 9) to carry further his novel about Dermot Trellis or indulge in other activities, such as a *"humorous or quasi-humorous incursion into ancient mythology"* (ASTB, p. 13). The two contrary motions bring about a multi-layered narrative structure, as is also the case with *Tristram Shandy*. *At Swim* can be divided into four "books". Firstly, there is the fragmentary biography of the UCD student, and, as he is a writer, this book may be considered a specimen of the artist novel. Many of the characteristics of this type can be traced in the respective sections of *At Swim*, the most obvious being the "outsider" position of the hero. These characteristics, however, are rendered in an exaggerated manner to form a parody of the artist novel. The UCD student composes a book about Dermot Trellis, who in turn is working on a novel about "the terrible cancer of sin in its true light" (ASTB, p. 36). Trellis is determined to teach a moral lesson to the world. He has realised "that purely a moralising tract would not reach the public" (ASTB, p. 35). Therefore he is putting "plenty of smut into his book . . . seven indecent assaults on young girls and any amount of bad language" (ASTB, p. 35). The plot is quite simple: "two examples of humanity – a man of great depravity and a woman of unprecedented virtue. They meet. The woman is corrupted, eventually ravished and done to death in a back lane" (ASTB, p. 36). Trellis betrays himself to be a tyrant who seeks "absolute control" (ASTB, p. 35) over his characters, who, in turn, call for a right to a private life, for "self-determination and a decent standard of living" (ASTB, p. 25). They conspire and revolt against their creator, drug him into sleep and lead a life to their liking. Furriskey, the intended central villain of Trellis's piece, does not corrupt and ravish his female counterpart; instead he falls in love with Peggy, a domestic servant (ASTB, p. 61), and the two arrange to lead virtuous lives, "to stimulate the immoral actions, thoughts and words which Trellis demands of them on pain of the severest penalties. They also arrange that the first of them who shall be free shall wait for the other with a view of marriage at the earliest opportunity" (ASTB, p. 61). The revolt culminates in a plan of the two characters: Shanahan and Lamont. Fearing that Trellis would soon become immune to the drugs and realising that Orlick, illegitimate child of Trellis's with the heroine of his piece, has inherited his father's gift for literary composition, they persuade Orlick to write a book in which Trellis is severely punished and put on trial for maltreating his characters. This *opus* constitutes the third narrative layer of *At Swim*.

It is possible to establish yet another level. This depends on whether one considers the tale about Finn MacCool, who in turn tells the romance about Mad King Sweeny, as part of the Trellis book. Such a view is corroborated by the narrator's remark that "Mr McCool [sic], a hero of old Ireland' (ASTB, p. 35), is living with the other characters Trellis has borrowed in the Red Swan Hotel. Furthermore, Finn is hired "to act as the girl's [i.e. Peggy's] father and chastise her for her transgressions against the moral law" (ASTB, p. 61). Some critics, on the other hand, regard the Finn part as a "book" in its own right for the sole reason that, unlike in the other "books", they do not detect any parodist element in the Sweeny romance.[15] This exegisis, however, is open to doubt.

The unifying device for the different books-within-the-book is the cluttered mind of the UCD student. All the digressions are interrelated in the prescience of the narrator. *At Swim* is thus also a stream-of-consciousness novel,[16] albeit somewhat contrived to fit the aesthetic theory of the narrator. The Chinese-box pattern, supported by an intricate counterparting of motifs,[17] lends it a more easily accessible structural order than does the associate compositional scheme of *Tristram Shandy*.

A further parallel between *At Swim* and *Tristram Shandy* is significant in this context. *At Swim* is also an anti-novel. The Trellis piece may, for good reasons, be considered a specimen of the conventional popular melodramatic, moralistic novel flourishing in the nineteenth century. By putting his alternative theory of fictional writing into practice, the UCD student lays bare the deficiencies of this type of novel and demonstrates the impossibility to go on writing in this medium. In fact, when Trellis is put on trial by his characters, he is tried as their maltreator, but he is also tried as "member of the author class" (ASTB, p. 91). Most crimes he is accused of take their origin in his capacity as omniscient, omnipotent, God-like author. The trial, then, is finally the trial of the traditional author of the conventional nineteenth century novel.

A fourth level of narration is established to make the Chinese-box pattern complete by O'Brien's telling the story of the UCD student. We have, all in all, O'Brien's novel about the UCD student who tells about his life, in which he indulges in "spare-time literary activities" (ASTB, p. 9); these bring forth the book on Trellis, which results in the book by Orlick.

II

A number of Sternesque elements may be grouped under the heading: "laying bare the methods and conventions of fictional writing", or: *artis est patefacere artem*. In his perceptive essay on *Tristram Shandy*, the Russian formalist Viktor Sklovskij[18] has discussed a variety of devices employed by Sterne to emphasise the artificiality of his work. Through them Sterne says to the reader: "Look how I did it". Both, *At Swim* and *Tristram Shandy* have a self-conscious narrator, who – as defined by Wayne C. Booth – intrudes into his novel to comment on himself as a writer and on his book as a deliberate fabrication.[19] The difficulties of the creative process are a permeating theme in these intrustions. Tristram is constantly engaged in discussing these problems; unable – or shall we say unwilling – to solve them in the conventional way, he eventually demands: *"let people tell their stories their own way"* (TS, IX, p. 602). In *At Swim*, such difficulties are reflected on the three main narrative levels. Trellis runs into trouble by infringing the "democratic" rules of his creator; Orlick, who is composing his counter-story in the style of a mythological romance, is critised by the other characters for the "fancy stuff" (ASTB, p. 167), which is "a bit too high up for [them] (ASTB, pp. 166f.). They want a "nice simple story with plenty of the razor" (ASTB, p. 169). Orlick has to start three times until he has an appropriate grip on his material. Whereas Tristram is often complaining about his inability to master the material, feeling "that things have crowded in so thick upon [him]" (TS, IV, p. 332):

> O ye Powers! ... which enable mortal man to tell a story worth the hearing, – that kindly shew him, where he is to begin it, – and where he is to end it, – what he is to put into it, – and what he is to leave out, – how much of it he is to cast into shade, – and whereabouts he is to throw his light! (TS, III, p. 215)

the UCD student is driven to admit:

> The task of rendering and describing the birth of Mr Trellis's illegitimate offspring I found one fraught with obstacles and difficulties of a technical, constructional, or literary character –so much so, in fact, that I found it entirely beyond my powers (ASTB, p. 144).

A most intriguing device for cutting across the (widely held) illusion of the "realness" of the events and characters in a novel is to take the "realness" of the events and characters literally and thus to achieve a *reductio ad absurdum*. In *At Swim*, this involves the ingenious invention of "aestho-autogamy" (ASTB, p. 40), the demand for a private life of the characters and their *non-serviam* attitude. *Tristram Shandy* anticipates O'Brien's dazzling quirk in a rudimentary form. Only after completing two and a half volumes of his "history-book" does Tristram find the time to write his preface: "All my heros are off my hands: – 'tis the first time I have a moment to spare, – and I'll make use of it, and write my preface" (TS, III, p. 202). This remark implies that the characters are real people with individual interests to be accounted for and thus with a certain amount of control over their author's activities. An even better example, in which the behaviour of the characters aspires almost to a form of revolt, is when Tristram tries to describe how his father and uncle Toby go down a flight of stairs. Steeped in a discussion with his brother, Walter Shandy steps down from the landing, halts for a moment, and draws his leg back. After an unsuccessful attempt over four chapters to have the two proceed to the bottom of the stairs, Tristram cries out in despair:

> HOLLA! – you chairman! – here's sixpence – do step into that bookseller's shop, and call me a *day-tall* critic. I am very willing to give any one of 'em a crown to help me with his tackling, to get my father and my uncle Toby off the stairs, and put them to bed (TS, IV, p. 285).

These instances are only rudimentary anticipations of what O'Brien undertakes in *At Swim;* especially the first quotation is more characteristic of Tristram's inability to minister a firm grip on his material. The second example, however, manifests a limited degree of wilfulness on the parts of the characters.

O'Brien was very fond of taking metaphors literally. His *Cruiskeen Lawn* columns offer ample proof for his predilection. The Circle-N-cowboy episode, in *At Swim,* for instance, owes its existence to a literal rendering of the phrase "the horse-play of corner-boys" (ASTB, p. 59). So when Trellis is unable to find a suitable villain, depraved enough for his purposes, in existing literature and therefore has to create Furriskey, *"ab ovo et initio"* (ASTB, p. 35) – this basic rule for the *ordo artis,* born out of Horace's admiration for Homer,[20] is one to which Tristram also whole-heartedly subscribes (TS, I, p. 38) – the birth of the villain is treated as if a real human being were born. An extract from a newspaper report on the "happy event" is incorporated in the text to demonstrate the "actuality" of the character's arrival:

We are in a position to announce that a happy event has taken place at the Red Swan Hotel, where the proprietor, Mr Dermot Trellis, has succeeded in encompassing the birth of a man called Furriskey. Stated to be doing "very nicely", the new arrival is about five feet eight inches in height, well built, dark, and clean-shaven ... (ASTB, p. 40).

And to make the evidence complete, the "Medical Correspondent" of the paper competently comments on the matter. He explains that the creation of Furriskey is a case of "aestho-autogamy" (ASTB, p. 40), and that Trellis's ingenious achievement has made the dream to eliminate conception and pregnancy, cherished by "every practising psycho-eugenist the world over" (ASTB, p. 41), come true at last. He also points out that "aetho-autogamy" is a "very familiar phenomenon in literature" (ASTB, p. 40). We may add: not only "aestho-autogamy", but likewise the notion that the characters are "real" persons, who have a right to self-realisation and who often are engaged or revolting in a Pirandelloesque manner against their author. A number of writers have voiced opinions easily to be fitted into the UCD student's aesthetic theory. Two examples may suffice. E. M. Forster maintained in *Aspects of the Novel*:

> The characters arrive when evoked but full of the spite of mutiny. For they have these numerous parallels with people like ourselves, they try to live their own lives and are consequently often engaged in treason against the main scheme of the book. They "run away", they "get out of hand" ...; if they are given complete freedom they kick the book to pieces, and if they are kept too sternly in check, they revenge themselves by dying ...[21]

Harold Pinter's attitude towards his characters — at least as described by him – reads almost as an ideal observation of the UCD student's rules:

> ... there is no question that quite a conflict takes place between the writer and his characters and on the whole I would say the characters are the winners. And that's as it should be, I think. Where a writer sets out a blueprint for his characters and keeps rigidly to it, where they do not at any

moment upset his applecart, where he has mastered them, he has also killed them, or rather terminated their birth, and he has a dead play on his hands.[22]

Usually, writers discuss such issues outside their work only. E. M. Forster did everything at his disposal as a writer to prevent treason among his characters; and Pinter has, so far, successfully inhibited his *dramatis personae* from upsetting his applecart. O'Brien, like the other meta-novelists, takes such issues into his novel, and by ridiculous exaggeration offers a burlesque of conventional modes to achieve life-like effects, thus deliberately breaking the reader's illusion.

Some of the quotations from Sterne's novel have shown that Tristram feels vexed by the problem of organising the different subject matters into an intelligible whole. Following Horace's prescription, he starts *ab ovo*, that is, with Tristram's conception. The subsequent chapters and books prove how justified he was to begin thus, since his mother's unseasonable question brought up unfavourable "humours and dispositions" in her husband and "scattered and dispersed the animal spirits" in him. That question started off the series of misfortunes which were to overshadow Tristram's entire life (cf. TS, I, p. 40). The reader learns to appreciate the ingenuity and significance of the beginning only after he has gone a good way into the first book. His initial reaction is one of puzzlement and irritation. For, in the way of facts, he learns comparatively little about the conception. Instead, having somewhat cryptically expressed his wish that his father and mother "had minded what they were about when they begot [him]" (TS, I, p. 35), Tristram digresses into an elaboration on "humours and dispositions", "animal spirits" (TS, I, p. 35), "the HOMUNCULUS," (TS, I, p. 36), "my uncle Mr Toby Shandy" (TS, I, p. 37), "the sagacious Locke" (TS, I, p. 39) and other matters, the relevance of which the reader is unable to see at this stage. It appears to him that Tristram's is exactly the method to begin a book advocated by himself in Volume VIII:

> The thing is this. That of all the several ways of beginning a book which are now in practice throughout the known world, I am confident my own way of doing it is the best – I'm sure it is the most religious – for I begin with writing the

first sentence – and trusting to Almighty God for the second (TS, VII, p. 516)

When he has read Volume VIII, the reader knows, of course, that the digressions are due to the association of ideas in Tristram's mind, and he has long realised their function in the compositional scheme of the novel.

The UCD student, too, has his own ideas about how to begin a book. With the principle: "one book, one opening" (ASTB, p. 13), he does not find it possible to concur. "A good book", he claims, "may have three openings entirely dissimilar and interrelated only in the prescience of the author ..." (ASTB, p. 9). Consequently, he gives his narrative "three separate openings" (ASTB, p. 9); the first is concerned with "The Pooka MacPhellimey", the second with "Mr John Furriskey", and the third is about "Finn MacCool" (ASTB, p. 9). Strictly speaking, there is still another opening. Whereas the three quoted relate to the novel-within-the-novel, the fourth, where the narrator speaks of his retiring "into the privacy of his mind" (ASTB, p. 9), is the actual beginning of the novel as well as of the narrator's biographical account, which frames the products of his "spare-time literary activities" (ASTB, p. 9).

As regards the ending of *Tristram Shandy* and *At Swim*, there, too, are interesting parallels. Sterne completes his novel by Obadiah's curious report of his cow that would not calve. Tristram's mother, failing to make head or tail of the story, asks: "What is all this story about?" And Yorick explains: "A COCK and BULL, ... – And one of the best of its kind, I ever heard' (TS, IX, p. 615). Yorick's words can, of course, be read as an ironic verdict by the author on his fabrication. *Tristram Shandy* is, to a considerable extent, a cock-and-bull story, and certainly one of the best. In the "Conclusion of the book, ultimate" (ASTB, p. 216), O'Brien discusses the difficulties of drawing a line between sanity and madness. He enumerates cases of people, all of them fictitious, who in one respect were quite normal and sane, while in another they showed manifest symptoms of madness. As prototypes, he names Mad King Sweeny, Hamlet, and Claudius (ASTB, p. 217) and links them to Trellis, asking: "Was Hamlet mad? Was Trellis mad?" (ASTB, p. 217), and concluding: "It is extremely hard to say."

He also expounds the diagnosis of an eminent German neurogolist who believed that Trellis was suffering from "an inverted sow neurosis wherein the farrow eats her dam". This is, evidently, an allusion to Stephen Dedalus's statement: "Ireland is the old sow that eats her farrow",[23] meant to characterise the situation of the artist in Ireland. Trellis's position as a writer in the novel-within-the-novel is equal to the artist's in Ireland; he is metaphorically eaten by his farrow. The subject of the last chapter, the evocation of Hamlet's name, and the allusion to yet another case of insanity in Hamlet, viz. to Ophelia by the three good-byes, reminiscent of her repetitive "Good night",[24] establish an ironic comment on the book. They imply that the whole novel, at least, however, the Trellis *opus* may be considered the fabrication of an abnormal mind. Yet, the allusion to Hamlet also carries the implication that it may be a case of feigned madness only and that the reader is well-advised to look for "the method in't".[25]

III

A third group of parallels between Sterne and O'Brien falls into the category of "narrative strategies and stylistic idiosyncracies" (in the narrow sense of the two terms; in an extended one, most of the devices discussed above may also be classed as such). To begin with, Tristram indulges in recurrent dialogues with fictitious readers. In most instances, these conversations are concerned with subjects of Tristram's "biographical" account. Very often, these readers request additional information or call for explanation as to what Tristram may mean by such and such a passage. One lady reader, for instance, is quoted as asking: "But pray, Sir, what was your father doing all December, – January, and February?" (TS, I, p. 39f.); and Tristram counters in a somewhat indignant manner: "Why, Madam, – he was all the time afflicted with Sciatica" (TS, I, p. 40). In *At Swim*, comparable discussions between the author and his audience may be found in the novel-within-the-novel. In his efforts to compose the "revolutionary" counterplot, Orlick is repeatedly interrupted by his employer-audience. They are dissatisfied with the way he is telling the story, which is a pastiche of the

Finn style. They demand that he abandon the long-winded "fancy stuff" (ASTB, p. 167) and get down to the business of punishing Trellis. Later, when Orlick lays down his pen for a moment to go to the "parochial house" (ASTB, p. 180), they even take it upon themselves to continue the narrative and give Trellis a thorough thrashing. Similarly, on "popular" demand, the apparently incessant flow of Finn's Sweeny legend is brought to a temporary stop, when Furriskey calls upon the working-class poet Jem Casey – a name that inevitably reminds one of Sean O'Casey – to recite his "pome" "Workman's Friend", which, so Jem has it, is "A PINT OF PLAIN" (ASTB, p. 76f.). After Jem Casey has ended his recital, Shanahan, acting as spokesman for "popular" literature, comments on the superior quality of the "pome" in contrast to "the real stuff of the native land" (ASTB, p. 75), represented by the Sweeny legend. As Clissmann has argued,[26] this *laudatio* bears the mark of unequivocal criticism by O'Brien on his fellow-Irishmen for being too atrophied in their sensibility to appreciate the value and richness of their native traditional folk literature.

Direct addresses to the reader by the author are also contained in the biographical frame-narration, where they take on the quality of a game with the reader. Again, this is equally typical of many of Tristram's conversations. In Volume I, for instance, he blames his fictitious lady-reader for being "so inattentive in reading the last chapter", in which he allegedly told her *"That my mother was not a papist"* (TS, I, p. 82). The lady-reader's remonstrances are futile; Tristram insists that she "turn back ... and read the whole chapter again" (TS, I, p. 82). Later on, when he is writing about Uncle Toby's "good-nature" (TS, II, p. 132), he points out that the following "is to serve for parents and governors instead of a whole volume upon the subject" (p. 131). Likewise, the UCD student wants to spare his reader the inconvenience of putting up with the "necessary drudgery of the novelist"[27] in the form of elaborated descriptions by inserting plot-synopses "of what has gone before", thus enabling a new reader to enter midway into the novel (ASTB, pp. 60f., 150, 164). At another point in his book, the narrator tells his reader in a "Note" to turn back "to the Synopsis or Summary of the Argument on Page 60" (ASTB, p. 103) before proceeding. The only difference between Tristram and the UCD student is that whereas the former insists, the latter "respectfully advises" to do so.

Tristram's strategy of narration has been characterised as "taking the reader by surprise",[28] this is to say that, throughout *Tristram Shandy*, the reader is confronted with matters he cannot understand, because he is first presented with an effect and afterwards with an explanation. Thus, for example, the initial sentence of *Tristram Shandy* strikes the reader as cryptic: "I wish either my father or my mother, or indeed both of them ... had minded what they were about when they begot me ..." (TS, I, p. 35). It is only after he has read on for some pages and has been given information about "animal spirits" and related matters that he is able to attach the appropriate meaning to this statement. This giving away of an effect before its causes have been named is also a way of playing with the reader. For in employing the device, the author invites the reader to specualte about possible solutions, only to prove him wrong afterwards by offering his own very different solution. O'Brien, too, uses this strategy. The opening of *The Third Policeman* is comparable to the opening of *Tristram Shandy* inasmuch as here the reader is equally taken unawares: "Not everybody knows how I killed old Philip Mathers, smashing his jaw in with my spade ..." (3P, p. 7).[29] In Sterne's, but even more so in O'Brien's novel, this device, in addition to its riddle or surprise effect, generates tension; it appeals to the reader's curiosity; he wants to know, how the presumable "Whodunnit" will be continued. The narrator of *The Third Policeman* is quick to suggest that he better "speak of [his] friendship with John Divney because it was he who first knocked old Mathers down by giving him a great blow in the neck with a special bicycle-pump ..." (3P, p. 7), and because he "was personally responsible for the whole idea in the first place" (3P, p. 7). There are a few more facts now, to be true, yet the secret is far from being explained. The reader is still deliberately kept guessing; even more so, because the narrator continues with a lengthy *curriculum vitae*. Eventually, the murder is explained, but – and this is significant – in a few paragraphs only. The reader is taken by fresh surprise when he realises that the murder-plot is only of secondary importance to the novel and that the book is not at all of the 'Whodunnit' class.

One of Sterne's most significant narrative strategies to win him much admiration from his critics is his "hobby-horsical" character drawing. After considering the advantages and disadvantages of conventional methods to picture a *persona* in a work of fiction, Tristram decides to draw "my uncle Toby's character from his HOBBY-HORSE" (TS, I, p. 98). He applies this technique, however, not only in respect to uncle Toby, but to most of his prominent figures. Almost everyone of them is drawn by delineating his mental obsessions or by repeatedly showing him in situations where he behaves in a stereotype manner. Uncle Toby, a soldier to the marrow, takes great pleasure in carrying out military sand-model exercises, after retiring from active service. His mind is completely filled with military matters, so much so that he is able to understand certain words and phrases only in their military meaning. This gives rise to a large amount of misunderstandings between Toby and his partners. Walter Shandy is characterised by his inevitable theorising on any issue in life. Having recourse to the infinite wisdom of ancient philosophers, he seeks to explain everything and solve all problems. To his distress, the vicissitudes of fate invalidate his logical reasoning by presenting him with unaccounted-for solutions. In having Tristram draw the characters "from their HOBBY-HORSE", Sterne, anticipating Peacock and Dickens, fills his novel with oddities and cranks. His idiosyncratic way of experiencing life and of telling his story let the narrator become a crank himself. Tristram has been called one of the first anti-heroes in literature,[30] for one thing, because he is "the continual sport of what the world calls fortune" (TS, I, p. 40), and, for another, because he plays a comparatively minor part in his own book. Tristram calls himself a "small HERO" (TS, I, p. 40).

O'Brien similarly fills his novel with oddities and cranks by drawing his characters in a "hobby-horsical" way. The UCD student is an anti-hero and a crank of a narrator, who ventilates "funny" ideas about literature and has an eccentric way of telling his tale. His hobby-horse is to spend most of his time in bed; for the remaining part, he is engaged in "putting glasses of stout into the interior of his body" (ASTB, p. 38). His uncle's obsession is to tease him with the recurrent question: "Tell me this, do you ever open a book at all?" (ASTB, p. 10, *passim*). Trellis is "another great bed-bug" (ASTB, p. 99), and he can read and write only green books, because "all colour except green he [regards] as symbols of evil" (ASTB, p. 99). Collopy, one of the heroes in *The Hard Life*,[31] is throughout the book associated with the plan to institutionalise ladies' conveniences in Dublin. And "the brother" in the same novel rides the hobby-horse of making money out of fantastic inventions. The capacity of a genius for devising bizarre machines and weird technical contrivances is also the sole characteristic of Policeman MacCruiskeen in *The Third Policeman*. At one time, he surprises the narrator by a spear the point of which is too thin to be seen, by his invisible chest-within-a-chest and by a curious musical instrument which produces "vibrations of the true notes ... so high in their frequency that they cannot be appreciated by the human earcup" (3P, p. 65). At another time, he shows him a mangle with which light can be stretched until it becomes sound (3P, p. 94f.). Sgt Pluck, MacCruiskeen's superior, has a pathological prediliction for bicycles and for picking his teeth; the latter is due to his belief that "nearly every sickness is from the teeth" (3P, p. 47). And, finally, the narrator resembles Walter Shandy in that his hobby-horse is also philosophy. He is obsessed by the ideas of the savant de Selby, who has influenced his life to the extent that he even commits his "greatest sin", the murder of old Mathers, for the learned man (3P, p. 9). Whatever the narrator does or whatever happens to him brings to his mind the corresponding de Selby theory. Thus, the body of the savant's wisdom forms a running commentary on his existence, in particular on his journey through the Dantesque *inferno* of the policemen. An even more striking parallel is established between the narrator and uncle Toby. When faced with what appears to them an unbearable situation, both resort to whistling a tune.

Another of Sterne's narrative habits is to give a studied precision to descriptions of physical postures in scenes where the composed effect is grotesque. The spotlight is directed in such a way as to heighten the trivial. Sterne is probably the first to introduce such delineations into literature as well as to incorporate insignificant details into his work.[32] An example of this sort of descriptive strategy is to be found in Vol. IV, Ch. ii:

My father lay stretched across the bed as still as if the hand of death had pushed him down, for a full hour and a half, before he began to play upon the floor with the toe of that foot which hung over the bed-side ... In a few moments, his left hand, the knuckles of which had all the time reclined upon the handle of the chamber-pot, came to its feeling ... (TS, IV, pp. 275f.)

"Slow-motion" technique and the heightened precision of rendering physical postures is a prominent feature of O'Brien's style. The UCD student watches his uncle and Mr Corcoran listen to "a thin spirant from the *Patience* opera" (ASTB, p. 95), and he observes:

My uncle, his back to me, also moved his head authoritatively, exercising a roll of fat which he was accustomed to wear at the back of his collar, so that it paled and reddened in the beat of the music (ASTB, p. 95).

A portrayal of Furriskey acquires in its minuteness a grotesque-like effect:

Furriskey sat opposite in a downcast manner. His flat hands were fastened along his jaws and, being supported by his arms on the table, were immovable; but the weight of his head had caused his cheeks to be pushed up into an unnatural elevation on a level with his eyes. This caused the outside corners of his mouth and eyes to be pushed up in a similar manner, imparting an inscrutable oriental expression to his countenance (ASTB, p. 207).

An equally grotesque, or surreal, impact emanates from the portrayal of the teeth-picking Sgt Pluck in *The Third Policeman* (3P, p. 47; see also 48).

Owing to the association of ideas dominating his narrative progress, Tristram is frequently compelled to break off one thread of argumentation and embark on another. He begins (Vol. VIII, Ch. ii) as if reflections on "LOVE" and "CUCKOLDOM" (TS, VIII, p. 516) were to follow; but before he has even finished the first section, he discontinues this line, because he "has long had a thing upon [his] mind to be imparted to the reader, which, if not imparted now, can never be imparted to him" (TS, VIII, p. 516). At times, Tristram freezes, as it were, an action to bring in additional information necessary for the reader to appreciate it or to give a delineation

of what has happened elsewhere in the meantime. He arrests
uncle Toby's "knocking the ashes out of his tobacco-pipe"
(TS, I, p. 88), then spends nine chapters on other matters, said
to enable the reader "to enter a little into [Toby's] character"
(TS, I, p. 87), and after several promises to return to the pipe-
knocking uncle, again suddenly drops a scene and changes "for
the parlour fire-side" (TS, II, p. 118) to relieve uncle Toby.[33]
Although for a different reason, namely that he finds it entirely
beyond his powers to describe "the birth of Mrs Trellis's
illegitimate off-spring" (ASTB, p. 144), the UCD student
decides

> to abandon a passage extending over the length of eleven
> pages touching on the arrival of the son and his sad dialogue
> with his wan mother on the subject of his father, the passage
> being, by general agreement, a piece of undoubted
> mediocrity (ASTB, p. 144).

One of the logical extensions of the strategy to break off at a
certain point in the narrative is to confess to the reader that a
chapter, or, maybe even more, has been lost beyond retrieval.
Both novelists under discussion indulge in this practical joke.
In Vol. IV, Ch. xxv, Sterne has Tristram complain: "There is
a whole chapter wanting here – and a chasm of ten pages made
in the book by it" (TS, IV, p. 311). But in the way of a
consolation for the reader, Tristram expresses his firm belief
that "the book is more perfect and complete by wanting the
chapter than having it" (TS, p. 311).[34] One day, the UCD
student goes through his manuscript and discovers that a
considerable portion is lost, in particular "one of the four
improper assaults required by the ramification of the plot or
argument" (ASTB, p. 60). Consequently, there is a "chasm in
the pagination" (ASTB, p. 60). To make good for this loss, he
decides, "to delete the entire narrative and present in its place
a brief resume (or summary) of the events which it contained"
(ASTB, p. 60). As for the deleted passage on the birth of "Mr
Trellis's illegitimate off-spring" the student, following
Tristram's attitude towards the missing chapter in his work,
consoles the reader that the book is no less perfect in
construction without the respective passage, as "the omission
of several pages at this stage does not materially disturb the
continuity of the story" (ASTB, p. 145).

Besides a comparable interest in linguistic grotesqueries – Sterne's neologisms, e.g. "ambidexterity", "hobbyhorsical" etc.; O'Brien's puns, e.g. "Kant's *Kritik der reinischen Vernunst'* (ASTB, p. 192) – there are two further stylistic parallels in the form of graphical signs and typographical arrangements. To begin with the latter, Tristram tries to define the nature of "LOVE", and he does so by speaking "alphabetically" (TS, VII, pp. 526f.):

> Love is certainly . . . one of the most
> A gitating
> B ewitching
> C onfounding
> D evilish affairs or life – the most
> E xtravagant
> F utilitous
> G alligaskinish
> H andy-dandyish
> I rancundulous (there is no K to it) and
> L yrical of all human passions [and so on up to the letter "R"]

In the counterplot of *At Swim*, Orlick seeks to enumerate Trellis's vices. The other characters, fearing that this is going to be a long, tedious list (ASTB, p. 170), suggest that he carry on in the manner of a catalogue; and Orlick continues thus:

> ANTHRAX, paid no attention to regulation governing the movement of animals affected with.
> BOYS, corner, consorted with.
> CONVERSATION, licentious, conducted by telephone with unnamed female servants of the Departments of Posts and Telegraphs.
> DIRTINESS, all manners of spiritual, mental and physical, gloried in.
> ELECTICISM, practised amorous (ASTB, p. 171).

Orlick breaks off here, because he believes that (1) "the completion of this list in due alphabetical order ... [requires] consideration and research"; and (2) "this is not the place ... for scavenging in the cess-pools of iniquity" (ASTB, p. 171).

As for the graphical signs, Sterne, or for that matter, Tristram makes repeated use of them, in the form, for instance, of two black pages representing Yorick's tombstone (TS, I,

p. 61f.), a number of bizarre curves to demonstrate the progress of his narrative (TS, VI, pp. 453f.), or a curved vertical line to stand for Corporal Trim's flourish with his stick. These graphical curiosities, although they have something of a clownish aspect to them, point to a serious issue of the eighteenth century philosophy of language. As H. Rauter has convincingly argued,[35] Sterne voiced substantial doubt as to the validity of Locke's rules, especially because the relation between ideas and words (= marks or signs for ideas) was considered occasional and arbitrary. The language of mime and gesture, on the other hand, was believed to be of unequivocal semantic value. It was understood that non-communication is a disadvantageous effect of using the language of words. As Corporal Trim puts it, the language of gesture is superior to the language of words insofar as "the eye ... has the quickest commerce with the soul, – gives a smarter stroke, and leaves something more inexpressible upon the fancy, than words can either convey – or sometimes get rid of" (TS, V. p. 356). The use of graphical signs in *At Swim* lacks these philosophical implications. When the UCD student incorporates in his novel "three dials or clock faces" (ASTB, p. 191) of a gas-meter to help Furriskey explain how one should read them, he does so merely for the sake of a practical joke.

IV

In regard to subject matter – again in the limited sense of the term as opposed to the extended reference, which would include many of the meta-aspects previously dealt with – there are very few Sternesque elements in O'Brien's writings. The most obvious are the "learned wit" passages. *Tristram Shandy* abounds in them. Every now and then, Tristram himself takes occasion to show off his apparent knowledge by quoting, in various contexts, the opinion of learned authorities or by expounding facts from a variety of scientific disciplines. Mainly, however, "learned wit" is linked with the "Shandean hypotheses", put forth in Walter Shandy's pathological theorising, whether about names (TS, I, xix); the residence of the soul (TS, II, xix); the effect of improper midwifery on the "chief sensorium" supposed to be somewhere "about the *medulla oblongata*" (TS, II, p. 163); about curses (TS, III, xii), noses (TS, III, xxxiv) or a rich number of other issues. The savant whose views Walter Shandy most often exploits is one Slawkenbergius. Sterne – as did many other authors who belong to the tradition of wit, most notably Robert Burton[36] – utilised such encyclopedic knowledge to parody scientific approaches and methods of the time as well as to satirise the belief in the usefulness of pedantic thoroughness and abundance of detail, showing in the case of Walter Shandy's resorting to the theoretical wisdom of assorted savants that the world of learning is often at variance with the world of human affairs and thereby pointing to the essential uselessness of this type of erudition.[37]

The UCD student incorporates in his writing extracts from learned books. This strategy conforms with the rule of his aesthetic theory, vaguely reminiscent of Eliot's "mature poets steal",[38] that every discerning author should make use of the "entire corpus of existing literature" (ASTB, p. 25). There are, for example, an *"Extract from Literary Reader, the Higher Class, by the Irish Christian Brothers"* on the question of "What is alcohol?" (ASTB, p. 21f.); the erudite explanation of aestho-autogamy by a reputed medical correspondent (ASTB, p. 40f.), or the discourse on *"the origin of the distinctive adjective [i.e. the chiefest wisdom], being the wise saying of the son of Sirach"* (ASTB, p. 96f.). These passages have certainly an aspect of parody to them, either as a parody of erudition or as a parody of a particular style of writing, designed to fit into the grand parodist scheme of the book, which includes parodies of some thirty different styles. At the same time, they are just another means to prove how the narrator's theory of the novel may be put into practice. There is, however, one example of erudite discourse, the sole function of which is to provide O'Brien with an opportunity for poking fun at a certain type of (scholarly) learning which consists merely of a useless accumulation of facts. This passage has Furriskey, Lamont, and Shanahan try to outdo one another by stringing together ever more curious data until the entire conversation resembles a travesty of some "Book of Records". Furriskey begins:

It is not generally known, ... that the coefficient of expansion of all gases is the same. As gas expands to the extent of a hundred and seventy-third part of its own volume in respect of each degree of increased temperature centigrade. The specific gravity of ice is 0.92, marble 2.70, iron (cast) 7.20 and iron (wrought) 7.79. One mile is equal to 1.6093 kilometers reckoned to the nearest ten-thousandth part of a whole number.

True, Mr Furriskey, remarked Paul Shanahan .... True knowledge is unpractised or abstract usefulness. Consider this, that salt in solution is an excellent emetic and may be administered with safety to persons who are accustomed to eat poisonous berries or consume cacodyl, an evil-smelling compound of arsene and methyl. A cold watch-key applied to the neck will relieve nose-bleeding. Banana skins are valuable for imparting a gloss to brown shoes ... (ASTB, p. 189).

The conversation rambles on in this fashion; it showers "pearls of knowledge" (ASTB, p. 192). By far the best specimens of "learned wit" are contained in *The Third Policeman,* where they are bound up with the name of de Selby. In the course of his journey through the Dantesque inferno of the policeman, the narrator acquaints his reader with a wide variety of de Selby views, e.g. "on the subject of houses" (3P, p. 19); "on the subject of roads" (3P, p. 33); that "a journey is an hallucination" and human existence is "a succession of static experience each infinitely brief" (3P, p. 44) – reminiscent of Zeno's paradox; on "the nature of time and eternity" (3P, p. 56); "that the earth ... is sausage-shaped" (3P, p. 81); "that darkness was simply an accretion of "black air", i.e. a staining of the atmosphere due to volcanic eruptions ... and also to certain "regrettable" industrial activities involving coal-tar products and vegetable dyes" (3P, p. 101). It is beyond doubt that O'Brien, who revelled in making up fantastic theories and outlandish inventions, as evinces from his "Research Bureau" and the pieces involving "the brother",[39] employed these theories for their comic effects. It is equally indisputable that they are intended as "learned wit" parodies on scholarly theorising, which O'Brien came the more to despise the older he grew. The question that has to be answered, however, is whether these passages are there only "for a laugh" or whether they fulfil a function in the compositional whole of the novel.

On close inspection, it becomes evident that they are of substantial semantic value. They gain their justification from the fact that the narrator is addicted beyond cure to the theories of the fictitious savant. So, naturally, any event in his life directs his thoughts to the corresponding view of de Selby's. Thus when he approaches Old Mathers's house, de Selby's theory "on the subject of houses" (3P, p. 19) comes to his mind. Further, de Selby regards "a row of houses ... as a row of evil" (3P, p. 19). Significantly, in Old Mathers's house, it is evil that the narrator encounters: he is blown to death by the bomb his friend has planted there. When walking towards the police barracks, he is forced to think on de Selby's theory "on the subject of roads" (3P, p. 32). In Chapter v, he explains the philosopher's "investigation of the nature of time and eternity by a system of mirrors" (3P, p. 56), which means that de Selby looked at himself when of middle age in a series of mirrors, with each mirror reflecting the impression of the former, and since light takes a certain time from one mirror to the next, this has a rejuvenating effect on the initial reflection. Through this contrivance, de Selby managed to see in the most distant of these mirrors "the face of a beardless boy of twelve" (3P, p. 57). In correspondence to this theory, Policeman MacCruiskeen, in the same chapter, acquaints the narrator with his box-within-the box invention. And, to give a last example, de Selby's notion that a journey is an hallucination (3P, p. 44) is in accordance with what happens to the narrator, while he is journeying through the "wonderland" of the policeman. All the events there have a hallucinatory quality. The de Selby passages, then, have a direct bearing on what the narrator experiences. Their absurd content reflects the absurdity of his position. And as the novel is, to a great extent, concerned with the mental activities (= mental agonies) of the narrator, the de Selby passages fit in perfectly well, because they are an integral part of his consciousness.[40]

Interrelated with the "learned wit" pieces in the text proper are the footnotes to the passages, which add up to a corpus of considerable size. The device of using footnotes to the text again finds its counterpart in *Tristram Shandy*, even though Sterne employs it more sparingly. Footnotes serve him, or a second authorial *persona* besides the narrator Tristram, to point to a mistake for which the latter is to blame (TS, II, p. 164).

This is a device that Beckett was to adopt to the same effect in
Watt. The bulky footnotes in *The Third Policeman* serve several
purposes. They deal with the opinions of outstanding critics
and thus resemble the apparatus of footnotes demanded of
every scientific work. And by voicing scholarly criticism on
de Selby, they seem to prove that de Selby is a real person, in
whom critics from France, England, and Germany take a
lively interest. Yet, the more the critical material is unfolded,
the more it becomes clear that, firstly, de Selby is a lunatic, or,
for that matter, that all his theories are "a forgery" and de
Selby does not at all exist (an opinion expressed by the critic
Hatchjaw, cf. 3P, p. 126); and, secondly, that de Selby
criticism leads itself *ad absurdum*, with the critics accusing one
another of being impostors and proclaiming untenable views.
The footnote apparatus is in the end as absurd as de Selby's
theories and as the "wonderland" of the policemen. The
absurdity of the narrator's journey through hell is thus
reflected on two additional levels, which proves the "learned
wit" passages as well as their appertaining footnotes to be
semantically functional parts in the novel.

Another example of "learned wit" should finally be
mentioned, because there seems to be a direct influence of
Sterne on O'Brien here. At one time during his stay in the
police barracks, Sgt Pluck explains a so-called "Atomic
Theory" to the narrator:

> Everything is composed of small particles of itself and they
> are flying around in concentric circles and arcs and
> segments ... These diminutive gentlemen are called atoms
> (3P, p. 73).

And, according to this theory, if two things are in direct
contact for some time, the "diminutive gentlemen" mingle.
Sgt Pluck sums up:

> The gross and net result of it is that people who spent [sic]
> most of their natural lives riding iron bicycles over the rocky
> roadsteads of this parish get their personalities mixed up
> with the personalities of their bicycles ... (3P, p. 74)

This theory appears to be indebted to Tristram's HOBBY-
HORSE theory: "By a long journey and much friction, it so

happens that the body of the rider is at length as full of HOBBY-HORSICAL matter as it can hold" (TS, I, p. 99).[41]

*

Tristram Shandy, just as Joyce's *Ulysses,* has been regarded as a novel *sui generis,* and the two works have been characterised as "ingenious dead-end streets".[42] On the surface, this seems to be a well-observed verdict; it, however, ignores the fact that there is a whole tradition of comic-experimental, or, as has been suggested in this essay, meta-novelists. The many parallels which it is possible to draw between Sterne and O'Brien, while pointing to a certain influence of Sterne on O'Brien, establish him firmly in the ranks of the meta-novelists. And even though O'Brien has employed many of the Sternesque devices to the same purpose as in *Tristram Shandy,* the way in which he has utilised them is often different. *At Swim* is, therefore, not a cheap imitation of the Sternesque type of novel; it is rather an example of how the constitutive narrative strategies of this type can be exploited to form another original instance of the meta-tradition. More interestingly still, a number – albeit a very small one – of contemporary novelists in England, who, compared to O'Brien, belong to the next generation of writers, have given evidence in their writings that the Sternesque tradition is alive and prospering. B. S. Johnson is a case in point: and it is significant that he himself has acknowledged his debt to *Tristram Shandy,*[43] while he employs many of the ideas and devices as characteristic of O'Brien.

Generally speaking, these meta-novelists are dissatisfied with the state of the novel; quite frequently, they choose as a point of reference for their own books particular types of novels, which they then debunk, undercutting the validity of accepted norms and strategies of fictional writing by parodying or burlesquing them; problems of creating a novel are openly discussed; the possibilities of writing fiction are taken into consideration, and alternative theories of fiction are advanced; many of the meta-novelist devices serve to demonstrate that *artis est patefacere artem.* All of these narrative techniques and stylistic idiosyncrasies as well as particular kinds of subject matter have a comic effect upon the reader, but they can be evaluated in their full semantic significance only if the reader sees behind the comic. There is no denying that *Tristram Shandy* and *At Swim* are basically comic works of literature. But then a work of literature is a multi-layered artifact. The level on which the comic operates is fairly close to the surface. To stop there in assessing is to enjoy merely half of its fascination. The essentially serious endeavours of the meta-novelists to infuse new vigour into the art form of novel-writing, so often proclaimed to be at the end of its tether, would not be given their due if the reader failed to take into account the multiple non-comic implications of the devices and strategies with which the present paper has been concerned.

From *Anglo-Irish Studies*, IV (1979), pp. 59-90.

DE SELBY DISCOVERED

Since little is known of the critical work of de Selby in his later period, the publication of the following fugitive piece found in the de Selby Archive may not be without interest to students of *At Swim-Two-Birds.*

The original is typed with a violet ribbon on four sheets of high-acid, short-fibre paper, 10″ x 8″ with printed journal ruling, headed in letter-press *Lilac Dairy / J. Halvey, prop. / Milk Roundsman / Cream to order.* The many errors in typing have been heavily corrected in indelible pencil of the type known as "copying ink". Damp has caused extensive staining of these manuscript additions but fortunately without loss of text. Accordingly in the following transcript it has not been felt necessary to reflect the varying states of de Selby's text and the text as here presented may be safely accorded the status of a fair copy of that originally composed, including footnotes.

While the piece is unsigned, in style and content it bears the characteristic marks which distinguish all of de Selby's writing and thought – the charming fusion of vast erudition with gross misunderstanding. Three of the sheets have scribblings on the

verso which may be either *probationes pennae*, obscene drawings
of the well-known de Selby logo or mandala "88".

While the review was clearly prepared for publication in one
of the learned journals, search for the appropriate literature
has failed to discover a published form.

Alf Mac Lochlainn,
Curator.

✳

With the passing of her late majesty some years ago one might
have hoped for an end to thinly-veiled moral tracts archly
masquerading as literature. But no. The distinguished name of
Mr J. G. O'Keeffe and the august sponsorship of the Irish Text
Society have now been lent to yet another effusion of the
Women's Christian Temperance Union, published under the
title *Buile Shuibhne or the Frenzy of Suibhne Geilt*.[1]

As the unknown author, perhaps the enthusiastic Mr
Nangle of Achill or one of his followers, realises that the odious
modern realism of Zola may already have sufficiently
disgusted us, he resorts to the allegorical device of placing his
"hero" in medieval Ireland. This device has so beguiled Mr
O'Keeffe that he has equipped the tract with all the scholarly
apparatus – *variae lectiones, stemmata* and the rest – which the
ponderous school of German Celtophiles has led us to expect.

The narrative commences *in medias res*, i.e. after the excesses
of drinking have already caused the mental, moral and
physical transformation of the main *persona*. (The use of the
name 'Sweeney' for this character, obviously echoing that of a
notorious pathological murderer of Victorian melodrama, is in
very doubtful taste, as indeed is the use of the name
'Loingseachan', a barely disguised version of the name of an
equally notorious fugitive western criminal, for 'the brother'.)

Indecent exposure, murder and sacrilege, personal, local
and real, are the first crimes of the alcoholic Sweeney and the
blame is clearly laid on the demon drink.

Demhan agat th'aidhmillidh
ro millis fadhéin (p. 73)
(A demon is ruining thee, thou hast ruined thyself.)

As é sin an banna dobheir an fer co lár. (p. 53)
(That is the drop which brings a man to the ground.)

Prolonged abstinence (*Gan lionn is gan brách,* "without drink without food"[2], p. 27) brings on symptoms of withdrawal and ultimately *delirium tremens,* described in terms which may be of interest to the alienist but which do not normally disfigure the pages of polite literature. *Ata crioth ar mo lamha ... Domeccad ialla omhain* (p. 31). (There is a palsy on my hands ... the bonds of terror came upon me.) Again: *Ro fhéch Suibhne suas iarum co rolíon nemhain 7 dobhar 7 dásacht 7 fúoinnel 7 fúalang 7 foluamain 7 udmaille, anbsaidhe 7 anbhoistine* (p. 15). (Sweeney looked up, wherepon turbulence and darkness and fury and giddyness and frenzy and flight, unsteadiness, restlessness and unquiet filled him.)

With Home Rule, as we write, already on the statute book and the day not far distant when the old house in College Green will have its rightful tenants, the introduction of the political note in *Buile Shuibhne* is to be deplored. Mr O'Keeffe's suggestion that Gleann Bolcáin, the glen beloved of the madmen of Ireland and in which each of them spent his year's asylum, is to be located in Co. Antrim can prove only divisive. And if our text attacks the brewers of Dublin[3] it lays its lash with an even hand on the industrious distillers of the north. *As misi Suibhne mac Colmáin ó Bhuais bhil* (p. 103). (Sweeney son of Colman am I from the pleasant Bush.) O'Keeffe's translation of *bhil* as *pleasant* hides the careful word-play on the doublet *mhil* which cleverly makes the reference to Bushmills whiskey all too obvious.

Sweeney's foregoing identification of himself is given in the course of an exchange with Fer Cailli, the outlaw, the champion madman of England, whom he meets during what must be called a flying visit to Britain. The lunatic British outlaw gives his name as Ealadhan, so suspiciously close to the oblique form (dative, e.g. giving vernacular nominative) of the word commonly used for art, craft, skill, that one can only interpret the whole passage as a heavy-handed attack on Mr George Moore, self-consciously importing "art" from Britain to Ireland.[4]

The narrative leads on to the social consequences of intemperance and having begun with the ineffectual attempt of Eorann, Sweeney's wife, to restrain his sacrilege, an attempt which merely removes his cloak and leaves him naked, it later shows us Eorann "dwelling" with another man, Guaire. Delicacy does not permit a more correct explanation of the Irish *Robhuí Eorann an tan sin an ffes le Guaire* (p. 45).

Loingseachan, "the brother", finally reduces Sweeney's powers of resistance and puts him under restraint. *Rochuir cuibhreach fora lámhaibh* (p. 58) and after six weeks of the enforced abstinence *tainic trá a chiall 7 a chuimhe dhó a ffoircenn na ree sin* (p. 60) and some measure of reason returns to the patient. Not without relapse, however, and further adventures are followed by a most horrific attack of the hallunications attendant on the advanced stages of *delirium tremens*. "A strange apparition appeared to him at midnight; even trunks, headless and red, and heads without bodies, and five bristling rough-grey heads without body or trunk among them, screaming and leaping this way and that about the road" (pp. 123-5).

References to water throughout give some hint that the author has an intimation of the primordial essentiality of the element but unfortunately true metaphysical insight is clouded by temperance polemics of the 'Adam's ale' type.

A uisce iodhan gan gheis
Ní liom-sa roba miosgas (p. 111).
(It's pure water without prohibition, 'tis not I that hated it.)
As e mo mhiadh mh'uisce fúar (p. 87).
(My mead is my cold water.)
Gidh maith libh-si i ttighibh óil
Bhar ccuirm leanna go n-onóir
Ferr lium-sa deogh d'uisge i ngiod
D'ol dom bais asin tiopraid (p. 153).
(Though goodly you deem in taverns your ale-feasts with honour, I had liefer drink a quaff of water in theft from the palm of my hand out of a well.)

At an early point in the narrative (p. 11) aspersion of water elicits the typical alcoholic's response: *Agus andar leis-sion bá da fhochuidmedh rocruithedh an t-uisge fair.* (Thinking it was to mock him that the water was sprinkled on him.) But towards the end, in true evangelical fashion, pure water (in the form of the holy well at St Mullins, Co. Carlow)[5] and the Bible (in the form of St Kevin's psalter) combine to effect a near-miraculous cure. The moral tract requires expiation, however, and a typical swineherd's wife of the order of St Moling is daily giving Sweeney the full of her footprint in a dunghill of new milk; this is misrepresented as an infidelity on her part and the swineherd murders Sweeney.

While the narrative structure, as will have been seen from the foregoing, is conventional and the use of language including the archaic verse-forms skilful to a degree not adequately represented in the translation, a disturbing innovation remains to be noted. During the conversation with the champion British madman, Sweeney is asked what his fate will be and the text continues: *Ro-innis Suibhne dhó iarum fébh atféd an sgél síosana* (p. 105). (Sweeney then told him as the story relates below.) We have here, then, a statement by a narrator that the subject of the narrative is himself a narrator and is already dead (since the narrative "below" concludes with his own death) at the time when he is reciting a narrative of events which include his death. It is to be hoped that this ridiculous story-form will find no imitators.

NOTES

Introduction

1. *London Review of Books*, II, 22 (1980), p. 5.
2. Cf. René Wellek & Austin Warren, *Theory of Literature* (Harmondsworth, repr. 1970), p. 241.
3. For the biographical sketch I shall be drawing on my article "Flann O'Brien" in J. Kornelius, E. Otto, and G. Stratmann (eds.), *Einführung in die zeitgenössische irische Literatur* (Heidelberg, 1980), pp. 161-79.
4. *New Ireland* (March 1964), p. 41.
5. In a letter to Stephen Ashe of 7 October 1955; repr. *The Journal of Irish Literature*, III, 1 (January 1974), p. 76.
6. Anne Clissmann, "Flann O'Brien", *Ireland Today*, 892 (September 1976), p. 4.
7. Not in 1910, as the Penguin edition of *At Swim-Two-Birds* maintains, nor in 1912, as Seamus Kelly asserted in his obituary "Brian O'Nolan. Scholar, Satirist and Wit", which appeared on 2 April 1966, one day after O'Nolan's death, in the *Irish Times*, and which was reprinted without correction in the special O'Nolan issue of *The Journal of Irish Literature*, III, 1 (January 1974), p. 3.
8. This anecdote is related by Niall Sheridan in "Brian, Flann and Myles" in: Timothy O'Keeffe (ed.), *Myles: Portraits of Brian O'Nolan* (London, 1973), pp. 36f.
9. Cf. Jack White, "Myles, Flann and Brian" in: T. O'Keeffe (ed.), *Myles: Portraits of Brian O'Nolan*, p. 71.
10. Cf. Niall Sheridan, "Brian, Flann and Myles", p. 47.
11. *Kavanagh's Weekly* (14 June 1952), p. 5.
12. Cf. Jack White, "Myles, Flann and Brian", p. 68.
13. Cited in Anne Clissmann, *Flann O'Brien. A Critical Introduction to His Writings* (Dublin, 1975), p. 328.
14. *At Swim-Two-Birds* (Harmondsworth, repr. 1971), p. 38. All references to *At Swim-Two-Birds*, which will be included in the text, are to this edition.
15. Niall Sheridan, "Brian, Flann and Myles", pp. 41f.
16. Jacket-note of Alf MacLochlainn's *Out of Focus* (Dublin, 1977).
17. Scholars of Irish literature like to distinguish between Irish literature written in Gaelic, which is termed "Irish" literature, and Irish literature written in English, which some call "Anglo-Irish literature", for which they are attacked by others who, because they consider the term "Anglo-Irish" to have strictly historical referents, wish to propose a different epithet. This, in turn, is reason enough for the former group of scholars to attack the latter party. Thus if one wanted to participate in the terminological squabble and take sides with what appears to be the more influential group of Hibernophiles, one would have to identify the writers mentioned here as "Anglo-Irish" writers. With so many excellent Irish

writers — others than those who inevitably figure high in any handlist of work in progress — still waiting, so far in vain, to be studied, the whole terminological controversy is an unpardonable waste of time and energy.

18. Letter to Ethel Mannin, repr. *The Journal of Irish Literature*, III, 1 (January 1974), p. 69.

19. Letter to Brian Inglis, repr. *The Journal of Irish Literature*, III, 1 (January 1974), p. 76; see also the extract from the letter in this collection.

20. Letter to Timothy O'Keeffe, cited in Anne Clissmann, *Flann O'Brien*, p. 82.

21. Letter to Ethel Mannin, repr. *The Journal of Irish Literature*, p. 69.

22. Aldous Huxley, *Point Counter Point* (Harmondsworth, repr. 1975), pp. 297f.

23. O'Nolan may have been influenced by the Ithaca episode in *Ulysses*.

24. Cf. Anne Clissmann, *Flann O'Brien*, pp. 106ff. reprinted here.

25. Cf. E. U. Klein, *Die frühen Romane Flann O'Briens: "At Swim-Two-Birds" und "The Third Policeman". Ein Beitrag zur Geschichte des englischen Romans* (Diss. Münster, 1971), p. 51.

26. This observation has by now obtained proverbial status in Ireland, with the majority of people quoting it having no idea where it has come from.

27. Cf. Vivian Mercier, *The Irish Comic Tradition* (Oxford, 1962), p. 28.

28. "Scenes in a Novel", *Comhthrom Féinne*, VIII, 2 (May 1934); repr. *The Journal of Irish Literature*, pp. 15ff; also in this collection.

29. E. M. Forster, *Aspects of the Novel* (Harmondsworth, repr. 1963), p. 72.

30. For a more detailed study of the metafictional aspects in *At Swim-Two-Birds* see my "Two Meta-Novelists. Sternesque Elements in Novels by Flann O'Brien", reprinted in this book.

31. Cf. V. Shkolvsky, "Der parodistiche Roman, Sternes *Tristram Shandy*" in: J. Striedter (ed.), *Russischer Formalismus* (München, 1969), p. 245.

32. Cf. Wayne C. Booth, "The Self-Conscious Narrator in Comic Fiction Before *Tristram Shandy*", *PMLA*, LXVII (1952), pp. 163-85.

33. Thomas Kilroy, "Tellers of Tales", *TLS* (17 March 1972), p. 301.

34. Cf. Anne Clissman, *Flann O'Brien*, p. 80.

35. Cf. the view of Richard Watts, Jr., which is cited in Anne Clissmann, *Flann O'Brien*, p. 81.

36. Cf. jacket-note to the Penguin edition.

37. Cf. my review of Anne Clissmann's *Flann O'Brien* in: *Etudes Irlandaises*, 2 (1978), p. 266; and my article "Flann O'Brien" in J. Kornelius *et al.*, *Einführung in die zeitgenössische irische Literatur*, pp. 170-74, 178.

38. B. S. Johnson, *Travelling People* (London, 1963), p. 11.

39. B. S. Johnson, *Christie Malry's Own Double-Entry* (London, repr. 1974), p. 49.

40. Anthony Burgess, *Earthly Powers* (London, Melbourne, Sydney, Auckland, Johannesburg, 1980), p. 520.

41. Raymond Federman, *Take It or Leave It* (New York, 1976).

42. Gilbert Sorrentino, *Mulligan Stew* (London, 1980).

43. Flann O'Brien, *The Third Policeman* (London, repr. 1974), p. 7.

Scenes in a Novel by Brother Barnabas

1. "Truagh sin, a leabhair bhig bháin
   Tiocfaidh lâ, is ba fíor,
   Déarfaidh neach os cionn do chlâir
   Ní mhaireann an lâmh do scríobh."

2. Who is Carruthers McDaid, you ask?

The Three Faces of Brian Nolan by Bernard Benstock

1. *Critical Writings of James Joyce*, ed. Ellsworth Mason and Richard Ellmann (New York, 1959), p. 69.
2. "'To Write for My Own Race': The Fiction of Flann O'Brien," *Encounter*, XXIX (July 1967), pp. 71-85.
3. Joycean echoes in the Flann O'Brien canon, particularly in *At Swim-Two-Birds*, are sometimes intentional, often incidental and as often coincidental, and most often delightful. Wain continually interrupts his "appreciation" of O'Brien to spot a borrowing: "the techniques of superimposition and palimpsest" found in *At Swim-Two-Birds* are basic to *Finnegans Wake* (as well as *The Waste Land* and the *Cantos*); the "wild, farcical poignancy" of one of its scenes he likens to *Ulysses*, but finds it superior; the overlay of mythic figures with contemporary characters has previously been attempted in *Ulysses* (and again in *The Waste Land*); the trial scene recalls Nighttown (as well as Kafka); Hackett is termed "a kind of scaled-down Buck Mulligan"; of *The Hard Life* Wain says: "This is Catholic writing, about Catholic matters, no less so than a full-scale attack like *A Portrait of the Artist as a Young Man* or a full-scale affirmation like the novels of G. K. Chesteron"; even Joyce's subtle use of the milk-woman in the first chapter of *Ulysses* as a personification of Ireland is duplicated in the servant Teresa who burns Trellis's manuscript. The last point shows Wain at his weakest: Joyce's crone is designated by her creator through his use of the popular epithets for Ireland, so that the Poor Old Woman has an ironic identity; Wain's attempts to imbue Teresa with as much is gratuitous, since O'Brien makes no visible attempt to aid his critic in making any further identification. Teresa is actually closer to the slavery in "Two Gallants," but even there Joyce paves his own path to such relationships, since the slavey wears the sailor's hat that shows her to serve the Empress of the Seas.

   Flann O'Brien openly invites the spectre of Joyce to sit at his feast; from the early pages of *At Swim-Two-Birds*, where the narrator's books range from "those of Mr. Joyce to the widely-read books of Mr. A. Huxley," to the use of James Joyce as an important character in *The Dalkey Archive*, James Joyce makes his presence felt. Other elements might be recalled to the reader's attention: the degree to which O'Brien's "uncles" resemble Simon Dedalus, particularly the uncle of *At Swim-Two-Birds* (Mr. Collopy of *The Hard Life* is actually a bit too ludicrous; his plan to dot Dublin with lavatories for women seems the sort of humanitarian scheme that Bloom entertained); the first uncle is the pompous head-of-family that Simon was, and he is as sentimental a lover of song. O'Brien's description of him is apt: "Rat-brained, cunning, concerned-that-he-should-be-well-thought-of. Abounding in pretence, deceit." Si Dedalus, like John Joyce, was "something in a distillery," while the uncle here is "holder of Guinness clerkship the third class." Also noteworthy in *At Swim-Two-Birds* are casual inclusions of some of Joyce's prime shibboleths: The Pooka is credited with sowing in Orlick's heart "the seeds of evil, revolt, and non-serviam"; Trellis is credited with an "inverted sow neurosis wherein the farrow eat their dam"; and the Pooka causes "a stasis of the natural order and a surprising kinesis of many incalculable influences." The Joycean method is comically pinpointed when the narrator admits, "I continued in this strain in an idle perfunctory manner, searching in the odd corners of my mind where I was accustomed to keep words I rarely used. I elaborated the argument subsequently with the aid of dictionaries and standard works of reference." And what are we to make of the cryptic assertion that "Finn is without honour in the breast of a sea-blue book"? (Joyce had the original edition of *Ulysses* bound in blue; in the *Wake* it is referred to as "his usylessly unreadable Blue Book of Eccles."

In *The Hard Life* the colloquy between Father Fahrt and Mr. Collopy embodies the love of disputation that is found so often in Joyce's works, but whereas *At Swim-Two-Birds* abounds in monstrous ignorance being passed off as gospel truth, the reverse is true in the second novel. Mr. Collopy's facts are precise, astonishingly so for a layman, so that although his tone suggests prejudice, his information remains accurate. The discussion held by Lamont, Shanahan, and the Furriskeys is intended as burlesque ("Homer finished his days on earth with his cup of poison. He drank it alone in his cell," says Lamont. "That was another ruffian, said Mrs. Furriskey. He persecuted the Christians"); the religious dialogue in *The Hard Life* is double-burlesque when the accuracy of the accusations is paralleled with the desultories of the conversation itself. Between the two discussions rests a resemblance to the bedside blather that Joyce records in "Grace,' and Mr. Collopy has the odd distinction of being a Simon Dedalus in reverse when he attacks the Jesuits and upholds the Christian Brothers.

The Dalkey Archive has the coincidence of an opening scene located at a bathing area just outside Dublin, an opening familiar to readers of *Ulysses*, the Dalkey site being only a few miles from the Forty Foot at Sandycove where Mulligan and Haines go for their swim. Later, an anecdote told by Father Cobble depends for its effect on a priest's emergence from the sea, indicating that O'Brien is consciously echoing the first chapter of Joyce's novel. (His employment of Dalkey's Vico Road seems almost gratuitous.) The tribute paid to Joyce in *The Dalkey Archive* is a relevant one: Mick Shaughnessy comments, after dismissing *Exiles* and the Joyce poems as undistinguished efforts, "But I have an admiration for all his other works, for his dexterity and resource in handling language, for his precision, for his sublety in conveying the image of Dublin and her people, for his accuracy in setting down speech authentically, and for his enormous humour." These indeed seem to be the aspects of Joyce's work that Brian O'Nolan sought to emulate.

4. As himself (as Brian Nolan, that is), our man has contributed a bizarre evaluation of James Joyce in the coterie-conceived James Joyce Special Number of *Envoy* (April 1951). His essay, "A Bash in the Tunnel," is not quite as cranky as Patrick Kavanagh's poem, "Who Killed James Joyce?" (as yet no poem called "Who Killed Brian O'Nolan?" has emerged from the league of Dublin wits), but it reflects a similar attitude: that Joyce has escaped our wrath through exile, that his genius makes him almost invulnerable and he must therefore be accepted, and that American critics deserve to be attacked instead for making a cult out of *our* Joyce. In *The Dalkey Archive* Mick makes the same sort of statement, but with none of O'Nolan's wit and little of his vituperative fervor: "I've read some of the stupid books written about Joyce and his work, mostly by Americans." When Joyce himself appears as a character in the novel, he disclaims *Ulysses* and never heard of *Finnegans Wakes* (*Dubliners* he acknowledges, claiming Gogarty as co-author); he even adds that a "fellow named Gorman wrote that 'he [Joyce's father] always wore a monocle in one eye'. Fancy!" He does not mention, however, that a fellow named Nolan or O'Nolan passed off a non-existent interview that he claimed to have had with John Joyce, having it published in *A James Joyce Yearbook* (Paris, 1949) — this is the story still making the rounds of Dublin pubs. (In *Exiles* Richard Rowan argues for the "faith of a master in the disciple who will betray him.")

5. The conflict between the escaped exile and the resident Irish writer is an important one, and in the light of O'Nolan's condition as a stay-at-home, the following dialogue from *The Dalkey Archive* is pertinent:
— It's a pity, Mick ventured at last, that most of us haven't the money to go and

live abroad. Our sort of people seem to flourish in an alien clime. One reason
may be that this country's too damp.
— It's too full of humbugs and hypocrites, Crabbe said.

6. The pronounced inferiority of the two later novels rests with the loss of Flann
O'Brien's strongest attributes, his fanciful manipulation of language and his
ability to structure a complex novel to exist on four or more levels simultaneously;
both of these are Joycean skills, and O'Nolan may have learned something of the
first from *Work in Progress* but he could hardly have divined the second without
access to the completed *Wake*. In comparison with *At Swim-Two-Birds* the
succeeding O'Brien novels are flat and prosaic, and the effort to handle more than
one plot line proves clumsy. The Finbarr-Manus aspect of *The Hard Life* — the
Bildungsroman portion — never quite interlaces with the comic situation of
Collopy's quest and collapse; in *The Dalkey Archive* the Joyce plot is introduced in
the second half and never gels with the De Selby conspiracy (Mick's own
tendencies toward frequent summation lack the magnificent humour of similar
attempts by the narrator of the first novel, so much so that Mick's call attention to
a failure of the portions to intermesh coherently: "It was strange how fast
somewhat grisly spices were accumulating on his platter. First, the central menace
of De Selby, and his own plan to foil him. Then the baffling Saint Augustine
episode. Next, the accidental Father Cobble complication, to be enacted on the
morrow. And now this Joyce phantasm." O'Brien's try at the picaresque never
quite comes off; interlinked segments prove to be badly joined fragments.

7. A nod to Samuel Beckett can be noted in *The Dalkey Archive,* where Mick considers
his own relationship to Hackett: "Hackett's mind was twisted in a knot identical
with his own. They were two tramps who had met in a trackless desert, each
hopelessly asking the other the way."

8. Patrick Kavanagh states the case for myth over reality in his petulant dedication
speech on Bloomsday 1967, as quoted in the *Irish Times* of June 17, 1967: "I don't
like Richard Ellmann's piece telling us what so-called real person lived at No. 7
Eccles Street, for such alleged realism and research clouds the myth. And this
myth is all that is real. And this door is as famous in the mythology of Dublin as
221b Baker Street is to London."

Literalist of the Imagination by J. C. C. Mays

1. "Brian, Flann and Myles", *Irish Times* (1 April 1971), p. 10.
2. Possibly an allusion to triadic motifs in Joyce, possibly to the triadic logic of the
Nolan himself (Giordano Bruno).
3. Reference is to *At Swim-Two-Birds* (London: Longmans, 1939; and MacGibbon &
Kee, 1960).
4. "An Aristophanic Sorcerer", *Irish Times* (2 April 1966), p. 7.
5. In his review of *At Swim-Two-Birds* ("Secret Scripture"), *Irish Times* (30 July
1960), p. 6.
6. This is not to deny that seemingly arbitrary details do not yield up a significance.
Heine's *Die Harzreise,* which the narrator wants to buy but never gets round to
buying, deals with students, is full of puns and epigrams, shifts to fairy-tales,
legends, descriptions of nature, etc., in much the same way as *At Swim-Two-Birds.*
7. Or with the English translation by J. G. O'Keeffe also included in his edition of
Buile Suibhne, Irish Texts Society, XII, David Nutt, London 1913. Cf. *AS2B,*
pp. 91-2 with *ed. cit.,* pp. 12 and 13, for instance, or *AS3B,* pp. 124-5 with *ed. cit.,*
pp. 136 and 137.

8. "Scel Lem Duib", *The Lace Curtain*, No. 4 (Summer 1971), p. 47. For versions of the lay that Sweeny sang, cf. *Buile Suibhne, ed. cit.*, pp. 33 and 35; John Montague, "Sweetness (from the Irish). I.M. Flann O'Brien, who skipped it", *A Chosen Light* (London: MacGibbon & Kee, 1967), p. 65.

Forms of Gloom by Stephen Knight

1. See J. G. O'Keeffe's edition and translation. *The Adventures of Suibhne Geilt*. Irish Texts Society, XII (London, 1913). For Finn, see Standish O'Grady's *Silva Gadelica* (London, 1892) and *The Book of the Lays of Finn*, Irish Texts Society, VII, XXVIII and XLIII (London, 1908-1953), edited by Eoin MacNeill and Gerard Murphy.
2. " 'To Write for My Own Race': The Fiction of Flann O'Brien", *Encounter*, XXIX (July 1967), pp. 71-87; I quote from p. 75.

The Story-Teller's Book-Web by Anne Clissmann

1. *Comhthrom Féinne* (now called *The National Student*) XI, 3 (June 1935), pp. 62-3.
2. Niall Sheridan, 'Brian, Flann and Myles', *Irish Times*, (2 April 1966).
3. BON to C. H. Brooks, 31 January 1938.
4. A. M. Heath to BON, 22 September 1938.
5. BON to A. M. Heath, 19 October 1938.
6. BON to Longmans, 15 January 1939.
7. Eóghan Ó Tuairisc in *The Encyclopaedia of Ireland*, p. 122.
8. Niall Sheridan to TOK, 4 March 1960.
9. A. M. Heath to BON, 14 April 1939.
10. Richard Watts, Jnr to Anne Clissmann, 12 March 1968.
11. BON to TOK, 25 November 1961.
12. BON to TOK, 1 September 1959.
13. BON to TOK, 15 October 1965.
14. BON to TOK, 18 December 1965.
15. John Wain, 'To Write for My Own Race', *Encounter* XXIX, 1 (July 1967), pp. 71 ff.
16. Richard Harrity, 'A Comic Masterpiece of Irish Fantasy', *New York Herald Tribune* (11 March 1951).
17. Vivian Mercier, 'At Swim-Two-Birds', *Commonweal*, LIV. 3 (27 April 1951), pp. 68, 70.
18. James Meenan (ed.), *A Centenary History of the Literary and Historical Society of University College, Dublin, 1855-1955*. (Tralee 1957), pp. 240-1.
19. The uncle is undoubtedly based on the uncle in Joyce's *Dubliners*. In *Araby* he is the fictive counterpart for Joyce's father; he disappoints the young boy and then becomes complacent and clichéd.

    My uncle said he was very sorry he had forgotten. He said he believed in the old saying: 'All work and no play makes Jack a dull boy.' He asked me where I was going and, when I told him a second time, he asked me did I know *The Arab's Farewell to his Steed*. When I left the kitchen he was about to recite the opening lines of the piece to my aunt. (*Dubliners*, p. 31).

    The uncle also appears in *The Sisters*, but here O'Brien seems to be basing the narrator's response to his uncle on the boy's response to Mr Cotter rather than to his uncle.

'It's bad for children,' said old Cotter, 'because their minds are so impressionable. When children see things like that, you know, it has an effect ...' I crammed my mouth with a stirabout for fear I might give utterance to my anger. Tiresome old red-nosed imbecile. (*Dubliners*, p. 9).

20. The committee's discussion on this point is probably based on a row in UCD in 1934 which developed when the SRC decided to hold a céilí on St Patrick's Day. There was bitter opposition to the scheme on the grounds that Irish dances were 'primitive'. The Gaelic League often overreacted to such statements by banning all dances other than reels and sets, etc. as non-Irish and, therefore, harmful to Irish purity. O'Brien was to return to this kind of topic in *An Béal Bocht*.

21. Joyce, *A Portrait*, p. 100.

22. *Ibid.*, p. 67.

23. There are several other places, notably in the section where the 'learned' discussion between Shanahan, Lamont and Furriskey takes place in Orlick's manuscript, that the 'Ithaca' episode is parodied. The parody of legalistic language is very prevalent in O'Brien's work. It is this that leads one to label it an 'Anatomy' even as a distrust of 'abstract' talk can be seen to be an aspect of Celtic literature.

24. The influence of *Dubliners* may, possibly, be discerned also in the Circle N episode of the book where the idea of associating the Dublin environment and the 'wild west' may have been inspired by *An Encounter*. 'The adventures related in the literature of the Wild West were remote from my nature but, at least, they opened doors of escape.' (*Dubliners*, p. 17) 'We walked along the North Strand Road till we came to the Vitriol Works and then turned to the right along the Wharf Road, Mahony began to play the Indian as soon as we were out of public sight.' (*Dubliners*, p. 20).

25. *A Portrait*, p. 203.

26. In an article in *Dublin Doings* (Christmas 1940) O'Brien, while criticising the cultural pretensions of the Irish speaker, also speaks of the Irish language as 'an instrument of beauty and precision'.

27. 'A Bash in the Tunnel', *Envoy* V, 17 (May 1951), pp. 5-11.

Flann O'Brien's Theory of Fiction by Ninian Mellamphy

1. See Anthony Burgess, *The Novel Now*, second edition (London: Faber and Faber, 1971), p. 78.

2. Joyce, in conversation with Niall Sheridan; see Anne Clissmann, *Flann O'Brien: A Critical Introduction to his Writings* (Dublin: Gill and Macmillan, 1975), p. 79.

3. See Burgess, *The Novel Now*, pp. 78-80; Wain, " 'To Write for my Own Race': The Fiction of Flann O'Brien," *Encounter*, 29 (1967), pp. 71-85; Mercier, *The Irish Comic Tradition* (Oxford: Clarendon Press, 1962), pp. 38-40, and Pritchett's review in *The New Statesman* (20 August 1960).

4. First published by Longmans, Green and Co., March 1939; re-published by MacGibbon and Kee, July 1960. Penguin edition 1967. An American edition appeared in 1951; reviews were good, sales bad (Clissmann, pp. 80-81).

5. Citations and references are to the Penguin edition (Harmondsworth, 1967) because of its general availability.

6. The novel opens with a biographical reminiscence, which brings the total to eleven — possibly an extension into the structure of the Pooka's concern with numerology ("truth is an odd number," etc.). The opening page is likewise the beginning of the ending(s): the *"penultimum continued"* heading to the description of Orlick's entry into society presupposes an *incipit penultimum*.

7. E. M. Forster, *Aspects of the Novel* (London: Edward Arnold, 1927), pp. 111-12.

8. "To write a book or to make a book," p. 24.

9. "The Art of Fiction" (1884): see Leon Edel (ed.) *The House of Fiction: Essays on the Novel of Henry James* London: Rupert Hart-Davis, 1957), p. 31.

10. *Aspects of the Novel*, pp. 132-35.

11. Aldous Huxley, *Point Counter Point* (London: Chatto and Windus, 1928), p. 408.

12. For a description of the plot of *The Cream of the Jest* (London: Bodley Head, 1923), see Clissmann, pp. 93-95.

13. *Buile Shuibhne*, a twelfth-century tale in prose and verse, recounts the ordeals of Suibhne Geilt (Sweeny the Madman), who went insane at the battle of Magh Rath (Moira), 637 A.D., where the forces of his king, Dónal Brecc of the Dal Riada, were routed by those of the High King of Ireland, Dónal Mac Aedha. A full translation by J. G. O'Keeffe was published by the Irish Texts Society (Vol. XII) in 1913. O'Brien provides his own translation.

14. The theme of failure informs even the one happy ending. The student gets a good honours degree and wins the respect of his delighted uncle, who presents him with an antique watch. He first consults the timepiece when the angelus bell peals; his watch tells him the time is 5:54 p.m. (p. 215). If the reader doesn't notice the six-minute deviation from the Greenwich ideal, then the failure is his.

15. On 17 March 1690 appeared the first number of *The Athenian Gazette* (thereafter *Mercury*), a twice-weekly folio sheet of advice for the middle classes published by members of the Athenian Society until 1695. *The Athenian Oracle*, a three-volume collection of "all the valuable questions and answers" in the old journal, was published in 1703-1704. Though he does not tell us so, it is Vol II (1703) which O'Brien uses as "the old book purchased ... upon the quays" by Michael Byrne, who one evening amuses the narrator and other guests by reading excerpts thereform (p. 102). The excerpts are mainly from the "Alphabetical Fable" of contents at the end of the volume; only two are from the 552 pages of the actual text.

16. The forty buckskin volumes of Dr Cowper's *Conspectus of the Arts and Natural Sciences* (Bath, 1854) which adorn the narrator's mantelpiece (p. 11) are elusive. I have failed to find even a bibliographical mention of this work.

17. See "Preface to *Portrait of a Lady*" in *The Art of the Novel* (London: Scribner's, 1934), p. 53.

18. In Act 1 of *Six Characters in Search of an Author*, the Father addressing the actors says: "I marvel at your incredulity, gentlemen. Are you not accustomed to see characters created by an author spring to life in yourselves and face each other?" Edward Stover's translation, from which I quote, had been available since 1923 when Dent published Pirandello, *Three Plays*.

Two Meta-novelists by Rüdiger Imhof

1. A. Clissmann, *Flann O'Brien. A Critical Introduction to his Writings* (Dublin, 1975). pp. 106-15, *passim;* John V. Kelleher, 'Dublin's Joyce and Others', *Virginia Quarterly Review*, Vol. 33, No. 1 (Winter 1957), pp. 132-5; Sighle Kennedy, ' "The Devil and the Holy Water" — Samuel Beckett's *Murphy* and Flann O'Brien's *At Swim-Two-Birds*', in R. J. Porter and J. D. Brophy (Eds.), *Modern Irish Literature* (New York, 1972); J. C. C. Mays, 'Brian O'Nolan and James Joyce on Art and on Life', *James Joyce Quarterly*, Vol. 11, 1974, pp. 238-56; J. C. C. Mays, 'Brian O'Nolan: Literalist of the Imagination', in T. O'Keeffe (ed.), *Myles: Portraits of Brian O'Nolan* (London, 1973), pp. 77-115; D. Powell, 'An Annotated Bibliography of Myles na Gopaleen's "Cruiskeen Lawn Commentaries of James Joyce" ', *James Joyce Quarterly*, Vol. 9, 1971, pp. 50-62.

2. A. Clissmann, *Flann O'Brien*, p. 81.

3. See S. Kennedy, "'The Devil and the Holy Water" ...'; T. Hilton, 'Ireland's Great Cyclists, *New Statesman* (8 December 1967), p. 815; B. Cosgrove in his review of A. Clissmann's monograph, *Irish University Review*, Vol. 6, No. 1 (Spring 1976), pp. 122-4.

4. A. Clissmann, *Flann O'Brien*, p. 352; Niall Sheridan, 'Brian, Flann and Myles', in T. O'Keeffe (Ed.), *Myles*, p. 51; J. C. C. Mays, 'Brian O'Nolan', p. 92.

5. A. Clissmann, *Flann O'Brien*, p. 155.

6. A. Clissmann, *Flann O'Brien*, p. 94.

7. For instance: A. Clissmann, *Flann O'Brien*, pp. 99, 352f.; B. Kiely, *Modern Irish Fiction: A Critique* (Dublin, 1950), p. 76; E. Klein, *Die frühen Romane Flann O'Briens: 'At Swim-Two-Birds' und 'The Third Policeman'. Ein Beitrag zur Geschichte des englischen Romans* (Diss. Munster, 1971), pp. ix. 99.

8. Wayne C. Booth, 'The Self-Conscious Narrator in Comic Fiction Before *Tristram Shandy*', *PMLA*, Vol. 67 (1952), pp. 163-85.

9. O'Brien's opinion on *At Swim* expressed in a letter to Ethel Mannin of 10 July 1939, repr. in *The Journal of Irish Literature*, Vol. 3, No. 1 (January 1974), p. 69.

10. Cf. *Laurence Sterne: The Critical Heritage;* for early reviews of O'Brien's novel see T. O'Keeffe, 'A Bibliographical Note', in T. O'Keeffe (Ed.), *Myles*, pp. 122-34.

11. M. H. Abrams, *A Glossary of Literary Terms* (New York, 1971), p. 114.

12. All quotations from L. Sterne, *The Life and Opinions of Tristram Shandy, Gentleman,* Ed. Graham Petrie (repr. Harmondsworth, 1974).

13. All quotations from Flann O'Brien, *At Swim-Two-Birds* (repr. Harmonsworth, 1975).

14. N. Sheridan, 'Brian, Flann and Myles', pp. 45f.

15. Cf. for instance A. Clissmann, *Flann O'Brien*, pp. 126ff., 131, 133; St. Knight, 'The Novels of Flann O'Brien', in D. Anderson and St. Knight, (eds.), *Cunning Exiles: Studies of Modern Prose Writers* (Sydney, 1974), pp. 101f.; J. C. C. Mays, 'Brian O'Nolan: Literalist of the Imagination', p. 88.

16. Cf. A. Clissmann, *Flann O'Brien*, p. 86f.

17. To name but a few of these counterparts that unit the different levels of narration: Trellis resembles Sweeny; he, too, is punished and has to live on trees. The bourgeois Furriskey household bears comparison to the bourgeois home of the UCD student. The narrator, like Sweeny, begins in anger and ends in reconciliation. Finn, the ancient folk hero, finds his counterpart in the Ringsend cowboys, the modern folk heroes. The leaps of Sgt Craddock are reminiscent of Sweeny's leaps. Orlick's literary style recalls Finn's style of narration. And the College students of the biographical reminiscences echo by their 'horse-play' the activities of the Ringsend cowboys. Trellis resembles the UCD student, because he, too, is a 'great bed-bug' (ASTB, p. 99). And, finally, the UCD student, Trellis, and Orlick are alike in that they are writers, thus the situation of the writer is established on the three major levels of narration.

18. V. Sklovskij, 'Der parodistische Roman. Sternes *Tristram Shandy*', in J. Striedter (ed.), *Russischer Formalismus* (Munich, 1971), pp. 245-99.

19. Cf. W. C. Booth, 'The Self-Conscious Narrator . . .', p. 165.

20. *De Arte Poetica Liber* (Zurich/Swiss, 1961), pp. 146f.: 'nec reditum Diomedis ab interitu Meleagri,/nec gemino bellum Troianum orditur ab ovo.'

21. E. M. Forster, *Aspects of the Novel* (Harmondsworth, repr. 1963), p. 72.

22. H. Pinter, 'Speech: Hamburg 1970', *Theatre Quarterly*, Vol. 1, No. 3, 1971, p. 4.

23. J. Joyce, *'A Portrait of the Artist as a Young Man'*, in *The Essential James Joyce*, Ed. Harry Levin (Harmondsworth, repr. 1965), p. 212.

24. W. Shakespeare, *Hamlet* (Longmans, London, 1973), p. 165.

25. *Hamlet*, II, ii, p. 71; assessments of the structural method have been provided by A. Clissmann, *Flann O'Brien*, pp. 90f.; E. Klein, *Die frühen Romane ...*, pp. 57ff.; J. C. C. Mays, 'Brian O'Nolan: Literalist of the Imagination', pp. 86f.

26. A. Clissman, *Flann O'Brien*, p. 133.

27. V. Woolf, 'Mr. Bennett and Mrs. Brown' in V. Woolf, *Collected Essays*, ed. L. Woolf, Vol. 1 (London, 1975), p. 329.

28. Cf. for instance L. Borinski, *Der englische Roman des 18. Jahrhunderts* (Frankfurt, Bern, 1968), p. 255.

29. Reference here and in the following quotations is to Flann O'Brien, *The Third Policeman* (London, 1974).

30. B. Fabian, 'Sterne. *Tristram Shandy*', in F. K. Stanzel (ed.), *Der englische Roman. Vom Mittelalter zur Moderne*, Vol. 1 (Düsseldorf, 1969), p. 267.

31. Flann O'Brien, *The Hard Life* (London, 1976).

32. D. W. Jefferson, '*Tristram Shandy* and its Tradition', in B. Ford (ed.), *Pelican Guide to English Literature*, Vol. 4 (Hardmondsworth, repr. 1966), p. 342. V. Sklovskij, 'Der parodistiche Roman ...', p. 257. L. Borinski, *Der englische Roman des 18. Jahrhunderts*, p. 253.

33. Cf. also *Tristram Shandy*, III, xxix - IV, ii, and V, v - V, xii.

34. Cf. also *Tristram Shandy*, IX, xviii and xix.

35. H. Rauter, *Dies Sprachauffassung der englischen Vorromantik in ihrer Bedeutung für die Literaturkritik und Dichtungstheorie der Zeit* (Bad Homburg v.d.H., Berlin, Zurich, 1970); see especially pp. 125-35.

36. K. J. Holtgen, 'Robert Burton's *Anatomy of Melancholy:* Struktur und Gattungsproblematik im Licht der ramistischen Logik', *Anglia*, Vol. 44 (1976), pp. 388-403.

37. Cf. D. W. Jefferson, '*Tristram Shandy* and Its Tradition'.

38. T. S. Eliot, *On Poetry and Poets*, pp. 64f.

39. Cf. *The Best of Myles*, Ed. Kevin O'Nolan (London, 1975), pp. 41-78, 112-37.

40. E. Klein, *Die frühen Romane ...*, pp. 153ff.

41. A. Clissmann, *Flann O'Brien*, p. 11; it is less probable that a comment on him in the student magazine *Comhthrom Féinne* gave O'Brien the basis for his theory: 'Mr Brian Ua Nuallain regrets the fact that he is becoming lantern-jawed from riding his bicycle in the dark.'

42. K. Otten, *Der englische Roman vom 16. zum 19. Jahrhundert* (Berlin, 1971), p. 89.

43. B. S. Johnson, 'Introduction', in B. S. Johnson, *Aren't You Rather Young to be Writing Your Memoirs?* (London, 1973), p. 22.

De Selby Discovered by Nicholas de Selby and Alf MacLochlainn

1. *Buile Shuibhne (the frenzy of Suibhne) being The Adventures of Suibhne Geilt, a middle-Irish romance*, edited with translation, introduction, notes and glossary by J. G. O'Keeffe. London: Nutt (for the Irish Text Society), 1913.

2. In presenting *brách* and *food* as equivalents Mr O'Keeffe seems to be relying on Dinneen's *brachán, broth, pottage, stirabout, gruel*. Dinneen gives, however, two further meanings, one of which (the filth in frieze after tucking) we can ignore, the other — *fermented matter* — being the more important and presumably to be related to Dinneen's *brachadh, malting, fermentation, act of fermenting*. (Also *corrupt matter in the eyes*.) This in turn must be related to Dinneen's *brach, the hop plant, hops*, and the real meaning of the text becomes clear.

3. The inclusion among the names of Sweeney's kinsmen of one dubbed Aongus the Stout (p. 15) is naive in the extreme and can only give offence to a family in Dublin who rank among the capital's largest and most enlightened employers, whose principal product is the Dublin working-man's favourite the 'pint of plain' and whose name derives historically from the illustrious family of MacAonghusa.

4. The low opinion of British standards implied here is reinforced when we differ from O'Keeffe in his interpretation of *brughaidh, Mac brughaidh mé ar an gheill Breathnach* (p. 103) (I am the son of a landholder, said the British fool.) One is surely entitled here to rely on Dinneen's *brughaidheacht, hostel-keeping,* and translate rather 'I am the son of a publican'.

5.   *Tiubra na Gealta súd thall,*
   Ionmuin cách dar tradh a barr,
   Ionmuin lium a gaineamh glan,
   Ionmuin a husige iodhan (p. 157).
   (Yonder is the well of the madman, dear was he to whom it gave food, dear to me its clear sand, dear its pure water.)

Mr Nicholas Kavanagh, lock-keeper of Tinnehinch Lower on the Barrow Navigation, some two and a half miles N.W. of St Mullins, tells me his grandmother, the late Mrs Nellie McMurrough, was cured of a 'bad leg' (the usual peasant euphenism for a suppurating varicose ulcer) by standing barefoot in the well at St Mullins for three hours during the 'pattern' in July 1888. The Rev. Mordecai O'Morphie, now living in retirement in Bury St Edmunds and sometime rector of the Church of Ireland parish of Glin in which St Mullins is situated, tells me that at the same 'pattern' in July 1888, it was reported that whiskey diluted with water from the well was increased rather than diminished in intoxicating power.

SELECTED BIBLIOGRAPHY

1. Works

O'Brien, Flann. "A Man and His Bicycle" [extract from *The Dalkey Archive*], *Queen* (13 August 1964), pp. 43-9.

At Swim-Two-Birds (London: Longmans, 1939; New York: Pantheon, 1951; London: MacGibbon & Kee, 1960; London: Four Square Books,1962; New York: Walker, 1966; Harmondsworth: Penguin, 1967; New York: Viking Press, 1967; Harmondsworth: Penguin, repr. 1975). Adapted for the stage by Audrey Welsh and staged at the Sugawn Theatre, London (in the pub "The Duke of Wellington"), in June 1977; cf. B. Levin, "Deep in the Heart of Tennessee", *The Sunday Times* (12 June 1977), p. 37.

— "At the Crossroads", *Irish Times* (20 February 1965).

— "Behan, Master of Language", *Sunday Telegraph* (22 March 1964).

— "Can a Saint Hit Back?", *Manchester Guardian* (19 January 1966).

— "Enigma", *Irish Times* (16 June 1962).

— "Gael Days", *Manchester Guardian* (6 May 1964).

— "George Bernard Shaw on Language", *Irish Times* (23 January 1965).

— "Going to the Dogs", *The Bell*, I, 1 (October 1940), pp. 19-24; repr. in: Frank O'Connor (ed.), *A Book of Ireland* (London: Fontana/Collins, 1976), pp. 168-70.

— "John Duffy's Brother", *Story*, XIX, 90 (July-August 1941), 65-68; repr. in: *Antaeus*, 20 (Winter 1976), pp. 27-31.

— "Mad Sweeny *versus* Jem Casey" [extract from *At Swim*] in: V. Mercier and H. Greene (eds.), *1000 years of Irish Prose* (New York, 1952), pp. 563-82.

— "National Gallery: Sean O'Sullivan", *Development*, 16 (December 1959), p. 1.

— "Old Hat Re-blocked", *Irish Times* (14 March 1964).

— "Slattery's Sago Drama", *Fiction*, IV, 2 (1976), pp. 10–15.

— "Standish Hayes O'Grady", *Irish Times* (16 October 1940).

— "St. Augustine Strikes Back: De scribendi periculo", *Bookmark* (World Book Fair Special) (1964), p. 2.

— *Stories and Plays* [incl.: *Slattery's Sago Saga*; "The Martyr's Crown"; "John Duffy's Brother"; *Thirst, Faustus Kelly*; "A Bash in the Tunnel"] (London: Hart-Davis, MacGibbon, 1973).

— "The Cud of Memory", *Manchester Guardian* (15 October 1965).

— *The Dalkey Archive* (London: MacGibbon & Kee, 1964; New York: Macmillan, 1965; London: Picador, 1976).

— "The Dance Halls", *The Bell*, I, 5 (February 1941), 44-52; repr. in: Sean McMahon (ed.), *The Best from The Bell. Great Irish Writing* (Dublin: O'Brien Press, 1978), pp. 36-43.

— *The Hard Life* (London: MacGibbon & Kee, 1961; New York: Pantheon, 1962; London: Four Square Books, 1964; London: Picador, 1976); adapted for the stage by Pat Layde, and staged at the Peacock Theatre, Dublin, on 7 October 1976.

— *The Third Policeman* (London: MacGibbon & Kee, 1967; New York: Walker, 1967; New York: Lancer Books, 1970; London: Picador, 1974, 1976).

— "The Third Policeman" [extract from *The Third Policeman*], *Transatlantic Review*, 25 (Summer 1967), pp. 78-83.

— "The Trade in Dublin", *The Bell*, I, 2 (November 1940), pp. 6-15.

— "Words", *Development*, 9 (Spring 1959), p. 1.

Nolan, Brian. "A Bash in the Tunnel", *Envoy*, V, 17 (May 1951), pp. 5-11; repr. in: John Ryan (ed.), *A Bash in the Tunnel. James Joyce by the Irish* (Brighton: Clifton Books, 1970), pp. 15-20; *Antaeus*, 21/22 (Spring-Summer 1976), pp. 119-24.

— *Flight* (1962) unpublished TV play.

— "Small Men and Black Dogs", *Manchester Guardian* (14 October 1960).

— *The Boy from Ballytearim* (1955, rev. version 1962) unpublished TV play.

— *The Dead Spit of Kelly* [dramatised version of the story "Two in One"] (1962), unpublished TV play.

— *The Detective Fastidiosities of Sergeant Fottrell* (1966), unpublished TV series, 2 parts.

— *The Ideas of O'Dea* (September 1963 — March 1964), unpublished TV series.

— "The Man with Four Legs" repr. in: *The Journal of Irish Literature*, III, 1 (January 1974), pp. 40-55.

— "The Martyr's Crown", *Envoy*, I, 3 (February 1950), pp. 57-62; repr. in: Devin A. Garrity (ed.), *Irish Stories* (New York, 1961), pp. 216-21; *Antaeus*, 19 (Autumn 1975), pp. 42-6.

— *Th' Oul Lad of Kilsalaher* (September — December 1965), unpublished TV series.

— *The Time Freddie Retired* (1962), unpublished TV play.

O'Nolan, Brian. "After Hours", *Threshold*, 21 (Summer 1967), pp. 15-18; repr. in: Frank O'Connor (ed.), *A Book of Ireland*, pp. 172-5.

— "A Poem from the Irish" in: Timothy O'Keeffe (ed.), *Myles. Portraits of Brian O'Nolan* (London: Martin Brian & O'Keeffe, 1973), p. 9.

— "Notes on UCD and the Literary and Historical Society" in: *Centenary History of the Literary and Historical Society 1855-1955*, ed. James Meenan (Tralee, n.d.), pp. 240-46.

— "Pisa bec on Parnabus: Extractum O Bhark l bPragrais", *Ireland Today*, III, 2 (February 1938), pp. 138-65.

— "What is Wrong with the L. and H.?", *Comhthrom Féinne*, X, 3 (March 1935), pp. 58-9.

Ua Nualláin, Brian. "Are You Lonely in the Restaurant?", *Comhthrom Féinne*, V, 3 (March 1933), pp. 40-41; repr. in: *The Journal of Irish Literature*, III, 1 (January 1974), pp. 9-13.

— *Máiréad Gillan* [translation of Brinsley MacNamara's play *Margaret Gillan*] (Dublin, 1953).

Brother Barnabas, "Scenes in a Novel", *Comhthrom Féinne*, VIII, 2 (May 1934), pp. 29-30; repr. in: *The Journal of Irish Literature*, III, 1 (January 1974), pp. 14-18.

Count Blather, "Food Taxes of Free Trade? Or Handy Vocabulars", *Blather*, I, 3 (November 1934), p. 38; repr. in: *The Journal of Irish Literature*, III, 1 (January 1974), pp. 22-3.

— "There is Really No Excuse for This Sort of Thing", *Blather*, I, 2 (October 1934), p. 27; repr. in: *The Journal of Irish Literature*, III, 1 (January 1974), pp. 19-21.

Na gCopaleen, Myles. *An Béal Bocht* (Dublin: An Preas Náisiúnta, 1941; Dublin: Dolmen Press, 1964; Dublin: Dolmen Press, 1975); translated *The Poor Mouth* (London: HartDavis, MacGibbon, 1973; London: Picador, 1975).

— "A Christmas Garland", *The Harp*, IX, 4 (Christmas 1966), p. 19.

— "A Pint of Plain", *The Harp*, VIII, 2 (Summer 1965), p. 27.

— "Baudelaire and Kavanagh", *Envoy*, III, 12 (November 1950), pp. 78-81.

— "Christmas Time at Santry", *The Harp*, III, 6 (December 1960), p. 8.

— "Cruiskeen Lawn", *Irish Times* (4 October 1940 — 1 April 1966).

— *Cruiskeen Lawn* (Dublin, 1943).

— "Cruiskeen Lawn", *Nonplus*, 1-4 (1959).

— "De Me", *New Ireland* (March 1964), pp. 41-2.

— "Donabate", *Irish Writing*, 20-21 (November 1952), pp. 41-2; repr. in: *The Journal of Irish Literature*, III, 1 (January 1974), pp. 62-4.

— "Drink and Time in Dublin", *Irish Writing*, 1 (1946), pp. 71-7; repr. in: V. Mercier and D. H. Greene (eds.), *1000 Years of Irish Prose* (New York, 1952), pp. 509-12.

— *Faustus Kelly* (Dublin, 1943).

— *Further Cuttings from Cruiskeen Lawn*, ed. Kevin O'Nolan (London: Hart-Davis, MacGibbon, 1976).

— "How Are You off for Tostals?", *Kavanagh's Weekly*, I, 5 (10 May 1952), p. 4.

— "I Don't Know", *Kavanagh's Weekly*, I, 3 (26 April 1952), pp. 3-4.

— "Letter to the Editor", *Kavanagh's Weekly*, I, 10 (14 June 1952), p. 5.

— "Letter to the Editor", *Kavanagh's Weekly*, I, 6 (17 May 1952), p. 5.

— *More of Myles,* ed. Kevin O'Nolan (London: Hart-Davis, MacGibbon, 1976).

— "Motor Economics", *Kavanagh's Weekly,* I, 7 (24 March 1952), p. 6.

— *Myles Away From Dublin,* ed. Martin Green (London, Toronto, Sydney, New York: Granada, 1985).

— "Myles, by an Admirer", *The Harp,* IV, 5 (December 1961), p. 19.

— "Pots and Pains", *Irish Housewife Annual,* XIV (1963/64), pp. 70-71.

— "Public Taste and Decorum", *Hibernia,* XXIV (9 September 1960), p. 3.

— "Review of L.A.G. Strong, *The Sacred River: An Approach to James Joyce",* *Irish Writing,* 10 (January 1950), pp. 71-2.

— "Review of Patrick Campbell, *A Long Drink of Cold Water",* *Irish Writing,* 11 (May 1950), p. 73.

— *The Best of Myles,* ed. Kevin O'Nolan (London: Hart Davis, MacGibbon, 1968; New York: Walker, 1968; London: Picador, 1977).

— "The Fausticity of Kelly", *RTE Guide* (25 January 1963).

— *The Hair of the Dogma,* ed. Kevin O'Nolan (London: Hart-Davis, MacGibbon, 1977).

— *The Handsome Carvers,* unpublished TV play.

— *The Insect Play,* repr. in: *The Journal of Irish Literature,* III, 1 (January 1974), pp. 24-39.

— *The Lurch of Time,* unpublished radio script.

— "The Sensational New 'Phoenix'", *Kavanagh's Weekly,* I, 4 (3 May 1952), p. 4.

— "The Shanchie", *Fiction,* III, 1 (1974), pp. 1-3; extract from *The Poor Mouth.*

- "The Tired Scribe: A Poem from the Irish", *Poetry Ireland,* 4 (January 1949), p. 12.

— *The Various Lives of Keats and Chapman and The Brother,* ed. Benedict Kiely (London: Hart-Davis, MacGibbon, 1976).

— *Thirst,* broadcast Radio Eireann 1943.

— "This Job of Work", *Evening Mail* (12 October 1961).

— "Three Poems from the Irish", *Lace Curtain,* 4 (Summer 1971), pp. 46-7.

— "Two in One", *The Bell,* XIX, 8 (July 1954), pp. 30-34; repr. in: *The Journal of Irish Literature,* III, 1 (January 1974), pp. 56-61.

— "1961", *The Harp* (Winter 1961), p. 18.

Doe, John James. "A Weekly Look Around", *Southern Star* (Skibbereen) (15 January 1955 — 27 October 1965).

Knowall, George. "George Knowall's Peepshow", *Nationalist and Leinster Times* (Carlow) (early to mid-1960).

II. Critical Material

Adams, R. M. *Afterjoyce: Studies in Fiction After Ulysses* (New York, 1977), pp. 187-90.

Alter, R. *Partial Magic: The Novel as a Self-Conscious Genre* (Berkley, Los Angeles, London, 1975), pp. 223ff.

Alter, R. "The Self-Conscious Moment: Reflections on the Aftermath of Modernism", *TriQuarterly,* 33 (Spring 1975), pp. 209-30.

Anderson, D. "Comic Modes in Modern American Fiction", *Southern Review*, VIII, 2 (June 1975), pp. 152-65.

Anon., "Eire's Columnist", *Time*, XLII, pp. 8 (23 August 1943), pp. 90, 92.

— "Flann O'Brien, Novelist, 54 is Dead", *New York Times* (2 April 1966).

— "The Real Myles", *Irish Times* (8 June 1973), p. 10.

Benstock, B. "The Three Faces of Brian O'Nolan", *Éire-Ireland*, III, 3 (October 1968), pp. 51-65.

Bergonzi, B. *The Situation of the Novel* (Harmondsworth, 1972), pp. 234-6.

Boland, J. "Flann O'Brien in His Crazy Tunnel", *Hibernia* (1 February 1974), p. 12.

Bungert, A. "Das harte Leben", *Tagespost* (Würzburg) (26/27 April 1968).

Burgess, A. *The Novel Now. A Student's Guide to Contemporary Fiction* (London, rev. ed. 1971), pp. 78-80.

Burgess, Anthony. "Flann O'Brien. A Note", *Etudes Irlandiases*, No. 7 (December 1982), pp. 83-6.

Carroll, N. "Myles is Now in Full Bloom", *Sunday Press* (3 October 1965).

Cassen, B. "Redécouverte de Flann O'Brien", *Le Monde* (13 September 1969).

Cataldi, M. "Mito edenico, utopia e fantascienza nella narrativa di Flann O'Brien", *Utopia e Fantascienza* (Turin, 1976), pp. 142-58.

Clissmann, A. *Flann O'Brien. A Critical Introduction to His Writing* (Dublin, 1975).

— "Flann O'Brien", *Ireland Today*, 892 (15 September 1976), pp. 4-6.

— *Parody and Fantasy in the English Novels of Flann O'Brien* (unpubl. Master thesis, University of Dublin, 1971).

Comhthrom Féinne, I, 3 (Summer 1931), p. 55; III, 1 (29 January 1932), p. 140; III, 3 (17 March 1932), pp. 188, 193; IV, 1 (23 April 1932), p. 205; VII, 3 (January 1934), p. 46; XI, 1 (April 1935), p. 12; XII, 1 (July 1935), p. 23; XI, 2 (May 1935), p. 43.

Cronin, A. "An Extraordinary Achievement: Flann O'Brien", *Irish Times* (5 December 1975).

— "After *At Swim:* Flann O'Brien", *Irish Times* (12 December 1975).

Cronin, J. "The Funnel and the Tundris: Irish Writers and the English Language", *Wascana Review*, 3 (1968), pp. 80-88.

Dumay, Emile-Jean. " 'The Full Little Crock' ou la Religion de l'Ivresse chez Flann O'Brien", *Etudes Irlandaises*, 1 (December 1976), pp. 99-110.

Fackler, Herbert V. "Flann O'Brien's *The Third Policeman:* Banjaxing Natural Order", *South Central Bulletin*, 38 (1978), pp. 142-45.

Fallis, Richard. *The Irish Renaissance. An Introduction to Anglo-Irish Literature* (Dublin, 1978), pp. 218-20.

Fallon, G. "Copaleen O'Brien", *The Standard* (7 February 1943).

Felter, Mary-Anne. "Department of Interesting Authors: A Flash Through the Tunnel", *Journal of Irish Literature*, IX, 3 (September 1980), pp. 136-50.

Garvin, J. "Sweetscented Manuscripts", in: T. O'Keeffe (ed.), *Myles. Portraits of Brian O'Nolan* (London, 1973), pp. 54-61.

Heckard, M. "The Novels of Brian O'Nolan", *Dissertation Abstracts International* 37:986A-87A.

Hilton, T. "Ireland's Great Cyclists", *New Statesman* (8 December 1967), pp. 815-16.

Hogan, R. and G. Henderson (ed.), "A Sheaf of Letters", *The Journal of Irish Literature*, III, 1 (January 1974), pp. 65-92.

Hogan, R. and M. J. O'Neill (eds.), *Joseph Holloway's Irish Theatre, III: 1938-1944* (Carbondale, Edwardsville, 1967).

Hogan, Th. "Myles na gCopaleen", *The Bell*, XIII, 2 (1946), pp. 129-40.

Hughes, C. "Discovering Flann O'Brien", *America* (3 May 1969), pp. 523-5.

Imhof, R. "Flann O'Brien" in: J. Kornelius, E. Otto, and G. Stratmann (eds.), *Einführung in die zeitgenössische irische Literatur* (Heidelberg, 1980), pp. 161-79.

— "Two Meta-Novelists: Sternesque Elements in Novels by Flann O'Brien", *Anglo-Irish Studies*, IV (1979), pp. 59-90.

Jacquin, D. *Lecture de Flann O'Brien* (Diss. Lille, in progress).

— "Never Apply Your Front Brakes First, or Flann O'Brien and the Theme of the Fall" in: P. Rafroidi and M. Harmon (eds.), *The Irish Novel in Our Time* (Lille, 1976), pp. 187-97.

Jacquin, D. "Techniques et effets de la satire dans *An Béal Bocht* (The Poor Mouth) de Myles na gCopaleen", *Etudes Irlandaises*, 6 (December 1981), 61-71.

Janik, I. del, "Flann O'Brien: The Novelist as Critic", *Éire-Ireland*, IV, 4 (Winter 1969), pp. 64-72.

Johnston, D. "Myles na gCopaleen" in: J. Ronsley (ed.), *Myth and Reality in Irish Literature* (Waterloo, 1977), pp. 297-304.

Jones, St. (ed.), *A Flann O'Brien Reader* (New York, 1978).

Jude the Obscure, "The H.U. Business Section", *The Honest Ulsterman* (July/August 1971), p. 31.

Kearney, R. "A Crisis of Imagination", *The Crane Bag*, III, 1 (1979), pp. 58-70.

Kelleher, J. V. "Dublin's Joyce and Others", *Virginia Quarterly Review*, XXXIII, 1 (Winter 1957), pp. 132-5.

Kelly, S. "Brian O'Nolan. Scholar, Satirist and Wit", *Irish Times* (2 April 1966); repr. in: *The Journal of Irish Literature*, III, 1 (January 1974), pp. 3-5.

Kennedy, S. "'The Devil and Holy Water' — Samuel Beckett's *Murphy* and Flann O'Brien's *At Swim-Two-Birds*" in: R. J. Porter and W. Y. Tindal (ed.), *Modern Irish Literature* (New York, 1972), pp. 251-60.

Kennelly, Brendan. "*An Béal Bocht:* Myles na gCopaleen (1911-1966)", in: John Jordan (ed.), *The Pleasure of Gaelic Literature* (Cork, 1977), 85-96.

Kiberd, D. "Writers in Quarantine? The Case for Irish Studies", *The Crane Bag*, III, 1 (1979), pp. 9-21.

Kiely, B. *Modern Irish Fiction: A Critique* (Dublin, 1950).

— "The Whores on the Half-Doors or An Image of the Irish Writer" in: O. D. Edwards (ed.), *Conor Cruise O'Brien Introduces Ireland* (London, 1969), pp. 148-61.

Kilroy, Th. "Tellers of Tales", *TLS* (17 March 1972), p. 301.

Klein, E. U. *Die frühen Romane Flann O'Briens: "At Swim-Two-Birds" und "The Third Policeman". Ein Beitrag zur Geschichte des englischen Romans* (Diss. Münster, 1971).

Knight, St. "The Novels of Flann O'Brien", in: D. Anderson and St. Knight (eds.), *Cunning Exiles: Studies of Modern Prose Writers* (Sydney, 1974), pp. 104-28.

Lee, L. L. "The Dublin Cowboys of Flann O'Brien", *Western American Literature*, IV, 3 (Fall 1969), pp. 219-25.

Lodge, D. *The Novelist at the Crossroads* (London, 1971).

Long, Gerard. "Brian O'Nolan: His Life and Works", *Gaeliana*, 2 (1980), 109-20.

MacDonagh, D. "The Great Lost Novel", unpubl. manuscript (London: MacGibbon & Kee).

MacKillop, J. *The Figure of Finn MacCool. A Study of a Celtic Archetype in the Works of James Macpherson, Flann O'Brien, James Joyce and Others* (Ph.D. thesis University of Syracuse, 1975).

Magalana, M. and R. M. Kain, *Joyce. The Man, the Work, the Reputation* (New York, 1956).

Mays, J. C. C. "Brian O'Nolan and James Joyce on Art and on Life", *James Joyce Quarterly*, XI (1974), pp. 238-56.

— "Brian O'Nolan: Literarist of the Imagination", in: T. O'Keeffe (ed.), *Myles. Portraits of Brian O'Nolan*, pp. 77-119.

McCoy, R. E. "Manuscript Collections in Morris Library", ICarbS, I, 2 (Spring-Summer 1974), pp. 153-62.

McGuire, J. "Teasing After Death: Metatextuality in *The Third Policeman*", *Éire-Ireland*, XVI, 2 (1981), pp. 107-21.

Meenan, J. (ed.), *A Centenary History of the Literary and Historical Society of University College, Dublin, 1855-1955* (Tralee, 1957), pp. 206, 230, 241f., 249-50, 251, 261, 262, 266, 312.

Mellamphy, N. "Aestho-autogamy and the Anarchy of Imagination. Flann O'Brien's Theory of Fiction in *At Swim-Two-Birds*", *The Canadian Journal of Irish Studies*, IV, 1 (June 1978), pp. 8-25.

Mendilow, A. A. *Time and the Novel* (London, 1952), pp. 224-8.

Meneghelli, P. "L'Irlanda di Flann O'Brien", *Studie Inglesi*, II (1975), pp. 283-306.

Mercier, V. *The Irish Comic Tradition* (Oxford, 1962), pp. 38, 39-40, 46, 104, 182, 208.

Montague, J. "Sweetness", in: T. O'Keeffee (ed.), *Myles. Portraits of Brian O'Nolan*, pp. 120-21.

Montgomery, N. "An Aristophanic Sorcerer", *Irish Times* (2 April 1966).

Moss, H. "Tom Swift in Hell", *New Yorker*, LXIV, 32 (28 September 1968), pp. 174-80.

O'Brien, D. "In Ireland after *A Portrait*" in: Th. F. Staley and B. Benstock (eds.), *Approaches to Joyce's Portrait. Ten Essays* (Pittsburgh, 1976), pp. 213-37.

O'Brien, G. "Flann O'Brien", *The Cambridge Quarterly*, VII (1976), pp. 85-92.

O Conaire, B. "Flann O'Brien, *An Béal Bocht* and Other Irish Matters", *Irish University Review*, III, 2 (Autumn 1973), pp. 121-40.

O'Keeffe, T. "Bibliographical Notes" in: T. O'Keeffe (ed.), *Myles. Portraits of Brian O'Nolan*, pp. 122-34.

O Luanaigh, L. "Culra agus oige Bhriain Ui Nuallain", *Innui*, XXXI, 6 (n.d.), p. 5.

O'Nolan, K. "The First Furlongs" in: T. O'Keeffe (ed.), *Myles. Portraits of Brian O'Nolan*, pp. 13-31.

Orvell, M. "Entirely Fictitious: The Fiction of Flann O'Brien", *The Journal of Irish Literature*, III, 1 (January 1974), pp. 93-103.

— "Brian O'Nolan: The Privacy of His Mind", *ICarbS*, 2 (1975), pp. 23-38.

— and D. Powell, "Myles na gCopaleen: Mystic, Horse-doctor, Hackney Journalist and Ideological Catalyst", *Éire-Ireland*, X, 2 (Summer 1975), pp. 44-72.

Poirier, R. "The Politics of Self-Parody", *Partisan Review*, XXXV (1968), pp. 339-53.

Powell, D. "An Annotated Bibliography of Myles na gCopaleen's 'Cruiskeen Lawn' Commentary of James Joyce", *James Joyce Quarterly*, 9 (Fall 1971), pp. 50-62.

— "A Checklist of Brian O'Nolan", *The Journal of Irish Literature*, III, 1 (January 1974), pp. 104-12.

— and Mr. Orvell, *Flann O'Brien: A Genesis. A Biographical Study of Brian O'Nolan, Flann O'Brien, Myles na Gopaleen* (as yet unpublished).

— *The English Writings of Flann O'Brien* (Ann Arbor/Mich, 1971).

— "Who was Myles, and What was He?, *The Journal of Irish Literature*, III, 1 (January 1974), pp. 6-8.

Power, M. "Flann O'Brien and Classical Satire: An Exegesis of *The Hard Life*", *Éire-Ireland* (Spring 1978), pp. 87-102.

Power, P. C. "Climbing the Mountain", *Dublin Magazine*, IX, 1 (Autumn 1971), pp. 68-73.

Quidnunc (B. O'Nolan), "A Visitation", *Irish Times* (23 July 1960), repr. as: "The Author in Person", *The Bookseller* (8 August 1960).

Radin, V. "Wild and Willy at the Court", *The Observer* (17 December 1978), 19 (review of Allan McClelland's adaptation of *The Dalkey Archive*, performed by Hull Truck at The Bush theatre, London).

Rafroidi, P. *L'Irlande: Littérature* (Paris, 1970), pp. 17, 140-142, 160.

Ricciardi, C. "Aperture sulla letteratura irlandese contemporanea: Struttura e significato in *At Swim-Two-Birds* di Flann O'Brien", *Cultura e Scuola*, 52 (1974), pp. 80-97.

Ryan, J. "The Incomparable Myles" in: J. Ryan, *Remembering How We Stood* (Dublin, 1975), pp. 127-143.

Ryf, R. S. "Character and Imagination in the Experimental Novel", *Modern Fiction Studies*, XX (1974), pp. 317-27.

Sage, L. "Flann O'Brien" in: D. Dunn (ed.), *Two Decades of Irish Writing: A Critical Survey* (Cheadle, 1975), pp. 197-206.

Sainsbury, I. "Talking of Flann O'Brien", *Sheffield Telegraph* (14 August 1965).

Semmler, C. "The Art of Brian O'Nolan", *Meanjin Quarterly*, XXIX, 4 (December 1970), pp. 492-500.

Sheridan, N. "Brian, Flann and Myles", *Irish Times* (2 April 1966); repr. in: T. O'Keeffe (ed.), *Myles. Portraits of Brian O'Nolan*, pp. 32-53.

— "The World of Flann O'Brien", *RTE Guide* (13 November 1970).

Silverthorne, J. M. "Time, Literature, and Failure: Flann O'Brien's *At Swim-Two-Birds* and *The Third Policeman*", *Éire-Ireland*, XI, 4 (1976), pp. 66-83.

Simple, P. (i.e. Michael Wharton), "Myles na gCopaleen", *Daily Telegraph* (5 April 1966).

Sullivan, K. "Literature in Modern Ireland" in: O. D. Edwards (ed.), *Conor Cruise O'Brien Introduces Ireland* (London, 1969), pp. 135-47.

The Honest Ulsterman (January/February 1972), pp. 28-29; (September/October 1973), pp. 28-40; (November 1973 — February 1974), pp. 27-28.

Wade, J. A. *Irish Fiction and Its Background after 1922 with Special Reference to the Works of Liam O'Flaherty, Sean O'Faolain, Frank O'Connor and Flann O'Brien* (Master thesis London, 1965).

Wain, J. "The Genius Who Stayed at Home", *Le Monde* (1 October 1969).

— "'To Write for My Own Race': The Fiction of Flann O'Brien", *Encounter* (July 1967), pp. 71-85.

Wall, M. "The Man Who Hated Only Cods", *Irish Times* (2 april 1966).

Warner, Alan. *A Guide to Anglo-Irish Literature* (Dublin, 1981), 153-65.

White, J. "Myles, Flann and Brian" in: T. O'Keeffe (ed.), *Myles. Portraits of Brian O'Nolan*, pp. 62-76.

Wilk, W. "Die Macht der Phantasie: Der mysteriöse Flann O'Brien — Hinweise auf einen irischen Erzähler", *Tagesspiegel* (Berlin) (2 October 1966).